gift gale
3-77

LIGHTEN OUR DARKNESS

BOOKS BY DOUGLAS JOHN HALL

Published by The Westminster Press

Lighten Our Darkness: Toward
    an Indigenous Theology of the Cross

The Reality of the Gospel
    and the Unreality of the Churches

LIGHTEN OUR DARKNESS

Toward an Indigenous Theology of the Cross

by
DOUGLAS JOHN HALL

THE WESTMINSTER PRESS

Philadelphia

Book Design by Dorothy Alden Smith

Published by The Westminster Press
Philadelphia, Pennsylvania ®

PRINTED IN THE UNITED STATES OF AMERICA

Library of Congress Cataloging in Publication Data

Hall, Douglas John, 1928–
  Lighten our darkness.

  Includes bibliographical references and index.
  1. Christianity—20th century. 2. Theology—
20th century. 3. North America—Civilization.
I. Title.
BR121.2.H317   230   75-38963
ISBN 0-664-20808-8

To
Fritz Hufendiek and the *Studentengemeinde*
in Münster, Germany, who made the writing
of this book possible

Today, the only possible alternative to
the belief in progress would be total
despair.

SIDNEY POLLARD
The Idea of Progress

I know: the paths of the soul, overgrown,
often know only the night, a very vast, very
barren night, without landscapes. And yet I
tell you: we'll get out. The most glorious
works of man are born of that night.

ELIE WIESEL
The Town Beyond the Wall

Lighten our darkness, we beseech thee, O Lord;
and by thy great mercy defend us from all perils
and dangers of this night; for the love of thy only
Son, our Savior, Jesus Christ. Amen.

The Book of Common Prayer

CONTENTS

PREFACE

THE SUBJECT of this book is the failure of a people and the courage that can come to those who contemplate this failure in the perspective of the cross. The people are the North Americans.

In his Gifford Lectures, which coincided with the outbreak of World War II, Reinhold Niebuhr reflected in a footnote on the pertinence of Christian faith for comprehending the events that were occurring. The Christian, he insisted, is not permitted to regard the tribulations of a civilization with detachment. Neither is he obliged to identify the meaning of life with the preservation of his own culture. In the midst of that conflict, which Niebuhr wisely saw as a struggle against a "virulent form" of a more subtle corruption, the responsibility of Christians is clear: they must strive "to fashion our common life to conform more nearly to the brotherhood of the Kingdom of God." For no religious loyalty to an *eternal* meaning and destiny should deter Christians from their "historical obligations." "But," he continued, "*if we should fail,* as well we may, we can at least understand the failure from the perspective of the Christian faith. In so far as we understand the failure we will not be completely involved in it, but have a vantage point beyond it. We could not deny the tragic character of what we discern but we would not be tempted to regard it as meaningless." [1]

I could wish nothing more than that this present study be considered a commentary, three decades later, on these words of my great teacher. Since he wrote them, it has become increasingly evident that the failure he anticipated as a real possibility for our civilization has come among us. It is most pathetically present in that society which most consistently embodied the modern version of success: North America. Having successfully warded off that "virulent form of corruption" to which

15

Niebuhr referred in the early 1940's, we soon found ourselves, to our own dismay, identified throughout the world as perpetrators of the same variety of corruption. In these latter days we have been confronted by shameful evidence of that "more static corruption" of which Nazism was a vulgar external manifestation. The very foundations of our culture have been shaken, because by our own standards of success we have failed.

The pathos of our condition is not that we have failed. Our failure has *tragic* dimensions, to be sure. The pathos of it is that we cannot bring ourselves as a people to contemplate our failure. Therefore our condition is all the more problematic, dangerous, and infinitely sad.

By Niebuhr's account, this incapacity for the contemplation of failure would have to imply a failure of Christianity, also, as we have known it. For he regarded faith to be in its essence the courage to reflect on the tragic dimensions of existence without being "tempted to regard it as meaningless." [2]

But perhaps this very failure of what we have known as Christianity could mark the beginning of something more akin to faith in Niebuhr's terms. As Kierkegaard said out of his Pauline heritage, "In his failure, the believer finds his triumph." Perhaps real faith, like real wisdom, can only occur "at eventide" (Hegel). That is, it occurs in that darkness where human beings have come to the end of their know-how.[3]

If that is so, then the task of Christian theology in our time and place must be to help men *enter into* that darkness. Not to offer them refuge from it, although this has indeed been the principal function of religion among us; rather, to help provide a way into the darkness. Of course darkness could not be the last thing that faith had to pronounce about life in this world. Such a conclusion belongs, not to Christians, but to Gnostics and others; Christianity early rejected it. But the light to which the Christian gospel bears witness in every age presupposes conscious exposure to the darkness of that age. After all, it is light *for* that darkness. Whoever refuses to enter the darkness can have no glimpse of this light.

"Lighten our darkness . . . " Christians have prayed this in one form or another for centuries. Paradoxically, wherever it has been rightly prayed, it has meant two things: not only "Give us light," but "Give us enough comprehension of our real darkness that we may see this light." *Lighten* our darkness . . . Lighten *our darkness*.

It is my conviction that light *can* be discerned by those, whoever they be, who enter deeply enough into the encroaching darkness of our civilization. I am speaking especially of our "America." There is more real light in our darkness than in the bright fantasies of the Enlightenment upon which we were founded; more promise in our failure than in the chimera of success to which we still cling. We could become wise, but only if we are ready to meditate long and deeply on the folly of so much of what we have thought, dreamed, and done.

The initial ideas for this study were expressed in much-abbreviated form in the book *Hope Against Hope*, published by the World Student Christian Federation in Geneva.[4] I am grateful for the support given me by the WSCF in their desire to publish those "working papers." I am grateful as well to W. A. Visser 't Hooft, John C. Bennett, Jürgen Moltmann, and many friends, students, and colleagues who have responded so helpfully to that publication. This ongoing dialogue has enabled me to develop in their present form the ideas broached in it. I have been especially indebted to Christians of the Third World, whose comments have indicated how surprised they are to hear from this continent both a theology which is intentionally "indigenous" and a theology of the cross. Above all, I am grateful to my wife, Rhoda Palfrey Hall, who remains my best partner in theological and human dialogue.

D.J.H.

Faculty of Religious Studies
McGill University
Montreal, Canada

INTRODUCTION

DIALOGUE, CONFLICT, AND CONTRADICTION

Human life is a dialogue between expectation and experience. The function of expectation is to deliver us from bondage to the past. When expectancy ceases, death occurs. The function of experience is to keep us tied to the life of the body, to history. When experience ceases to inform existence, the consequence is illusion. Human life is thus a perilous journey between death and illusion. Few are able to reach the end of the journey without capitulating to one or the other peril. Most human beings, before their time runs out, are well acquainted with both.

It is a peculiarity of this dialogue that it is almost always out of balance. Sometimes expectation takes hold of a person or a people. Dreams are dreamed and visions are entertained; there is little regard for the experiences of the past, with their implicit warnings of limits that must not be transgressed. This is the stuff out of which civilizations are made, if the moment is right. If it is not, the expectancy may be nothing more than the frantic Dionysian cavorting of a society in decay. At other times, experience becomes the master of the discourse. The sober god Apollo commences his rule. Men speak then of stability and reason, and they say to one another, "Remember!" On occasion this has been the very tonic that saved men and nations from foolish illusion. Sometimes it is just the dry and cautious prating of cynicism cloaked as wisdom, the fruit of disillusionment and bitterness. The musty smell of death is in it.

Conscious of the dangers on either side, cautious persons conclude that security, if not salvation, lies in balance. They conceive the ideal state, whether of individual or communal life, to lie in an equilibrium between

19

expectancy and experience. But in fact the whole idea of balance is absurd. Balance could only mean that state of dreadful equipoise where expectation is continuously fulfilled in experience—where nothing more is expected. Clearly such a condition is not descriptive of life in this world. When it is offered *pre*scriptively, as an ideal to be striven for or a program to be launched, it is dangerous and misleading. The state of fulfilled expectancy must be either a fabrication of the imagination or an enigma beyond the limits of time, either a lie or the Kingdom of God. Since the Kingdom of God is a mystery not even revealed to the saints and martyrs in its depths, it can be assumed forthwith that those who give us systems by which such a balance can be achieved are giving us lies.

As for life in this world, it is a *dialogue* between expectation and experience, and therefore dependent upon their differentiation and *im*balance. Without this variance there could be no dialogue, no movement, no life. Because of the perils of the journey—death on the one side and illusion on the other—men do indeed long for places of permanent rest. In political ideologies, in philosophical systems, in their loves, and (above all!) in their religions, they seek the comfort of a perfect balance, the realization of all longings, the aseity of the gods. The city is the symbolic manifestation of this entirely human desire to end the discrepancy between expectation and experience, to reach the goal of the journey, to exchange tents for houses, to have *securitas*. But in spite of our impressive efforts, this security is forever denied us. Our walled cities, our sanctuaries, our systems in which everything has been accounted for, our bourgeois morality so serene and predictable—every bid of ours for fixity is attacked. Always the most devastating invasions occur from within. Because life is itself the invader: it will not be contained. It constantly renews the dialogue, setting expectancy and experience again at loggerheads with each other. Life enters, and the affluent homes of executives are found to have bred gypsies and revolutionaries. The ivy-covered monuments to rationality become the scenes of orgies of love and war, and in Jerusalem not one stone is left standing on another.

But already we have moved beyond the initial observation that life is a dialogue between expectation and experience. By itself, the word "dialogue" hardly conveys the truth about the dynamics of this process. It too readily suggests the amiable discourse, with a certain willingness to give and take, a certain well-bred geniality. It is indicative of the quite different character of the dialogue in question that it has been necessary, so early in this discussion, to use words of a very different color to describe it. Some of them are almost bellicose: discrepancy, invasion, loggerheads.

Such language anticipates what we must now make quite explicit, namely, that the dialogue of which life partakes is essentially a *conflict.*

In one degree or another, the meeting of expectation and experience always involves struggle, for the two are not easily compatible. Each demands of the other what the other cannot possibly give. Expectancy demands of experience that it actually offer what is longed for. Experience requires of expectancy that it provide the guarantee that evil would not come of what it desires.

Conflict is not a condition that human beings find comfortable. It is, no doubt, a sign of sanity to wish that all conflict should at last be resolved. Yet what emerges or may emerge out of the conflict between expectation and experience is of the very essence of life. Just because expectancy is never satisfied but keeps requiring that experience transcend itself, the category of the new is never quite lost to us, Koheleth's testimony notwithstanding. Impregnated by expectancy, time again and again brings forth the *un*expected. What the past does not itself beget, what experience seems not even to permit, nonetheless occurs. Thus the quality of wonder is kept alive in the race, and men are moved to search for possibilities where nothing new has ever been found—to go even unto Bethlehem! Such wonders could not sustain themselves, however, unless experience, always skeptical of genuine novelty, chided and conditioned hope to ground its fantasies in history. Without the hard demands of experience, expectancy is prone to weave Edens out of thin air; where those demands have been heard, it is sometimes capable of creating less fabulous gardens in the wilderness.

Because of what emerges out of this conflict, those who celebrate life do not attempt to resolve it. For the sake of the glory that is always hidden within the conflict, they accept the pain of it. They know, besides, that resolutions nearly always betray those who cannot avoid the pain. Solutions, including religious ones, are usually accessible only to those who have been able on other grounds (normally economic) to rise above the fundamental conflict of existence.

It is indeed the aim of religion, whether in its more obvious forms or in subtle, secular dress, to overcome the persistent conflict between expectation and experience. The bourgeois religion that meets us today under the usual guise of Christianity is kept going by its overestimated reputation for delivering people from this conflict. Through the reduction and domestication of hope, on the one hand, and by accentuating the positive aspects of experience, on the other, it smooths the unrest in the souls of the affluent and gives them peace of mind.

As distinct from religion, Biblical faith refuses to heal the people lightly.

It too announces a resolution of the conflict, an eschatological denouement which is both "already" and "not yet." It offers this resolution, however, only to those who sit in darkness and in the shadow of death; and it offers it as the object of faith, not of sight. Moreover, the resolution to which Biblical faith points is gained, not by minimizing the character of the conflict, but by an exposure of man—and of God!—to the core of its aboriginal pain. This faith knows that the Spirit of God fans the struggle between hope and history into a very flame. Out of it arises a dissatisfaction so monumental that it will not be stilled until all men sit at banquet together and death itself is overcome. For faith in the God of Abraham and of Jesus Christ is the celebration of life. There lies in it the awareness that abundant life can be tasted only when the conflict of expectancy and experience has been brought to full consciousness, refined by suffering, and enlarged to encompass the whole, groaning creation.

We have been thinking, however, about conflict, not about *contradiction*. They are two different conditions. Conflict between what is expected and what actually *is,* is necessary to life and is life. Contradiction is deadly.

There is of course an element of contradiction in conflict. It belongs to the state of conflict that the correspondence between expectation and experience be always tenuous, a correspondence in tension. It is always something of a miracle when experience actually offers what is longed for, when "the hopes and fears of all the years" are met in Bethlehem, of all places. Every lover, every parent who wills parenthood, recognizes this miracle. The songs of every culture are filled with testimony to it. Nevertheless, in the state of conflict, at least the *possibility* of a correspondence between hope and history is entertained. I, even I, could be loved! It is in fact only on account of this anticipation of "impossible possibilities" that the conflict persists. Men give themselves over to the conflict, not because they enjoy struggle (most human beings do not), but because they dare to believe that what they hope for might really come to pass.

A state of contradiction has been reached at the point where that possibility is no longer believed in or sought after. The dialogue between expectation and experience has been virtually closed. The logical thing would be to admit its end. But the essence of the contradictory state is that such an admission is precisely what cannot occur. In any case, in the moment of such an admission one would have stepped out of the state of contradiction into something else again—perhaps cynicism or nihilism. To admit that the possibility of a correspondence between hope and history is no longer looked for would constitute a deliverance from the contradiction, eliminating one of the two contending elements, expectation. The courage to make such an admission—if it is courage—is rare.

To admit that they expect nothing, or that what they have claimed to expect was an insincere claim, is simply not an alternative for most human beings. As for communities, the moment of such a confession, even if it were feasible, would signal their end. Societies are organized around expectations.

In the state of contradiction, on the contrary, there is a determined concern to preserve expectation. Sensing that they are suspended over an abyss, that their expectations are no longer credible, individuals and societies in a state of contradiction make all the more effort to vindicate their aspirations. Primarily they do this by allowing their expectations to persist without meeting the actualities of experience. In fact, everything is done to prevent such an encounter. Expectation and experience are divorced, and each is given an independent role: the speeches of political candidates on the one hand, the news broadcasts on the other. Dialogue is replaced by two monologues. Somehow, people in societies where such a thing occurs are able to keep the monologues from being overheard by one another. There is a tacit agreement among the citizens to refrain from giving in to the natural demand for a confrontation.

On the surface, individuals or societies in which this state pertains may even seem strangely calm. This calm is in reality not difficult to explain. Living in the same house, running into each other at every turn, expectancy and experience engage in noisy conflict. When they are divorced and apart, the pain that is present in the state of conflict seems to have been healed. In reality it has only been replaced by a suffering more insidious.

The suffering engendered by the state of contradiction, however, does not fall most conspicuously upon those who invoke the divorce of expectation and experience as a way of preserving themselves. It is borne, rather, by the relatively innocent, who for one reason or another find themselves in proximity to the deceivers. They become the pathetic victims of the deception. Their agony is the price that is paid for the superficial calm of the others, who will do anything to avoid facing the contradiction in which they are living.

The Repressive Society

The whole world suffers today because its most powerful societies desperately retain expectations that can no longer stand the test of experience.

These expectations belong to an image of man inherited by the dominant societies from their past. According to that image, man is a high and noble being, and history is the progressive march toward the realization of his grandeur. But the characteristic experience of human beings within these societies is marked, increasingly, by intimations of man's apparent ignominy and the meaninglessness of the historical process.

From the social sciences it is possible to derive a language to use to discuss the suffering that results from this contradiction. But it is better to speak concretely. Modern history has provided many names for this suffering, the most notorious of which are Auschwitz and Hiroshima. No doubt other specific terms will arise. In the immediate past—if it is past—the suffering that arises from the contradiction at the heart of Western civilization bears the name Vietnam. Whoever makes it his business to understand today who man is must reckon with that name. The responsibility to do so, as some in our society are insisting, has only increased with the reputed cessation of overt warfare in Southeast Asia.

To fathom something of the depths of the suffering called Vietnam it is necessary to grasp the nuances of what we have designated a state of contradiction. In such a state the most decisive factor is *the energetic nonrecognition of the state itself.* Undoubtedly there would be suffering in the world even if its most powerful societies recognized the contradiction between expectation and experience. But it would be a quite different kind of suffering from that signified in the term Vietnam. As it is, the great bulk of human physical suffering in our time bears the unmistakable earmark of a spiritual sickness in the heart of the world's controlling empires. It can be traced without difficulty to concentrated efforts within these empires to keep from themselves the truth of their own condition.

The nonrecognition of something so basic as the gulf between our expectations and our experience is not easily managed. It requires tremendous effort to prevent these two fundamental constituents of life from seeking each other out. To maintain even an appearance of congruity requires great expenditures of material and psychic energy. To present expectations as though they were being realized, and, on the other hand, to minimize daily evidence of degradation and disintegration—such things cannot be successfully achieved without vast outlays of energy and resources (to wit: the space programs of the societies in question).

A terminally ill person who steadfastly refuses to alter his expectations in the light of his new existential situation consumes most of his energy in the effort to keep himself from acknowledging his contradictory state. He cannot for long hide from himself the fact that something is wrong. But to save himself from the prospect that *his expectations themselves are wrong,* and may always have been so, he flails out at those around him—doctors, friends, members of his family, even perfect strangers. He must locate the source of the problem outside himself. It is a well-known phenomenon in the psychology of illness.

Is there any reason to suppose that matters differ with the macrocosm? Would not a society engaged in the consuming task of hiding from its own self-destruction be a potentially paranoid society? Would not the need to preserve its own expectations intact drive it to seek the destroyer beyond its own horizons? And if it should be perhaps "the most advanced technological society ever to have been," would it not be a society greatly to be feared? Might not it prove, in fact, with a dread kind of inevitability, to be a society at war?

Goaded by such reflections, many of the most sensitive students of Western civilization have reached a conclusion: there is no more urgent political vocation today than to help Western man come to terms with the contradiction in which he lives. They rightly discern that, compared with the enormity of that task, most of the involvements to which we are urged by political activism are superficial. Political activity that does not concern itself concretely with this fundamental contradiction and its nonrecognition must be deemed irrelevant. Unless Western man in general and (let us say at once!) North American man in particular can be made aware of this contradiction, no conceivable alterations in the economic or political structures of his society will be able to save the world from the consequences of his anxiety and self-loathing.

All the same, many of the sensitive who have grasped these strange connections are lacking in that final degree of sensitivity to the human condition which makes for true wisdom. They are keen to bring the guilty to a clear, clean confession of their guilt: let the polluters acknowledge their polluting, and the wasters of earth's resources their greed, and the educators their insincerity, and the intellectuals their mediocrity, and the politicians their opportunism! Let us all face squarely the emptiness of our rhetoric, the vacuity of our hope! Behind these cries for honesty and authenticity, noble as they are on occasion, there is a naïve assumption. They assume that the recognition of the contradictory state is itself redemptive.

What is not comprehended is that nonrecognition of contradiction is a way of dealing with contradiction. Whoever wants to bring our civilization to the point of realizing the discrepancy between its expectations and its experience must be prepared to offer another way of coping with the state of contradiction. For the sake of the race and the future, it is necessary that Western man's self-imposed blindfold be removed. But whoever sets out to remove it must have something in his hands to replace the blindfold. Mere recognition of the contradictory state is no solution. It could quite conceivably lead to a state worse than contradiction. Because there *is* a state worse than contradiction, and it is not far from the surface anywhere in the Western world today. Nietzsche, who understood all of this while our forebears were still dreaming their bright dreams, had good reason for fearing the nihilists, who expect nothing, more than the "last men," who blink and say that they have invented happiness.

Who can contemplate with ease the spectacle of a society no longer able to maintain even the *semblance* of expectancy? In theory, overt cynicism may be more readily challenged than the cynicism that lives behind a screen of well-rehearsed platitudes. But in practice? Even where expectations no longer inform experience at the level of economic policy-making and foreign relations; even where the internal laws of technological "advance" are no longer answerable to goals announced in the purple prose of industrialists; even where public leaders are no longer motivated by noble ideals—even *defunct* hopes, still propagated as though they were alive, can sometimes function as a rallying point for protest. So long as a people claims to believe in freedom, peace, and equality, it may be possible to call into question its thwarting of these qualities. The more it is driven by antithetical experience to accentuate its highest ideals, the more sensitive it may become to the criticism that its avowed goals are betrayed by its daily performance. On the other hand, an openly nihilistic society is prepared to recognize nothing except sheer power. Therefore whoever wishes to cure our society of its "hypocrisy" and replace its rhetoric with truth and self-knowledge must at least reckon with the prospect of a culture that has no "values" at all, but only violence.

The question facing the critic of the society in which a state of contradiction exists is not only whether he can open men's eyes but whether he can give them a reason for seeing.

Only a fool or a misanthrope could be satisfied with exposing to men the absurdity of their past and present. Whoever is wise, and cares for humanity, must offer men a way into the future.

Reduction to Monologue

Beyond repression, the next most common way of dealing with a contradiction is by dissolving one of its components. It is not surprising, then, that the two greatest contemporary systems of thought which have offered ways into the future are Marxism and existentialism. The fundamental genius of both systems is their ability convincingly to eliminate one or the other of the factors constituting the state of contradiction in which modern Western man lives.

Marxism resolves the contradiction between expectation and experience by eliminating experience in the dialogue of existence. Experience in this system is made consistent *a priori* with expectation. History can only confirm what the system defines as hope.

Official Marxism refuses to admit any dimension of radical negation within human experience as such. Since the experience of negation is evidently the characteristic experience of twentieth-century Western man, Marxism is obliged to account for it on environmental grounds. This obligation becomes embarrassing when the experience surfaces, as it continues relentlessly to do, within the Marxist state itself.

Marxism not only denies the experience of negation as a permanent feature of existence, it also denies that this experience inheres in some special sense in the modern vision, of which Marxism itself is of course a product. Rather, it insists that the experience of negation is the typical and inevitable consequence of a specific form of society, imposed on us by men and institutions enveloped in greed. It claims that the sense of futility testified to, for example, in the arts is native not to contemporary life as such but to life in those societies where men are alienated from one another by capital. It is a matter of "bourgeois decadence." Thus Marxism is able theoretically to retain the high expectations for man and history integral to the modern vision—and to retain them, indeed, in a form more extravagant than ever before. The way into the future, it announces, does not lie in the direction of obtaining more modest expectations. On the contrary! If the oppressive systems and institutions that have fouled our corporate life are discarded, the ideals of brotherhood, peace, and progress present in the best of our Renaissance tradition will prove more accessible than ever before.

Existentialism attacks the opposite component of the contradiction—expectation. Existentialism wants to save us—for what end it is difficult to say—by enabling us to reject the hopes we have been conditioned by our civilization to entertain. Contrary to common opinion, these expectations are not confined by existentialists to hopes associated with the tradition of Jerusalem. In any case, God had already ceased to inform the expectations of many in our culture before modern existentialism came on the scene. The expectations in question also belong to the tradition of Athens, revived in some form by the founders of the modern epoch. More particularly, these expectations have to do with man as the conscious center of a significance that precedes and transcends his existing. In its most consistent forms, existentialism insists that what men have called "essential" being is a construct superimposed on the raw stuff of existence in order to make it bearable. Whatever may be said about the past employment of this construct, it is no longer useful. It is experienced by honest modern men as quite untenable. One cannot be an "authentic" human being today if one pretends to be heir to an essence other than, greater than, and determinative of existence. The way to the future is open only for those who courageously dispense with the dream of essences and embrace existence in all of its indifference and objective purposelessness.

Marxism and existentialism are mortal enemies because each denies the reality of that element in the human dialogue which the other makes most of. They are united, however, in assuming that the way out of the contradiction into which our civilization has fallen is through the elimination of one of its constituents.[1] Both systems reduce the dialogue of experience and expectation to a monologue.

But a terrible price is paid by these systems for the solutions they offer. Their basic determination is right—namely, that the state of contradiction must be overcome. Humanity is probably being endangered more today by those who refuse to admit the contradiction than by those who insist on solving it. But solutions too, like overhasty surgery, can be dangerous. Too often the dilemma is overcome by removing not only the diseased part but the vital organ in which it is contained.

We have argued that *conflict* between expectancy and experience is vital. Without it existence becomes a static thing—no longer life, in fact. To resolve the state of contradiction by dissolving one of these conflicting elements is to rob existence of its dynamic. It may be admitted that sensitive representatives of both systems under discussion recognize this fact and adjust their thought accordingly. But the pull toward monologue is inherent in both systems. For the existentialist, hope inevitably tends to become unreal. No doubt this refers more directly to the specific historical hopes that have sustained Western man; but at bottom, consistent existentialism attacks the habit of hope as such. For the Marxist, what is unreal (or, more accurately, accidental and unnecessary) is the encounter with nothingness. Radical, ontological alienation is simply expelled from the account of life given by dogmatic Marxism. Actually, neither hope nor the experience of negation can be so easily dismissed from life, and there are both existentialists and Marxists who know it. But the very practice of responding to the state of contradiction by seeking to eliminate it drives to exaggeration. In the end, these accounts remove the distorted component not only from the problematic state but from life itself. The result is that the human condition is falsified which, especially when institutional-ized as in the case of official Marxism, becomes oppressive and even demonic.

The price paid by dogmatic Marxism for neutralizing experience is sheer irrelevance to the real problematic[2] of contemporary humanity. There is no better evidence of this irrelevance than that provided in those Western societies which have most consistently been adapted to the Marxist way. They maintain their exaggerated form of expectancy only by constructing the most artificial culture the world has ever known. It is a culture matched in this respect only by the most fanatical religious groups, past and present, to create ideal societies, and no doubt for comparable reasons. Those capable of giving the most sensitive accounts of actual human experience—artists and writers—have been systemati-cally controlled and suppressed in such societies. The one thing that cannot be permitted under this system of belief is that experience should have an independent and conflicting witness.

The strength of existentialism lies just at this point of official Marxism's great weakness. Existentialism gives a poignant and unflinching account of modern man's experience of the darkness. Experience in the existential-ist analysis is *not* neutral. Pain, "fall," "nausea" are inherent in it. Being is "being-towards-death" (Heidegger). To be human and to know it is to suffer: "Men die, and they are not happy" (Camus). Human suffering is more than the suffering of poverty, war, and inhumanity, which the Marxists have astutely chronicled. Existentialism points to a greater suffering which occurs in the depths of the human spirit. It knows that most of the physical suffering of mankind must be traced to this deeper malaise, especially in our own time. The spirit of modern man is dulled by his discovery of death. He has sometimes called this death the "death of God," because it is a death too overwhelming to be associated with a lesser being. The pious among the Christians took that announcement quite literally and became predictably defensive. They did not realize that the "death of God" reported by Nietzsche and the others was a way of speaking about the death of man—the discovery that "man as an idea is dead" (Wiesel).

> I looked anxiously around me: the present, nothing but the present. Furniture light and solid, rooted in its present, a table, a bed, a closet with a mirror—and me. The true nature of the present revealed itself: it was what exists, and all that was not present did not exist . . . : we have so much difficulty imagin-ing nothingness. Now I knew: things are entirely what they appear to be—and behind them . . . there is nothing.[3]

No Tree behind trees, no Justice to give substance to morality and make some deeds forever unjust, no Eternity behind time, no Man behind men.

Whatever must be said about its prescriptions for moving beyond the "nausea" of this discovery of the nihil, it is certain that existentialism has provided the most accurate statement of the characteristic spiritual experience of contemporary Western man. Obviously it is not, and it could not become, the official philosophy of our culture. This is evidenced by its conspicuous absence in the official halls of learning on this continent. But Karl Rahner and others are right in assuming that existentialism is nevertheless the *representative* philosophy of the age. No account of the human situation can afford to ignore it. Marxism suffers, as do many other versions of the human condition, because it has not come to terms with the existentialist report on the experience of modern man: namely, that he has not found existence positive, or merely neutral; rather, he finds it a relentless, gnawing negation of possibilities. Marxism offers a way into the future without taking seriously the present impasse.

Existentialism also pays an enormous price for its resolution of the contradiction. Is expectation any more susceptible to elimination than the experience of negation? Does "hope spring eternal" merely because we have been conditioned to hope by certain historical influences such as Christianity, the Enlightenment, the nineteenth century? Is man really capable of living *without* hope, as Camus once proposed we must? Is not the consequence of the loss of expectation exactly what Camus implied when he said that now the only legitimate "philosophical" question is whether suicide is the authentic response to existence? What besides that is the price for dispensing with the belief that man is somehow more than his acts? Experience alone does not produce the stuff out of which courage is made! The courage to "go on" (Beckett) depends on the prospect that something will occur that is not now, and does not seem inevitable. Again, are we ready to cease speaking about man, humanity—*der Mensch?* What sort of civilization could possibly emerge where it is no longer possible or permissible to assume these concepts which judge existing men and societies? If there is nothing but deed, nothing but the present, nothing but experience, nothing behind it all; if no "is" is there to bolster the "ought" of conscience but only the fear of anarchy and chaos, then is the way not clear for humanity and civilization? It should seek its way as quickly as possible back toward the primeval mud from which it emerged, as in the film play of Ionesco.[4]

If such a suggestion sounds merely literary, the observation of Nietzsche should be pondered carefully: Men will will nothing rather than have nothing to will. The will to oblivion is strong in the human race,

INTRODUCTION   31

especially when the species is confronted by what can seem insurmounta-
ble problems of survival, as is the case today. It can even be phrased in
attractive terms, as when it is associated with the new nature romanticism
born of the environmental crisis. Man is the problem; nature itself is pure;
let man immerse himself again in nature. In the words of Robinson
Jeffers:

> Turn outward, love things, not men, turn right away from
>   humanity,
> Let that doll lie. Consider if you like how the lilies grow . . .[5]

The thought appeals especially to these who are comfortably insulated
against the ravages of nature. The poor of the world, who live in greater
proximity to the mud, find it less convincing.

Against the existentialist elimination of expectancy, Marxism is right in
standing for the essential nature of hope. Apart from hope, there is no
chance for humanity. Existentialism is a sensitive account of modern
man's despair. But it does not provide a way into the future for man.
Certainly not for mankind, even though for some individual men it may
seem to open up a way beyond contradiction.

Both of these systems of thought are built on the nontheistic assumption
that man is alone. Existentialism is more consistently nontheistic than
Marxism, since it knows that if man is alone, it is no longer permitted
*pan*theistically to translate the gods that used to be above the historical
process into the historical process as such. The great question that
existentialism puts to Marxism is how the latter can dispense with
metaphysics and yet retain what is so patently a metaphysical basis for its
expectancy—i.e., the belief that the historical process itself is redemptive.
On the other hand, the very fact that Marxism seems to provide a way
into the future for many whose past experience precludes all hope throws
into question the existentialist determination that hope must be unlearned.

Something is missing in each of these accounts of the human condition.
Perhaps the reason why neither of them can be consistently or willingly
adopted by the majority in the Western world does not lie in their radical
social and moral consequences, after all, but in their being finally too
facile. In discounting one or another of the elements of the very
incongruity they seem to resolve, they limit their appeal to those who are
not living at the center of the contradiction. Perhaps it could be said that
they appeal more to the *victims* of Western man's contradictory state than
to those in whom that state is most acutely present. This seems especially
true of the Marxist alternative. Contrary to the expectations of Marx
himself, this alternative has been taken up by societies least representative

of the *spiritual* struggles of the modern epoch. In the same vein one must ask why existentialism has appealed to so few of those who have to assume responsibility in society. Why has it produced no political ethic? Wherever Marxist theory encounters the characteristic spiritual struggles of twentieth-century humanity, as in Czechoslovakia, it can survive freely only so long as it finds more convincing ways to speak about both human alienation and human transcendence than are provided in the official dogma. And wherever existentialism runs into elements of society where personal and political morality cannot be evaded (e.g., the resistance movement during World War II), it must introduce as ground for moral activity some sense of purpose, and will even go so far as to borrow this from the Marxists.

The Way of Transformation

What can be learned from observing the courses of Marxism and existentialism in the contemporary world? They have been able to offer men alternatives to the state of contradiction only at the expense of reducing man to something far less complex than he is. In effect, they save man from contradiction by persuading him that there is no contradiction. No real contradiction, but only one that has been created by historical circumstances and can be changed. But in eliminating one or the other of the factors constituting the contradictory state, these accounts of the human situation end in truncated versions of life.[6]

Is there a way to address the state of contradiction in which our civilization is caught, without falling into the trap of resolving it at the expense of the human soul? This study is based on the conviction that there is. Its aim must be, not the resolution of the contradictory state, but its transformation.

Logically, the most commendable approach to a contradiction must take seriously both of its constituents. If it is a genuine contradiction, it cannot be overcome by suppressing one of its elements, any more than by repressing the knowledge of both. Neither will succeed with a genuine contradiction. The only reasonable approach is to assume the reality of both elements, and to seek a more profound understanding of their sources and their relationship to each other. In popular introductions to formal logic, this approach is sometimes labeled "Taking the Bull by the Horns." It is the decision to descend into the heart of the contradiction itself. At the core of the dilemma, a new comprehension of its causes may come into view, and a way beyond the impasse opened up. In assuming this posture in relation to any dilemma, one risks the concomitant possibility that the contradiction is unresolvable. Nevertheless one proceeds in the hope that, by deeper exposure to it, it could be transformed and become creative of new possibilities.

To apply this logic to our situation it means, concretely, a readiness to take seriously the reality of both the expectations and the experiences of our culture. This must be done not only at the theoretical level but in the most practical sense. Neither expectations nor experiences are merely indefinite, mutually contending qualities of the human spirit. They are always manifest in particularities. To speak quite empirically, the decision to follow the way of transformation means a readiness to believe that most people in our culture still entertain great expectations for man and history, as these have been enunciated in the modern vision. On the other side, it means to take seriously that experienced negation which so threatens the expectations of persons in our society that the majority can only cope with life by repressing the dialogue.

Here and there it is fashionably cynical to assert that all belief in man's vocation to responsibility, dignity, and integrity has become "sheer rhetoric" in our time. If that were so, it would follow that whatever shock is being registered in our culture over the daily revelations of human insignificance and lowness must also be conjured up. If both of these things are true, then it would follow that what we have in this society is no contradiction at all, but merely a hangover of moral convention from another era. All that would remain, in that case, would be to demonstrate how the *seeming* contradiction will disappear as soon as our expectations have been adjusted to the new ontology—as outlined, perhaps, by a Desmond Morris!

Wise and sensitive persons live on the edge of that cynicism today. Listening to the calculated mediocrities of politicians and the thinly disguised nihilism of military and industrial spokesmen, even hardened optimists find themselves challenged by it. When before in history have so many good human beings been so tempted to find solace in a permanent retreat from history? And in an age when most men suspect that there is no place beyond history to retreat to!

In the last analysis, the cynic's account of our situation is also implausible. The notion that our "great expectations" are held *only* rhetorically—i.e., hypocritically—is simply not adequate to explain the intensity of our repression of everything that would bring us face to face with the contradiction of those expectations in everyday experience. Thousands are in jails and in jeopardy today on account of our desperate need to repress this contradictory state. Such intensity cannot be sustained by "sheer rhetoric." The posture called hypocrisy stoops neither to repression nor to passion, for it values nothing. As a way of attempting to cope with contradiction, repression exists only where something is still seriously valued. No astute observer of our culture could doubt that there is a great deal of empty rhetoric abroad. But there is also much desperate rhetoric. If there is hypocrisy in it, it is a hypocrisy that can still be made to feel shame (as Watergate demonstrated in its way). Behind this hypocrisy lies the anxious attempt of men and women to retain some vestige of the vision that inspired the builders, or at least the fear of the awful abyss of nothingness which opens up if some sort of vision is *not* sustained. Only because the expectations bequeathed to us by the framers of the modern vision persist, however improbable their realization becomes, are the events of the present so shocking to contemporary man. So shocking that they must be swept under the carpet, only to emerge in other grim corners of our superficially clean domicile—in Vietnam.

Every genuine attempt to save our civilization from the final humiliation of man inherent in the state of contradiction begins in recognizing this state as a distorted form of a conflict that belongs to the human condition. It is not wrong that men should entertain great expectations; nor is it unusual that their expectations should be called in question by their experiences. The distortion consists, rather, in the fact that the confrontation of what *is* and what is hoped for has been forestalled. All who want to avoid the ultimate degradation of the contradictory state must seek a means whereby that encounter can be reopened. An atmosphere must be created in which the anxiety that has closed off this dialogue might find the courage to resume it. Only in this way can the state of contradiction be transformed into a state of creative conflict.

Christianity has been discounted by many, no doubt by the majority, in the modern Western world. There are many good reasons why this has happened. In general, the reasons could be gathered up into a single observation: *Christianity ceased to be a forum for the meeting of experience and expectancy.*

Accordingly, the confronting question of this study is: Can Christianity provide for a new and creative meeting of these two elements whose dialogue is basic to human life and culture? What would be necessary by way of the transformation of *Christianity* for such a thing to occur?

These questions are not asked of Christianity in general, or of contemporary culture at large. While they imply the larger context, they are asked with specific reference to the Christianity and culture of the North American continent. The North American continent represents a special kind of problematic in connection with the question under discussion. This continent is the place where the expectations of the modern epoch were supposed to have been realized most fully; at the same time, it is the place where human beings seem least able and willing to face the contradiction of those expectations vouchsafed to them in their experiences. To abbreviate: it is the society whose activities have somehow focused in "Vietnam." Moreover, the Christianity of this continent has been notoriously incapable of providing an arena for the conflict of experience and expectation—largely because it has been so exclusively identified with the expectations of modernity.

Related to this is another reason for concentrating on North America: What happens in and to this continent today happens in and to the rest of the world. North America, which is most representative of the spirit of the modern experiment and at the same time the most complexly problematic society in the contemporary world, must become the focus of interest for all who address the possibility of salvation in a circumscribed planet. Here the expectations of the modern spirit came to rest, like the dove out of Noah's ark. Here these expectations have been allowed time to grow and flourish. And here they are bearing bitter offspring. Only from within the life of this continent is it possible to explore the failure of the modern vision, to come to know the darkness that it left out of account, and to seek the light that may shine in that deeper darkness.

PART ONE

POSITIVE CHRISTIANITY
AND THE EXPERIENCE
OF NEGATION

THE ARGUMENT

THE VISION that inspired North American society from the beginning has been reduced to an official philosophy. We may call it the positive outlook. As such, it is maintained at the level of exhortation and public rhetoric: we are an officially optimistic society. But the vision from which this "national philosophy of optimism" [1] was extracted has all but vanished. What remains—the sentiment, the imperative, the drummed-up determination to think positively—is wholly incapable of generating sufficient confidence to deliver us from the crisis of humanity in which we find ourselves, or even to face it. As we are driven by forces no longer answerable to any controlling vision, our most characteristic experience, the official optimism notwithstanding, is one of impending catastrophe, disintegration, chaos, negation. Of all earth's peoples we, the people of the New World, are least capable of encountering this abyss. Nothing in our cultural heritage, not the vision itself, certainly not the puerile and lifeless extract in which the vision has been transmitted to us, has prepared us for such an encounter. On the contrary, the thrust of that heritage has encouraged us to indulge our sense of expectancy along lines so unqualifiedly positive that no negative, not death itself, can be seriously admitted at the conscious level. The mere suspicion of an abiding negative has been enough to disqualify many who were regarded in other times or places as great and noble minds. Generation after generation, we have been admonished to think positively. We expurgate the word "can't" from our vocabulary. Those most scorned by us have always been persons who thought it their duty to bear witness to the limits of human power—who "said it couldn't be done." How can a people nurtured on such an outlook contemplate an omega so devastating that, beside it, medieval visions of

39

the apocalypse, still being enclosed within a framework of meaning, appear almost quaint?

The sense of chaos and of an ending causes some among us to turn to the churches and religion. But the Christianity typical of our culture is incapable of providing a vantage point from which even to contemplate, let alone enter into, a future from which the radical negative can no longer be expelled. To be sure, this Christianity is obligated to announce itself as a message of consolation to the afflicted. But it is in reality so thoroughly identified with the official optimism of the culture that it is constitutionally incapable of entertaining the affliction with which man in our time is really afflicted. Insofar as it permits itself to glimpse the negative in human existence, it is in order ever and again to hand it over to a predictably triumphant positive. Thus it operates in a manner strictly continuous with the general optimism of the culture. Its special contribution, if it may still be said to have one, is to transform into possibilities the reputedly few areas of life that the technological society still experiences as limits. Where the human machine flounders, the divine may be given another chance; where technology fails, there is yet a little room for the *deus ex machina!*

In short, the primary function of this Christianity is repressive. For a certain class of people, it serves, for the time being, to ward off the full effects of the experience of negation. It offers remnants of the vision that inspired our pioneer ancestors, thus perpetuating the assumption that our problems are no more complex than theirs. In the midst of an increasingly circumscribed planet, it keeps before the eyes of anxious parents, businessmen, and schoolteachers the picture of a limitless universe in which "all things are possible"—with God, of course. One can argue plausibly that it is better to help people retain their illusions than let them fall into despair. That illusion is at least better than death. But the price of the illusions the churches of our society are helping to maintain is the death of other men and other societies. Besides, unless this changes, it can only be a matter of time before the death which comes of these illusions embraces also those who indulge in them. More important, why should any Christian permit faith to be given over to the service of *either* death *or* illusion?

The question is whether Christianity can sufficiently disengage from the positive outlook to discover an alternative role. Are we relegated by our own past performance on this continent, or perhaps by our entire tradition, to play the role of insulators against the harsh reality of evil in our world? Is the church inevitably a "zone of untruth"? Must we be the hucksters of expectations that are forever contradicted by experience? Are we bound to be on the side of illusion? Or is it still possible for us to discern in our tradition the stuff out of which that sort of hope is made which does not have to look away from death in order to find the courage to live?

That is a survey of the argument of this section. We turn now to its elaboration.

I

THE OFFICIALLY OPTIMISTIC SOCIETY

A New Image of Man

The positive outlook to which we are trying so desperately to cling today is the product of a new image of man. It was born in the darkness of the thirteenth and fourteenth centuries, emerged into view in the sixteenth and seventeenth, was formalized in the eighteenth and mechanized for production in the last century.

Paul Tillich frequently said that the nineteenth century ended on August 1, 1914. He meant that that image of man was shattered by the "guns of August." While that was no doubt true for many sensitive European intellectuals such as Tillich, it is by no means universally true. As Marxism and its success in Europe and elsewhere makes abundantly clear, the disillusionment that followed in the wake of World War I was not sufficiently powerful to prevent men from being enticed by the same dreams. In North America, where neither the first nor the second world war was felt as a blow to the optimistic image of man, it is only now beginning to be realized that we have been living on the basis of such an image. At the point of its demise, the point where it has become inappropriate, some of those who have lived out of that *imago hominis* are beginning to understand that it is, after all, an image: It is not eternal but historically conditioned. It is not universal but geographically conditioned. It is not absolute but relative to the aims of a specific people. And those aims are not above question.

This is one of the strange properties of an image of man. When it is truly operative, it comes into the minds of only a few of those in whom it works its spell that they are living according to an *imago hominis*. The vast

majority think that what they believe, value, plan for, and fear is simply
natural, human, axiomatic. It does not occur to them that there could be
other, quite different images of man. If such a thought does happen to
cross the minds of some in the heyday of a given image, it is a sign of
madness to wonder whether some other image of man might be superior.
But in times of changing images, an important minority come to know
themselves as the inheritors of other men's answers to the question, What is
man? Revolutions—real ones!—are the products of this recognition.

We are living now in such a time. What we call North America—or
more often simply America—is the product of an earlier period of
transition.

A new *imago hominis* emerged at about the same time the New World
came into prominence. It was indeed responsible for the "discovery" and
"development" of that new world, with man at the center. It was anthropocentric, replacing an *imago hominis* that was specifically theocentric.

But here it is necessary to issue a warning. However critical we may
have to become of the "modern" *imago hominis,* this criticism ought not to
be interpreted as a lament for the passing of the older, theocentric image of
man. It is a temptation today to look with a certain nostalgic longing on
the Middle Ages. This temptation is felt not only by the religious but often
more acutely by those who no longer affiliate with organized religion. It is
a continuation of that nineteenth-century spirit of Romanticism, late in
coming to our continent. Apprehensive of the destructive propensity of a
society based on technicized, autonomous rationality, this romantic spirit
looks to an earlier period for another view of what it means to be a
"rational animal." We do not castigate the romantic. It is sane and
necessary for men in our time to seek for wisdom in other times. It is
natural that many turn to the medieval period. But the Christian in
particular has to avoid the suggestion that he is calling for a return to the
theocentric universe of the pre-modern epoch. His criticism of modernity
must be based on a commitment that transcends whatever commitments to
and interests in specific historical periods he may have. In the last
analysis, he is permitted to judge the image of man dominant in his own
epoch only from the vantage point of a view of man that has been realized,
according to his belief, only once: in the man Jesus. He accepts and fosters
historical images of man to the extent that they *approximate* that *imago,* for
he believes that in that man he has glimpsed "essential manhood." He
rejects images of man when they do not approximate that *imago,* when they
prevent men from being *imago Dei,* when they distort and belittle authentic
humanity. A theocentric image of man is just as open to such distortion as

an anthropocentric one. Conversely, there is no reason why an anthropocentric image of man may not, under certain historical circumstances, be more acceptable to the Christian than a specifically theocentric *imago*.

To speak historically: There is much in the image of man which governed the Middle Ages that was true, beautiful, and good, from the standpoint of its approximation of the manhood revealed in Jesus. But no one who studies the Middle Ages carefully, particularly not the Christian, can mourn the passing of the so-called age of belief. For the vast majority, the image of man under which they labored had become dehumanizing. It may have been theocentric, but the question is: In *what* God did it center? For countless tens of thousands, this theocentric image of man guaranteed, before they were born, that they would never even approximate the manhood promised in the gospel of Jesus Christ. For a privileged few it may have *seemed* to offer a veritable Kingdom of God in history, but only by a grave distortion of the Biblical concept of the Kingdom. The line between the theonomous and the demonic is a very fine one.

The new *imago* was a revolt against the domination of man by divine/demonic powers, and their earthly representatives. Instead of envisaging man under the control of arbitrary, external forces, the new image declared him to be autonomous, the determiner of his own destiny. Many of those who articulated the new image regarded themselves as Christians. And why should we doubt their sincerity? To deliver man from bondage to a dehumanizing image of himself—does that not belong to the gospel? If in the name of the God who makes men free one chases away a God who enslaves—is that not a work of Christian reformation? Even if the two Gods are called by the same name?

What follows by way of criticism of the modern *imago hominis* does not insist that that image *was* wrong, but that it *is* wrong. It is wrong for us today. It has become in turn a destructive image of man. There were certain flaws in it from the beginning, as there probably are in all the images that men and societies acquire for themselves. They contain the seeds of their own destruction and the destruction of those who live by them. The wise man will have some awareness of the flaw, the destructive potential, in every image of man. Thus he will never give himself unreservedly to any historic *imago hominis* or to the institutions in which it finds expression. He will not remain aloof and untainted! He will rather be on guard concerning his own bright pictures of himself, so one-sided, so unambiguous, so appealing if the time is right, and yet so fraught with danger.

It is strange and sad that so few of those in whom the new image of man began to take form, though Christian, were able to manifest that perspective, that wisdom. It ought not to have been so difficult for them to see the flaw in the new *imago*. At the very center of it lies an idea which is at best questionable to Christian belief, and at worst the essence of sinful presumption: the idea of man's mastery of nature and history. Indeed, such a concept is questionable to our Greek as well as to our Judeo-Christian foundations. Naturally, its questionableness was not unnoticed. But it was noticed by the wrong people. Those who resisted the revolt against the theocentric image had vested interests in maintaining the old world view. Wise men who knew well enough the traditions of Athens and Jerusalem, in their zeal for the new, liberating vision, neglected to criticize the image of man they championed. Their statements sound to us exaggerated, naïvely heroic. Yet we recognize in them the very stuff out of which this continent was made. Anyone over forty years of age in North America has heard without disbelief—often from pulpits:

> I am the master of my fate;
> I am the captain of my soul.

What is still more pathetic is that so few of us over forty have found anything to replace the idea of mastery—or even to confront our own sense of uneasiness in the presence of continued reiterations of that notion.

WAS IT REALLY NEW?

Was the image of man as master of his environment in fact a new *imago hominis?* Is it not, after all, applicable to earlier periods—for example, to Roman civilization? May it not even be said from a theological point of view that it is as old as Adam? Has not man from the beginning sought autonomy, mastery? Did not the Hebrews understand long ago that the search for mastery was of the essence of man and of historical existence?

Certainly the search for mastery is as old as history. It must be regarded as a primary ingredient in historical existence. Moreover, only when that search for mastery has been in some measure successful is it possible to achieve the human community that we call civilization. Babylon, Egypt, and Rome came into being because men were able to master certain natural and historical forces militating against human community.

In saying that the image of man as master is the foundation of modern Western culture, we are not saying that it belongs exclusively to this period. We are saying that in the modern period something integral to the idea of mastery became believable for the first time. It became possible during that period for a sufficiently great number of men to see *in themselves* the potential for mastery, so that it could become the formative image for a whole culture.

The concept of mastery implies that it lies within the power of the one who claims mastery to do what he wills. Civilizations prior to the modern one depended, certainly, upon man's ability to master. But never before had men been able to regard their mastery as the direct application of their wills to nature. Until the modern epoch, mastery could only mean manipulation of the forces—supramundane forces—which *are* in the controlling position. There was always something contradictory in it, and that contradiction lies at the heart of all religions, from the most primitive animism to the sophisticated "great religions" of the world. The aim of religion, as the Bible is forever telling us, is quite clearly *human* mastery over events. But ironically, this mastery can only be attained by those who acknowledge the ultimate mastery of what lies beyond man's control.

It is not accurate, then, to apply the image of man in terms of mastery to all historical existence. It belongs in the strict sense only to that period—what we are calling modernity—in which men began to find it possible to believe their own mastery immediate and ultimate. It is one thing to desire mastery, and another to think oneself in possession of it.

How Did It Arise?

Why did the idea of mastery become believable and powerful enough at this time to exert itself as the foundational image of man?

There is no simple answer to this question. Every attempt to answer presupposes a greater ability to perceive and correlate the many details of life than is humanly possible. How do new images of man come into being, anyway? Obviously they do not happen all at once. Nor are they consciously produced or manufactured. Advertisers think they are *creating* images when they are merely elaborating an image big and subtle enough to include the whole social fabric of which their agencies are part. Do new images of man begin to take shape in the thought of a few great men, as some people think, and from those minds spread to ever-wider circles? Or is the beginning to be sought in more nebulous constellations of events, which weave strange new patterns before even the most sensitive minds begin to find words for them? Certainly it is possible to notice the effects of the advent of a new image of man: in philosophy, in social and political changes, perhaps above all in works of art. But when it comes to the primary cause of images, as with every other act of creation, there is great mystery.

Without presuming to explain that mystery, we may nevertheless draw closer to it by making three generalizations: (1) The new image of man arose in response to the failure of the image of man that dominated the Middle Ages. (2) It was inspired from the outset by a new awareness of man's position within the natural universe. (3) It implied from the first, and soon made explicit, a view of the relationship between man and God that was clearly different from both the medieval view of this relationship and the Biblical view.

1. It is unlikely that images of man are ever replaced, in either corporate or individual life, unless they begin to fail. With respect to epochal images of man, it is probable that a dominant *imago* must fail notoriously. Not only is there a deeply psychic resistance to change in man, but dominant images are always incarnated in conventions and institutions. And there are always vested interests in maintaining them intact.

This negative prerequisite for the image that finally found expression in the idea of mastery is certainly present in the experience of the people in whom the new *imago* emerged. It is to be observed especially in the Europe of the fourteenth century. It was an apocalyptic era comparable, as Barbara Tuchman thinks, to our own.[2] People thought they were living at the end of the world. And no wonder! One third of Europe was carried off by the black plague. All the systems of order were breaking down. In particular, the church had ceased to give cohesiveness to existence. "Yet," writes Dr. Tuchman, "amidst the disintegration were sprouting, invisible to contemporaries, the green shoots of the Renaissance to come. In human affairs as in nature, decay is compost for new growth."[3]

2. The positive impetus of the new image that grew out of the decay and death of the old is certainly very much associated with a new awareness of nature on man's part—particularly an awareness of order in nature. Nature was seen not through the eyes of the Romantic (that came later) but through the eyes of the investigator, the measurer. We are speaking about the beginning of the age of science.

Certain well-known discoveries were made. *We* could suppose that many of these discoveries—or at least the cumulative effect of them all—might have produced an image of man, not as master, but as one infinitely small in a vast and "indifferent" (Camus) universe. That we could suppose this only belies our own predilections as twentieth-century men. That is, it belies how far the image of man about which we are thinking has already disintegrated. For us it seems true that the overall influences of the discoveries of science have been humiliating. But far from producing such an effect in our forebears, the world described by Copernicus, Kepler, Galileo, Newton, and their successors filled men with awe. The awe referred not only—not even primarily—to the vastness of the universe but to the vastness of human potential for comprehending and directing this universal vastness. It is true that the Copernican revolution had the effect of removing man's *earth* from the center of the universe. At the same time, it had the salutary effect of putting man at the center. It is man who discovers such things, man who can measure the world and discern its order and use it to his own ends. Man, uniquely in all the universe, possesses mind. He must therefore in some wondrous way participate in the creative mind behind the order. "What a piece of work is man!"

It is man, not nature, who thus becomes the locus of particular mystery and curiosity. As for nature, it (increasingly the feminine personal pronoun gave way to the impersonal "it") is no longer something to be held in awe, to be feared. The demons and gods that still inhabited the forests and lakes of medieval men have been exorcised. The mystery has gone out of it. It can be measured, quantified, objectified—and used!

> She [Nature] is no mystery, for she worketh by motion and geometry. . . . [We] can chart these motions. Feel then as if you lived in a world which can be measured, weighed and mastered and confront it with audacity. (Hobbes.)[4]

> I perceived it to be possible to arrive at a knowledge highly useful in life, and in room of the speculative philosophy usually taught in the schools, to discover a practical, by means of which, knowing the force and action of fire, water, the stars, the heavens and all other bodies that surround us, as distinctly as we know the various crafts of our artisans, we might also apply them in the same way to all the uses to which they are adapted, and thus render ourselves the lords and possessors of nature. (Descartes.)[5]

Such statements about nature are unthinkable as utterances of medieval men. The sentiment they express is the presupposition of the entire modern experiment: man is undoubtedly also a creature, but he so transcends his environment as to be, in relation to it, a veritable divinity.

3. The corollary of this assumption was that the more it asserted itself, the more necessary it was to qualify the divinity of God. That qualification did not take the form of an outright rejection—not, at any rate, in the earliest stages. It would be a mistake to think that God was "edged out of the world" (Bonhoeffer) by the cynicism of a Voltaire or the skepticism of a Shakespeare. The journey of God to the periphery is not chronicled by Voltaire's wit or Shakespeare's tragedies. Rather, it is told in the prayers and sermons of those who were not at all satirical or tragic

in their accounts of life. They edged God out, not in the name of anything so crass as agnosticism, but precisely in the name of God! God had to become more "godly," that is, more transcendent, more remote and rational. The simple Yahweh of the Hebrews had to become "Jehoveh"— quite another being in fact, despite the innocent attempt of the English to transliterate the Hebrew word for "God." The *theos* of the Greek New Testament, who manifests himself in a suffering *anthropos,* became *deus*—a divine Augustus, a refined Zeus.

The result was an entirely new concept of God—though not so new as to be without antecedents. The antecedents, perhaps strangely reintroduced by late medieval Scholasticism, are easily traceable to Greek philosophy, notably to Aristotle. Without this new/old image of God, the new image of man could not have been sustained. They are interdependent. Man could only envisage himself as master if God's mastery were totally reinterpreted. So it was. The God of the Deists no longer exercises in the world what could be called mastery in anything like the immediate, active meaning of that word. He no longer interferes in his world. He has created it; and it may be said that he governs it—but no longer in Calvin's sense, as One who upholds it moment by moment, who exercises personal rule over its movements, who sometimes sets its laws aside. He governs it, rather, by eternal laws, inherent in its makeup. The world is predictable. It is self-sustaining. Hence man, in order to be the "lord and possessor of nature," does not have to settle for a derivative mastery which in the moment of its realization has to recognize the final mastery of the Other. Man's mastery is henceforth not dependent upon magic, or ritual, or prayer. Finally not even upon moral uprightness—but upon measurement. He can discern the eternal, steady workings of things and, as the superior creature, exercise an immediate authority *within* nature.

THE TELEOLOGICAL BASIS OF THE IMAGE

To understand not only the positive outlook but also its *disintegration,* it is necessary to notice a carry-over from the old image into the new one that was displacing it. (Do successive images of man as a rule reflect this carry-over phenomenon?) While the new *imago hominis* was in a real sense a frontal attack on the concept of divine providence, as conceived both in medieval theology and in the thought of the Reformers, at the same time it was deeply dependent upon certain consequences of belief in divine providence. The image of man as master was in fact a viable image of man only so long as men could still entertain those consequences. What follows should be regarded as an elaboration of that assertion.

In order for man to regard himself as master of his destiny, the God who acts in history—who interferes, who is Lord!—had to be edged out. Man could not imagine himself master and lord of nature and at the same time retain the image of a God who might stop the sun in its track or change the laws of life and death because of a father's sorrow. This image of man requires that God retire from active involvement (interference!) in the affairs of men. At the same time, it retains the reasonableness and the purposefulness which were formerly identified, not with the world as such, but with God's *will* for the creation. This reasonableness and purposeful-ness is now written into the creation itself. It is expressed in the laws of movement governing nature and history. This is the teleological basis of the new *imago hominis*. Without this basis, the whole thing becomes tenuous. It is essential to the *imago* not only that man is master of his environment but that his mastery is exercised within a reasonable, purposeful universe.

The decline of the positive outlook is precisely concomitant with the awareness that this was an assumption. The image of man as master is a workable, confident image only so long as the assumption that the universe is reasonable and purposeful is not seriously questioned. For it makes sense to regard ourselves as masters only if we can believe that what is to be mastered is worth mastering. Seventeenth- and eighteenth-century men could possess a feeling of tremendous exhilaration, sometimes a blatant delight, in wresting the world from the hands of the medieval and Biblical God, and claiming it as their own proper sphere of dominion. This already begins to darken in the nineteenth century. Twentieth-cen-tury man, who has experienced the "indifference" of the vast universe that seventeenth-century man began so gleefully to measure, can have no joy in mastery. He knows no other way of conducting himself in the world than according to the rubrics of this image. But he can have no joy in it. His joy is at best prefabricated, at worst masochistic and fundamentally malevolent. There is a world of difference between the ecstatic claims made for man by Alexander Pope and those emanating from the American astronauts and their speech writers. "What a piece of work is man!" differs markedly from the same theme as it is sung in the musical *Hair*. The affirmation of man's grandeur has become entirely subjective. It is no longer sustained by that horizon of meaning which transcends man's existing and knowing and guarantees that his existing and knowing are unique and full of purpose. From the perspective of the twentieth century, it is possible to discern an almost inevitable movement from seventeenth- and eighteenth-century Deism to the modern man's aware-ness of an empty universe and a lonely life. At first it only seems that meaning *(telos)* is being taken away from God, as the active, purposing Agent, and built into his creation. But as soon as that occurs, the creation itself is given a burden and task that Biblical theology never assigned it. It has to "prove itself." It has to demonstrate its own purposefulness. What occurs within it, whether natural or historical, has to bear witness over the long haul to this purpose. It has to give evidence of being "the best of all possible worlds."

If Voltaire is in some respects a very modern man, it is because he discerned, long before most of his actual contemporaries, that this is not the best of all possible worlds; that it cannot demonstrate, either from nature or from history, a consistent purposefulness.

From Providence to Progress

The particular form assumed by *telos* in its transfer from God to the universe was the doctrine of progress. As George Grant has said, the doctrine of progress is the secularized version of the doctrine of *providentia Dei*.[6]

But in the transfer of providence from God to the historical process as such something significant happened. The belief in divine providence always maintained the mystery of God's dealing with and in the world. To be sure, it was always the temptation of official religion, whether Judaic or Christian, to reduce this mystery to knowable laws. But as the prophetic tradition of Israel and the reforming movements of Christianity always insisted, the providential dealing of God with man never means that man will always experience what happens to him as "providential"! The ways of God with man are unaccountable, according to that tradition; they cannot be predicted. God will love: that is the only certainty. It is never known in advance *how* he will provide for the beloved. "God moves in a mysterious way His wonders to perform."

It was this element of mystery, of unpredictability, that was offensive to the ordered minds in which the new image of man was taking shape. The doctrine of progress derives from the Biblical doctrine of divine providence the linear view of history, history moving toward a goal that can be recognized as good. What the doctrine of progress eliminates from the Biblical concept of divine providence is the element of mystery.

More precisely, it eliminates the strange and recurrent Biblical notion that the purposes of the loving God are being worked out in events which for the most part appear devoid of purpose and frankly evil! Beside the Biblical story of a people led by divine providence into slavery, the

wilderness, exile, suffering, crucifixion, the following statement of Lord
Acton seems to emanate from another world altogether:

> This constancy of progress, or progress in the direction of
> organized and assured freedom, is the characteristic fact of
> modern history, and its tribute to the theory of Providence.[7]

Biblical theology envisages history moving toward a triumph of God, the
God who is *pro nobis* ("for us"). But it is not necessary to resort to the more
lurid apocalyptic sections of either Testament to appreciate that God's
liberating triumph in our behalf may be something astonishingly different
from what we, according to our own lights, would readily recognize as
triumphant or liberating! Man's perfecting may certainly be a way of
speaking about the goal of the *providentia Dei* in Biblical terms. But when
Jesus gave this admonition, "Be perfect, as your heavenly Father is
perfect," he did not mean what Condorcet meant when he wrote, in the
full confidence of the eighteenth century:

> Nature has set no term to the perfection of human faculties. . . .
> The perfectibility of man is truly infinite; and . . . the progress
> of this perfectibility, from now on independent of any power that
> might wish to halt it, has no other limit than the duration of the
> globe itself upon which nature has cast us.[8]

The reinterpreted teleological basis for the new image of man leaves no
room for ambiguity or paradox. Progress is implicit in historical existence.
It is obvious, and it is assured!

PROGRESS AND WORK: A CONTRADICTION?

But if progress is assured, how are we to account for the clarion call to
work which permeates the thought of this period and is integral to the
whole idea of mastery? Does the new age herald *inevitable* salvation
through history, or does it call for men who will take their salvation into
their own hands and create it, amost, out of nothing? Is the "New World,"
America, in which this new age is going to occur, the scene of a new
beginning of creative cosmic forces transcending man's will and act? Or is
it a *tabula rasa* where man himself, no longer fettered by transcendent
powers either supramundane or mundane, will take his destiny by might
and right? Both themes are present. They can be heard, for example, in
this statement of Saint-Simon:

> The imagination of the poets placed the Golden Age in the
> cradle of mankind, in the ignorance and brutality of earlier

times. It is rather the Iron Age which should be relegated there. The Golden Age of the human species is not behind us, it is before us. It lies in the perfection of the social order. Our fathers did not see it at all. Our children will one day arrive there. It is for us to clear the path.[9]

Here, as in other statements already cited, is certainty of progress. It is fixed, inevitable: "Our children will one day arrive there." A kind of determinism is presupposed, which works in man's favor. It is hardly consistent with the popular conception of determinism or fate, which has a negative flavor. On the other hand, there is a clearly voluntaristic ring in the statement of Saint-Simon. One hears the characteristic call to responsibility, to mastery: "It is for us to clear the path."

That call is of the very essence of North America. The concept of preparing the way—the very metaphor of "clearing"—belongs to our experience. It is not possible to read our history books without running into it on every page. It still rings out, a clarion call from every high school valedictory address. But if nothing can stand in the way of that "Golden Age"—one wants to ask Saint-Simon—then why is it necessary to issue such a call, and to do so with such insistence and (today) desperation?

This contradiction between the deterministic and voluntaristic assumptions of the new *imago* touches our culture at every point. Modern Western man in general, and in particular North American man, has displayed a tremendous uncertainty in this respect. He cannot seem to make up his mind whether he is simply selected for greatness or whether he must work to attain it.[10]

There is, however, a certain logic in the relationship between the doctrine of progress and the doctrine of work. In the attempt to trace that logic, we may expose ourselves to the very essence of the positive outlook to which the new image of man gave rise, as well as to the basic cause of its present penury.

The doctrine of work has been an extremely powerful influence in our culture. It is almost impossible for persons whose roots are in North America to experience real leisure—in spite of the fact that, by comparison with most other peoples of the earth today, we have abundant "free time." [11] At least in terms of public notice—exhortation, education, talk—North Americans have seemed to emphasize the voluntaristic side of the image of man as master. "Work, for the night is coming"—incidentally a somewhat somber corollary: the laborer is goaded not only by the thought of reward but also by the reflection that his work must come to an end, or even that without his work chaos (the night) will take over. That emphasis, however, belongs more to the medieval than to the modern doctrine of work. It is carried over, as elements frequently are, by cultic associations. The more characteristically modern (and certainly North American) emphasis was positive: work will be rewarded!

There are a number of reasons for this apparent stress upon the doctrine of work in North America. For one thing, our culture is more the product of the new image of man than its producer. Few of those who engaged in the actual work of "clearing" on this continent participated, at the conscious level, in formulating the ideological basis of their work. The exhortation to work, the feeling for work's benefits, and the work itself have always characterized our continental experience more than has reflection on its philosophical or religious foundations. Moreover the ideological foundations of the call to work are questionable. This has meant that *contemporary* North Americans are apt to hear nothing besides the exhortation to work, for in the contemporary scene here, the questionableness of work's ideological basis is even more conspicuous.

The result of this vociferous emphasis on work obscures the importance of the other side of the matter, i.e., the deterministic basis of our culture. We are prone to believe that while earlier civilizations waited for the gods to act, our civilization has been founded on the principle of free, responsible human activity. It is as if the new image of man involved a simple transferral of power and initiative from the divine to the human agent. In fact, that is not at all the case. What made "North America" was not a new vision of man only, but a new idea of history. Conjuring up the typical pictures of our pioneers—sturdy men with axes clearing the forests; courageous women facing the perils of the wilderness, etc.—we forget that the vision which put confidence in their muscles and courage in their hearts was one that transcended their own individual efforts at "clearing." They saw themselves as part of a process. The same thing can be said, incidentally, of the equally sturdy and confident "workers" who are depicted in the official art of the Communist world—and for the same reasons! Not man's ingenuity and power to direct history toward a noble goal, but history's inevitable movement toward a goal thoroughly beneficial to man: that is what lies behind all this endeavor. "The dominant note in modern culture," wrote Niebuhr, "is not so much confidence in reason as faith in history. The conception of a redemptive history informs the most diverse forms of modern culture.[12]

It is instructive to regard the relationship of these two motifs, progress and work, as analogous to the relationship between gospel and law in Christian theology. The analogy is not arbitrary, since the idea of progress was nothing less than a "gospel" which virtually replaced the gospel of divine, providential grace.

In Christian belief, the gospel of the prior, freeing love of God gives the possibility of obedience to the "new" law of love for the neighbor. The law is "new" only in the sense that the condition necessary for obeying it—viz., the freeing from self-love—has been newly given in the act of God in Christ. Similarly, the "gospel" of historical progress functioned as the condition (the indicative) on which the exhortation to work (the imperative) could be issued with a certain conviction. The call to work is to the religion of progress what the call to discipleship is to the gospel of Christ. The commandment is to "make good" what has been and is being achieved, to realize what has been and is being realized. "Be what you are!" History is moving toward a glorification of man. The exhortation to work merely urges man to take upon himself the responsibility (or "the burden") of mastery for which history has selected him.

The analogy with gospel and law is, however, by no means satisfactory. It breaks down at many points, particularly because the context of the new "gospel" no longer is relational but is impersonal. What saves the Christian dialectic of gospel and law from contradiction is that it can only maintain itself authentically as a second-best way of describing the paradox of the divine-human relationship: i.e., God wants to be gracious to man without annihilating man's will. The Biblical dialectic is first of all a dialogue. In the dialectic of progress and work, however, the relational context has been removed. We are dealing, not on the level of "I and Thou," but on the level of impersonal forces. No matter how theoretically compatible these two motifs may be made to sound, they were never quite compatible in life.

One thing the analogy of gospel and law can clarify, however, is the extent to which priority belongs to the concept of progress. It is the metaphysic presupposed by the ethic of work. It is the "gospel" out of which man is able to derive a new enthusiasm for his own efforts. The pioneer with his ax in the endless forests pauses: life is hard, the forest seems limitless, infinite. Is it worth it? But he perseveres. For he remembers the ends toward which he is working. Probably he expresses this memory in religious, even in specifically Christian terms. But what he is expressing is nonetheless the doctrine of progress. That was the cult that built our culture. Work becomes problematic only in the contemporary period, when the cult of progress is in question.

THE DETERMINISTIC ROOTS OF THE POSITIVE OUTLOOK

For various reasons—some obvious, others obscure—optimism is normally associated with faith in man's capacity for overcoming obstacles, finding a way through complexities to simple goodness, or at least making the best of things. Pessimists, on the contrary, draw attention to man's propensity to evil, to his weakness, selfishness, and egotism. In short, one's attitude toward *man* and his potentialities determines whether one should be classified an optimist or a pessimist. For many, these are the only known possibilities!

This practice is called into question by the foregoing observations. For the conclusion to which we have been led is that the positive outlook that was the product of the new image of man as master is rooted not in a decision about man, but in a decision about time. The decision is that time unfolds an existence increasingly meaningful; the omega toward which the process moves is one that man can recognize as good, as wholly consistent with his best determination to master the earth. This decision about the character of time, i.e., "that historical development is a redemptive process," is the "single article of faith" which "has given diverse forms of modern culture the unity of a shared belief." [13] It has found expression in many ways: in rationalism, liberalism, romanticism, and communism. Some regard progress as gradual and steady, others think it sudden and revolutionary. But "the ultimate similarity between Marxist and bourgeois optimism, despite the provisional catastrophism of the former is, in fact, the most telling proof of the unity of modern culture." [14] *History* is redemptive.

But it is necessary to press beyond that observation to another. Many of the exponents of the new *imago hominis,* though not all, insist that this redemptive process in history is *inevitable.*

This means that the positive outlook depends, in its origins, upon a decision about a process that not only *transcends* man's will but that in effect *determines* it. Wherever such determinism is indulged, one has good reason to suspect that its adherents find themselves uneasy in contemplating the reliability of the human will. Thus it may be that the positive outlook has from the outset implied a negative assessment of man which was offset only by an exaggerated faith in the progressive movement of time. Such a view is essentially religious and carries far more "orthodox" Christianity than is usually admitted by secular exponents of progress! Whether such a negative assessment of man was assumed or not, it is impossible to ignore the inevitability of progress for the whole *imago.* As Robert Heilbroner has observed:

> The idea of the inevitability of progress sheds an important light on the philosophy of optimism. . . . It makes evident the fact that a hopeful orientation toward the future did not emerge solely from confidence in man's unaided ability to shape his own destiny. On the contrary, it came with the growth of historic forces which promised to shape his destiny for him. It was the dynamic potential of technology and of democratic aspiration, brought to fruition within a self-sustaining mechanism for economic growth, which first opened the future to optimistic expectation; and further yet it was the very blindness, the determinism of these forces which fortified men's faith in them.[15]

Heilbroner even raises the question whether optimism does not always depend on determinism:

> It is difficult to conceive of an optimistic philosophy which does not draw its faith from the ongoing momentum of historic forces. What optimism does assume about the future is not an *absence* of historic influence, but a *congeniality* of influence. Or to put it differently, a philosophy of optimism assumes that the direction in which we seek to venture as the heroic steersmen of our destiny will be compatible with the currents and tides set in motion by history's impersonal forces.[16]

Whether or not optimism always depends upon a deterministic base, it is indisputable that the positive outlook about which we are thinking was strongly informed by a sense of destiny. Even the voluntaristic expressions of this outlook, such as those of John Dewey, depended for their reception upon a favorable climate of opinion. That atmosphere was highly charged with the thought that history was moving inevitably toward the glorification of man.

Such was the end which gave zest to the age. So long as it could be envisaged, there was no need to apologize for the predominant language of exhortation which abounded, and which always *seems* to presuppose a voluntaristic base. Every North American whose childhood predates World War II knows there *was* an extraordinary amount of exhortation associated with the positive outlook. Children, citizens, educators, business executives, factory workers, nations, commonwealths, the white man, could be urged again and again, in ever more extravagant terms, to take up the responsibilities ("the burden") of mastery over nature and history. Editorials, novels, treatises, and sermons of the nineteenth century in particular are full of unadulterated exhortation. Part of the explanation for this is that the metaphysical basis of this world view was already beginning to give way. It is probably true that exhortation always increases in volume whenever the exhorters begin to be uncertain of their grounds! At the same time, by contemporary standards at least, we were all remarkably open to this exhortation. We did not deny it categorically, though we may have chafed under it sometimes. Children were obedient, laborers worked long hours and had few holidays, white men went off to India with their "burden." Surely it was not because men were then more docile than now. It was because the vision was still somehow real. For North Americans it continued to be real long after many sensitive (or "jaded") Europeans had abandoned it.

But every imperative requires an indicative; every command lives with an implicit, Why? If that Why? is no longer answered in the very atmosphere in which the command is given, then whoever commands must be ready to provide a reason.

Children today are not noticeably obedient; laborers are "overpaid and lazy" (*Time* magazine) and those who are sent off to civilize the East frequently return as drug addicts or in other ways demoralized, or sometimes even converted to Eastern ways! As can be seen everywhere (not least of all in the methods of warfare by means of which we are today giving expression to the white man's "burden"!), we have attained through advanced technology an apex of mastery which would have astonished even the most expectant of eighteenth-century prophets of the new era. Yet there is today, as never before in our history, and at every level, a great dis-ease. In accord with "the dictates of history" we have done all this—and hardly anyone can say convincingly what a phrase like "the dictates of history" could possibly mean! We are still urged on by the momentum of the past, and those institutions and persons who represent it. Now, we are to conquer space! The universe! But every command begs the question Why? from an increasing number of our people. Every achievement is full of irony—not least the achievements in space, as Norman Mailer so cleverly demonstrates.[17] In the words of George Grant: "Mastery comes at the same time as the recognition that horizons are only horizons. Most men, when they face that their purposes are not cosmically sustained, find that a darkness falls upon their wills." [18]

II

THE EXPERIENCE
OF NEGATION

An Omega Without an Alpha

We belong to a society that was assured it could hope. Hope would not disappoint us, for we were participants in a process and the end of the process was good. We belong to a people that was taught to think positively. We learned to eliminate radical negativism from our consciousness in a manner utterly unique in history. We did not dismiss the residue of evil in our midst; but we learned to dissociate this evil from our own essence, to believe that it would be eliminated, and to see ourselves in the role of its eliminators. The end of the process, where expectancy and experience would meet and embrace each other, was near. And it was good. Very good!

Suddenly the end we contemplate and by which we are drawn is not positive but negative, not light but darkness. It is not the point of departure for a wondrous new age of which the present has been merely an anticipation and preparation. Not a new beginning, but simply—the end: an omega without an alpha in it.

The New Omega

One thing has not changed: North America is still oriented toward the future. The future dominates our life. This can be seen in the advertisements of industries which promise that although technology may have introduced certain problems, technology will also save us from those problems. But the captivation of our thought by the future is to be seen even more tellingly where what appears on the surface is an apparently opposite preoccupation with the past. What "the conservatives" among us are really trying to conserve is not the past, but a vision of the future that belonged to the past. With the exception of certain minorities, let us remember, we have no past except the past that believed in that future. "The conservatives" want to preserve *that* "future" against the one that insists upon replacing it. *That* "future" was steeped in hope. The new future contemplates an omega which not only removes the substance of the hope but replaces it with the very data of despair. It is a future "shock"!

What is the end for us concretely today? What omega colors our expectation? Whether it means the end of civilization, or of the race, or of all life on earth, or of the planet itself, is doubtless important. Yet the psychological effect is not greatly altered by the specifics of the end envisaged. Unless a man can achieve the sort of dubious magnanimity that renders the perpetuation of his own species a matter of indifference to him (the silly boast of some of our more ecstatic ecologists), he will not find the contemplation of an end to human civilization or to the race less devastating than the prospect of a planet unable to support life of *any* kind. At least for the great majority of men in the West, the end of man raises the same questions as the end of life or of the planet.

The prospect of such an end is not only one of the many factors in our situation, it is the characteristic factor. Apart from it, much of our behavior is inexplicable—especially our painstaking and sometimes ludicrous repression of this "omega factor." Like children at play after the bell has rung, we have a peculiar intensity. In a way, everything continues as usual. But in reality everything is changed by the awareness that it will shortly be impossible to continue as usual. How could it be otherwise? For we have been conditioned by our whole continental experience to look to the future. All at once the question that appears on the horizon to which we have been looking so expectantly is the question, Does man have a future? Can man survive? We repress the question, but only as the children repress the memory of having heard just now the bell for their classes: with the dull awareness that it cannot be repressed for long. No doubt some are more and some less conscious of the new omega. There are countless ways of reacting, from panic to a programmed indifference. But this omega factor is the most conspicuous and unifying factor in our culture. It is shared by Middle Americans and hippies, hard-core conservatives and revolutionary groups, old and young, rich and poor.

Indeed, its presence is almost independent of our recognition or articulation of it. For by now the question concerning the future of man has objectified itself. It has overflowed the limits of human knowing and willing and has worked its way into the very fabric of the human environment. It is there in the air we breathe, in the water we drink. It is incarnate in our bodies and in the flesh of the creatures that sustain our bodies. It confronts us—in perhaps the most terrifying of all its forms—out of the eyes of our children. In a way that was not true for our forebears, the future dominates our life. The new omega is even more powerful than the old one, in which there was an implicit and desirable alpha.

The only forerunner of the new omega to have crossed the paths of most people on this continent has been some form of ancient or medieval religious visions of the Final Judgment. Our forefathers, whether religious or secular, had already reduced these visions either to art or to madness. The madness persisted, as madness will, in sectarian Christianity. It can be found in Protestant and Catholic orthodoxy even today, though in ever more modified and acceptable forms. But here in North America apocalypse was not very influential in our story as a people. It was recognized for what it really was: the remnants of a mythology of another civilization, a detail out of a previous *imago hominis.* Its queerest representatives, the strange, bearded, long-haired and robed figures, were never absent from our larger cities. Along with their signs announcing the end of the world, the whole conception could be dismissed with a smile by rational men in gray-flannel suits.

But suddenly thousands of such strange figures have appeared in our streets and parks. With or without signs, it doesn't matter: everything about them identifies with the apocalypse. To our utter dismay we have found them to be the sons and daughters of the rational men in gray-flannel suits.

Even more distressing for us, many of the eminently rational men in our society, whose credentials and clothing we cannot criticize, are writing the books, giving the lectures, and leading the parades by which these apocalyptic young have been influenced. The more paranoid among us naturally look for the menace behind the scenes. Naturally we find it in communism, drugs, and sexism. But the steadier and more reflective know that the question of the end is what lies in the background of much extravagant preoccupation with ideologies, drugs, and sex. Indeed, as Norman Mailer says, it is no longer as if the contemplation of the end were to be associated with insanity or abnormality; it has become the preoccupation of the sane:

A century devoted to the rationality of technique was also a century so irrational as to open in every mind the real possibility of global destruction. It was the first century in history which presented to sane and sober minds the fair chance that the century might not reach the end of its span.[19]

Reinhold Niebuhr had said the same thing in almost identical language.

Thus a century which was meant to achieve a democratic society of world-scope finds itself at its half-way mark uncertain about the possibility of avoiding a new conflict of such proportions as to leave the survival of mankind, or at least the survival of civilization, in doubt.[20]

Since Niebuhr wrote those words, another quarter of a century has elapsed. Far from providing evidence that his statement is exaggerated, it has merely expanded the terrifying character of the omega that we face. Now it includes not only the prospect of a final war, horribly magnified by new automated weapons, but a whole new dimension which may in some ways be more formative for us: the depletion of resources and the deterioration of the environment.

Can Man Survive?

One of the ways that men have of dealing with unmanageable problems is to reduce them to manageable proportions. This is eminently the case with those great, hardly imaginable threats which darken the horizons of today's world. The manner in which both the private and public sectors have recently fixed their moral and technical ardor upon the "pollution problem" reveals how reductionism, the most ancient of problem-solving techniques, can be used in the service of expectations no longer in touch with experience. It is therefore imperative to grasp that the question by which we are confronted today is indeed fundamental. It is not merely the question of pollution, but the question of survival. Can man survive? Will there be a future? We delude ourselves if we imagine that it is possible to get away with a less critical or less radical reading of the "signs of the times." The question indigenous to our era is the question of survival. It is as blunt, as basic, as that.

The temptation to regard the problem in less critical terms is almost too great. Behind it lies that optimism whose genius we have been attempting to fathom—the optimism of a people whose *Weltanschauung* has provided no point of reference for the prospect of such a crisis. This incapacity to meet so drastic a question has been aided by numerous other factors in our experience—most of which can be traced back to that same *Weltanschauung*.

Such a factor, for instance, is the very caution of our "scientific attitude" toward truth. It guarantees *a priori* that conclusions such as, "We face a crisis of survival," must be regarded as intemperate and high-strung. It is ironic that the scientists who have alerted us to the problems of the biosphere have almost without exception been able to do so only by forfeiting something of their reputations as scientists. For not only their colleagues but also the general public, well indoctrinated in the "scientific attitude," knows that science never draws conclusions about the totality. It is even doubtful whether the public is willing to grant any kind of social, political, or even moral function to science. The absolute objectivity of science is firmly assumed and regularly transferred to the scientist as a person. Is a scientist who takes up a cause credible as a scientist? If he takes up such causes as many ecologists and others have, he can easily seem to overstep altogether the limits of his knowing.

Another factor that tempts us to minimize our crisis lies in the compartmentalization of knowledge and reflection. It is not only among the scientists and intellectuals that specialization is manifest in our society. All of us have been indocrinated in that practice. We have been so conditioned to deal in facts, and to keep facts of various sorts from entering into contact with one another, that we are scarcely capable of drawing conclusions or making generalizations. We lack not only the symbols and language but also the imagination for comprehending "the whole." The question about survival is one that demands holistic thought.

A further barrier to forthright acknowledgment that we live with a crisis of survival is to be found in a fundamental assumption of the technological society. That assumption is that a "problem" must be defined from the vantage point of the technique, actual or potential, required for its solution. This assumption is deeply ingrained in our society. It is kept alive by the economic interests that benefit from it. It is really very difficult for many people in our society to reflect on problems that are not related to technique, or defy technical solution. An example is the problem of meaning, which is so significant for theological thought. The extent to which the "average man" has been able to eliminate the question of life's meaning from his consciousness has probably not been appreciated by most Christian intellectuals. As van Buren writes,

> There are . . . those, possibly the great majority of men today, who simply ignore the question, dismiss it, or even argue that it is illegitimate. The only questions men ask that are worth pursuing, for many today, are those which admit of clear answers. This attitude is part of what we have in mind when we use the word "secular" in a pejorative sense.[21]

Under these circumstances, it is not surprising that a great deal of human energy today is spent formulating the problematic of the future in ways that are less dramatic and alarming than the form in which we have stated it. So long as the crisis of the biosphere can be identified as the problem of a poisoned environment, limited resources, and even war, it can seem to admit of technical solutions. Thus no radical questioning of the *status quo* need accompany the admission of a problematic future. All that is needed is the wise application of technique, goaded into action by the rhetoric of responsibility. But as soon as the problem is linked with something more complex, like overpopulation, the crisis deepens. Some persons, it is true, are able to "solve" the population question also through technique—frequently without any recollection of the most ghastly experiments of our epoch in such problem-solving! Nonetheless, relative to the other great physical problems by which we are confronted, population has a way of conducting us into the dark places of our condition, where technology and the whole technocratic attitude toward existence are of no avail. As Garrett Hardin in his controversial essay "The Tragedy of the Commons" has rightly said, "The population problem cannot be solved in a technical way, any more than can the problem of winning the game of tick-tack-toe." [22]

We can reduce the problem of survival to its simpler constituents only at the level of conscious awareness. At the subconscious level, we live with more than enough data of despair to make us a conspicuously neurotic people. The mention of one or two facts about our physical situation brings to the surface our anxiety about the future. The report of an oil spill (an almost daily occurrence), or the outbreak of famine in a remote part of the world, or a crisis in the Middle East which invariably involves the great powers, can immediately conjure up in the minds of most persons the whole apocalyptic spectacle. Parents of small children cannot fail to contemplate that at the present rate of population increase the year 2026 marks the point at which—in theory—the population curve would begin to go straight up. (In practice, of course, such a thing could not happen; instead, nature would see to it long before 2026 that the world population was reduced!) Predictably, we have developed a kind of programmed indifference to much of the data of despair, particularly that associated with the pollution of the environment. We are no longer shocked to learn that cormorants off the coast of California are now laying eggs with no shells at all. Or that the breast milk of American mothers contains .2 parts per million of DDT, four times the safe level the Federal Government allows in cow's milk for human consumption. Or that a city like Montreal produces eight million pounds of garbage per day, much of it synthetic material which resists natural decay. Our very indifference to, and inactivity in the face of, such data constitutes perhaps the most serious aspect of the omega factor in our situation. Yet this is no genuine indifference. It is an apathy for which, both as individuals and as a people, we expend a great deal of energy. It is the very real recognition that we live within a crisis of survival that drives us to articulate our problematic in less frightening terms.

CAN MAN SURVIVE?

The new omega by which we are encountered is even greater, however, than the question of survival. That is, not only is it comprised of physical parts, it is also a spiritual question. The survival of the biological entity called *Homo sapiens* is one thing; the survival of the spirit of man that warranted his being called *Homo sapiens* is something else.

There are two key terms in the question about the future. So far, we have reflected only on one of them: "survive." We have been content to use that term in the biological sense to which our culture, ever since Darwin, has become accustomed. But the other term is infinitely more subtle: "man." Can *man* survive?

One of the great seers of our era, George Orwell, entered these words in his journal in 1940:

> Reading Mr. Malcolm Muggeridge's brilliant and depressing book, *The Thirties*, I thought of a rather cruel trick I once played on a wasp. He was sucking jam on my plate, and I cut him in half. He paid no attention, merely went on with his meal, while a tiny stream of jam trickled out of his severed oesophagus. Only when he tried to fly away did he grasp the dreadful thing that had happened to him. It is the same with modern man. The thing that has been cut away is his soul, and there was a period—twenty years, perhaps—during which he did not notice it.[23]

Some physical and social scientists have quite recently become concerned about the survival possibilities of the race and the planet. Another group of observers have for a much longer period of time been asking whether the species that our Western tradition has been pleased to name *Homo sapiens* has not already become extinct. Throughout this century and already in the preceding century, artists, dramatists, novelists, and some philosophers and theologians have asked whether it is any longer meaningful to speak of "man" (*der Mensch*). Can we presuppose when we use this term that we are speaking about the same being that Aristotle or Paul discussed? Some of the most influential of these "poets" would have us ponder whether the death of man has not already occurred. When we reflect on "the end," should we not perhaps speak *ex post facto?* May it not be a gratuitous question to ask whether man has a future?

We should not mistake this for poetic exaggeration. Such thoughts may appear surrealistic to those for whom realism has come to mean the most banal sort of empiricism. Is it not conceivable that the most *factual* kind of assessment of our period might name it a time in which the death of man had shaped the face of events?

If times are known by their most characteristic events (as they always have been), then it is not preposterous to propose that the death of man constitutes the rudimentary event by which our time is best chronicled. Or, as many have put it—rightly wishing to be historically concrete—ours is the time "after Auschwitz," "after Hiroshima." In an insightful variation, the Jewish novelist and scholar Elie Wiesel prefers to say, "between Auschwitz and Hiroshima":

> Our generation . . . is the generation of Auschwitz, or of Hiroshima, tomorrow's Hiroshima. The future frightens us, the past fills us with shame: and these two feelings, like those two events, are closely linked, like cause to effect. It is Auschwitz that will produce Hiroshima, and if the human race should perish by the nuclear bomb, this will be the punishment for Auschwitz, where, in the ashes, the hope of man was extinguished.

And he continues: "At Auschwitz, *not only man died, but also the idea of man*. . . . It was its own heart the world incarcerated at Auschwitz." [24]

So Wiesel has one of his protagonists cry, "There are no more men . . . !":

> "We are living in a time of madness. . . . It's a universal eclipse. Everything is falling apart; past, future, present, hope, humanity, progress, all these are nothing but words. Are you sure that there is a tomorrow? No, tomorrow has already been, is already extinguished. Time only exists in the measure to which man is there to endure or bless or deny. But there are no more men. . . . Here and there, a few, but they are hiding in caves, like frightened animals, while the others mistake themselves for gods because they are thirsty for blood." [25]

For a few witnesses like Wiesel the holocaust is regarded as an event of revelatory significance on the order of Sinai.[26] Among the majority, including many Jews, the names of Auschwitz, Dachau, Buchenwald, and the other extermination *(Entwesung!)*[27] camps of the Nazis are already almost forgotten. Many of the young today hardly recognize those names. That in itself may speak more eloquently than anything about the death of the human spirit. It is possible now in dictionaries of the English language to discover the term "extermination camp" defined without any reference whatsoever to those specific historical names: it has become a species.

Even if the symbolic and historic significance of those names has been lost (or was never comprehended in the first place, as is more likely the case) after a mere two decades, one has to reckon with the indelible connection between what transpired there and what has transpired since 1945: not only the obvious connections such as the racial dimension of the "American" activity in Southeast Asia and elsewhere but also those which are far more significant for the question of North American identity. Marcuse has identified these latter succinctly:

> Auschwitz continues to haunt, not the memory but the accomplishments of man—the space flights; the rockets and missiles; the "labyrinthine basement under the Snack Bar"; the pretty electronic plants, clean, hygienic, and with flower beds. . . . This is the setting in which the great human achievements of science, medicine, technology take place.[28]

In the same passage, significantly, Marcuse says something that may be unique in the annals of Marxist social commentary: "The real face of our times shows in Samuel Beckett's novels." His judgment was confirmed by Beckett's reception of the Nobel prize for literature in 1969. The significance of this award can hardly be overestimated. Anyone wanting to enter deeply into the problematic of our era could do no better than to contemplate that in the same year in which men walked on the surface of the moon, the most coveted award in the art of writing was presented to one who "had become the laureate of an age that feels suffocated by its own desolating sense of nothingness." [29]

There are many ways of dying. Biological death is only one of them. The death of expectancy, about which we reflected in the introductory statement, is a death far more terrible. The societies described in Huxley's *Brave New World,* Orwell's *1984,* Vonnegut's *Player Piano,* Bradbury's *Fahrenheit 451,* Frayne's *A Very Private Life,* and, the earliest and in many ways the best of this literature, Zamiatin's *We,* are societies that have managed remarkably well to avoid the final holocaust. They have even created what too many in our own culture should regard as almost perfect states: expectancy has been satiated by experience! But this has been achieved only because the spirit of man has been "cut away."

The new omega contains dimensions that are scarcely touched by the term "survival." Any attempt to reduce the omega factor to a purely quantitative one is either naïve or devious. At very least, the omega we encounter on our horizon raises the question not only of the *possibility* of survival but of the *quality* of survival. The scientist René Dubos, who grasps our predicament at that level better than most scientists, states it bluntly:

> My own view of man as a biological animal suggests that something worse than extinction is in store for us. Man will survive as a species for one reason: He can adapt to almost anything. I am sure we can adapt to the dirt, pollution and noise of a New York or Tokyo. But that is the real tragedy—we can adapt to it. It is not man the ecological crisis threatens to destroy but the quality of human life, the attributes that make human life different from animal life.[30]

Finally: we have not begun to appreciate the depths of the new omega factor until it has dawned upon us that precisely in man's attempts to meet and to solve some of his problems he may be abetting his own demise. This is so especially of the great physical problems usually associated with the word "survival." In his very effort to prevent an ending, he may bring about an end to man—to humanity—at least as abhorrent as death by war or famine. "The optimistic views [of the future] on the one hand and the gloomy ones on the other," says Josef Pieper, "cannot be separated so unequivocally as we may think. For example, it might be that the very success of the great humanitarian plans for a 'fulfilment society' is the more to be feared than their failure." [31]

What if, in order to save the bodies of men, it were necessary to strangle whatever the traditions of Athens and Jersualem have meant by their souls? Or perhaps the question should be stated in this more specific manner: What would sane men have to think about a society that instituted programs designed to alleviate the physical suffering of men *without so much as asking whether those very programs violated anything integral to man the spirit?* Might not the sane man be led to conclude that that society had indeed already submerged itself in death?

The Question Within the Question

Sometimes it is objected that the question about the end of mankind and of the world of man is not different in kind from the question that is faced by every thoughtful man about his own end. Does it make any difference, it is asked, whether a man is confronted by the end of his own participation in earthly existence or the end of earthly existence as such? In either case, it is claimed, a man has to come to terms with the omega factor.

That objection does not take into account the question that the prospect of the end of the world, or of the species, or of civilization, raises. It is the question of the *meaning* of historical existence which is not raised when the end in view is individual death. This is not for a moment to suggest that the question of meaning is *absent* from the contemplation of personal death, or of the fact of death in general. But the prospect of history coming to an end, whether with a "bang" or a "whimper," an end that is not a consummation, introduces a whole new dimension. It raises the question of meaning in existence in a way that it is not raised by the inevitability of one's own demise or by the phenomenon of death as such.

Indeed, so long as the history of mankind could be thought to be moving toward a *positive* omega, the individual facing his own death could take a certain comfort, perhaps even pride, in the belief that his life was contributing to that larger cause: "Our fathers did not see it at all. Our children will one day arrive there. It is for us to clear the path." [32] Purpose was visited upon the lives of individual men, who must all die, by the greater purpose of human history and destiny in which all were participants. Even today, wherever the concept of a meaningful human destiny is still alive, individuals can face their own ends with something like composure. Illustrations of this can be found not only among the religious, but in the post-religious world as well. In Marxist China, for example, the parable is told of a man who went out with buckets to remove a mountain that was in the way. Not with faith in God, but with buckets! He would not live to see it moved, nor would his sons, nor even his sons' sons. Still, one day the task would be complete, and they all, generation after generation, would have had a part in it. (Pious Christians who imagine that the nontheistic Marxist must be overwhelmed in the depths of his soul by the thought of his own pathetic mortality have not yet reckoned with the Marxist hope: "Man is mortal, mankind is immortal." [33])

By contrast, it could be said that the reason why personal death has become so difficult for the men of the West is that few of them can see their own brief lives in the context of a greater, purposeful history. Confronted by a whole spectrum of apparently meaningless possible ends, an untold weight of absurdity has been added to the existential problem of personal death in our society.

Yet Marxists and others who embrace an overarching historical meaning based on the perpetuity of the race are no better off. They must sustain their sense of purpose by force. This force is in reality directed not against nations and men but against time itself. The endless walls and barbed wire, the enormous armies and the unbelievable concentration of energy and money on technological advance, all have this purpose: to keep the new omega from entering their horizon; to keep out the twentieth century—the century of the death of man.

For no one who really lives in and with the spirit of this age can say that "mankind is immortal." It is exactly the mortality of *mankind* that has been borne in upon us by both external and internal history. Precisely the mortality of mankind is what is tallied up not only by the ecologists and demographers but also by the poets. Marxism is a twentieth-century miracle because it has been able to maintain the vision of nineteenth-century secularism for half a century after the decisive end of the nineteenth century. It has somehow succeeded in arresting time before time presented us with the new omega. But it is a miracle born, as most miracles are, of human need. It is dependent for its continued "curative" powers on blindness to its failure to effect any genuine cures—or even to present any real alternatives. Witness the fact that environmental problems are just as serious in Russia and other Communist lands as in the so-called free world—and perhaps more serious in view of the official refusal to acknowledge them.[34]

Just because what the twentieth century has raised into prominence is the death of man, the question within the question of human survival and its quality is the question of meaning. Men have always had to contemplate the prospect that death would put an end to their own labors, their striving, their loving. Never before in history have men in such numbers had to reckon with the prospect of an end that would render their labor, striving, and loving meaningless not only to themselves but to their progeny, their homeland, their race.

It is thus not accidental that of all questions the question of meaning has been repressed by so many with almost total success. People do not merely affect to know nothing of what is meant by this question; they really do not know what sort of question it is. And pains are taken to instruct the young, especially little children who *will* raise the teleological question, not to know what this question is all about.

We live in an age that has been visited by the teleological question in its most grotesque form. The terrible pathos of our situation is that, of all the ages of man, ours is perhaps least well equipped to deal with any form of the question of meaning.

III

THE OFFICIAL RELIGION
OF THE
OFFICIALLY OPTIMISTIC SOCIETY

CHRISTIANITY AS THE PROBLEM

We have proposed the thesis that our society is in a state of contradiction because its expectations and its experience no longer meet and inform each other. We have also attempted to elaborate and substantiate that thesis. The problem, as we have stated it thus far, comes to this: there is nothing in the operative traditions of our culture to enable us as a people to encounter, at the level of conscious reflection, the prolonged experience of negation. Our expectations are overwhelmingly positive; our experiences are increasingly and profoundly negative. The dialogue between expectation and experience upon which civilization depends has had to be stifled for want of courage to confront this discrepancy openly.

What is called for—the *conditio sine qua non* of all other, serious reform—is that our society discover ways of facing the experience of negation, including the recognition of the negative and indeed nihilistic factors implicit in its own expectations. Only when the experienced negative can be openly acknowledged and reflected upon truthfully will there be a renewal of the dialogue between expectation and experience. Only when the new omega of our experience is permitted to confront the old omega of expectations can there be for us the possibility of an alpha beyond the impossibilities that are imposing themselves upon us with dreadful haste.

The question that this situation raises for thoughtful Christians is whether Christianity can provide any help. Let us put it still more modestly: Can Christianity offer anything that might contribute to a

73

meeting ground for expectation and experience? Concretely, can Christianity provide a vantage point from which to acknowledge, reflect upon, and reckon with the encroaching nihil?

One wishes that it were possible to move straightaway to the theological foundations of Christian faith, to the Bible and the tradition, for an answer. It would indeed stand within the most common practices of Christian apologia to do so: Having identified the problematic character of the situation, then to turn to the gospel as the source of answers to every problem! Such a procedure, however, not only is questionable for theological reasons, but it would constitute a serious misrepresentation of the predicament in which we stand. Indeed, it would falsify beyond measure the character of the problem itself. We are simply not yet in a position to think of *answering* the question about Christianity's potential for providing light in this darkness. Because so far as the specifically *Christian* articulation of that darkness is concerned, the problem itself has not yet been adequately stated. Perhaps it has been satisfactorily characterized as a problem for the concerned citizen of this society. But for the Christian, who tries to work not only within general human categories but within the categories of gospel and church, a whole dimension of the problem has so far been left entirely out of account.

The truth of the matter is that for the Christian an integral part of the problem, perhaps the most problematic part, is—Christianity itself! As it has displayed itself in the life of this New World, Christianity is the greatest barrier to its becoming a redemptive force in such a society, a light for our darkness.

The reason for this is evident enough. The Christianity that has become manifest as the dominant religious institution of this continent is totally, perhaps inextricably, identified with the positive outlook whose character we traced in the first chapter. This Christianity is nothing more nor less than the official religion of the officially optimistic society.

For the Christian who sees the problem of our epoch in something like the terms outlined in the foregoing chapters, therefore, the problem itself is instantly complicated. The very faith toward which he looks for redemptive possibilities has been "established" in such a way on this continent as to make it almost inaccessible to us as light in the real darkness in which we find ourselves today. How could Christianity provide a way into that night, when it is so consistently identified with the light? How could Christianity become the battleground for the encounter of expectation and experience, when it so clearly belongs to those who have most successfully banned such an encounter from their consciousness? How could Christianity offer a place from which we can expose ourselves to the experience of negation, when the whole thrust of that religion in this society until now has been exactly the elimination of the negative? With important exceptions (whose importance lies partly in the sheer fact that they are exceptions!) the Christian churches of North America have been inactive and ineffectual as places of honest encounter with the great social issues of our epoch, such as Vietnam. Was there anything in the story that the churches told, or in what they represented to and in the world, which could have prepared us for the confrontation with evil, especially our own evil?

The question about the potential for Christian faith to be an effective agent for transforming the contradiction at the heart of our culture is not purely theoretical or theological. If we are asking for a redemptive Christian force *in society*, then we have to reckon with the Christianity that has actually been involved in our society from its inception, and long before. We have to ask specifically about the character of the redemption for which this Christianity has stood, and stands. For it is just the positive, unambiguously optimistic message of redemption testified to by this Christianity that makes Christian faith seem so inadequate, so frequently offensive and even ludicrous, when it is offered today as light for *our* darkness.

The Real Establishment

Early in the history of this continent, churches addressed the question of establishment. There were bitter struggles between those who coveted establishment for a particular church, those who resisted on account of other ecclesiastical loyalties, and those who questioned the whole concept. Ostensibly, the nonestablishmentarians won the fight. Christians of the "free church" tradition have always taken a certain pride in the fact that here there is no establishment. Our theologians, clergymen, and laymen are astonished over the state of the establishment in European countries, especially in strongly Protestant nations such as West Germany. We are amazed to learn that in some nations the state collects church taxes, ministries are ratified or established by governments, and high percentages of the population are officially members of the church, even though the churches are emptier than in North America.

Such comparisons blind us to our own situation. In reality, what is with us from one point of view *(de jure)* nonestablishment is from another *(de facto)* the most deeply entrenched kind of establishment. Relatively speaking, Christian churches in North America are independent of the state. But in the depths of their social relationships and cultural assumptions they are bound to the dominant culture. Establishment here is not a matter of taxes, official appointments, and ceremonial (though it is also that, in a measure). Rather, it is a fundamental unity with the established culture—a unity at the level of decisive values and goals. It is a real establishment, in so many ways more effective than the merely legal ones that somehow persist in old Europe.

The real establishment consists in the fact that from the outset, and with only peripheral exceptions, the Christian interpretation of life that was communicated and practiced in our society was at one with the whole spirit of the New World. The differences that have existed, apart from the witness of Christian minorities that were as much ostracized from the society at large as from the major denominations of the church, have been incidental rather than essential. There have been differences of language, differences of context, or—the most important category—differences of emphasis, intensity, and degree.

These latter require elaboration. What is meant is best illustrated by reference to morality. What is in reality a quantitative distinction has been regularly mistaken for a qualitative difference between Christianity and culture. The churches have enjoyed the reputation of standing for a morality much "higher," more "demanding," and more "critical" of personal and social evil. It could be regarded as a mark of significant differentiation between Christianity and the culture that this or that denomination went on record as totally opposed to the sale of alcoholic beverages, or critical of the "open Sunday," or in favor of greater censorship. However, without demeaning the significance of much that has been done in the name of this "higher Christian morality," it must be recognized that this morality has not usually represented a fundamentally different order from the general public morality. On the contrary, it achieved the reputation of being "higher," and the churches have come to be regarded as the "conscience of society," only because this morality is essentially continuous with the moral code that has informed our society at large. Society has aimed at producing men and women of the same general mold as the churches and Sunday schools hoped to produce. "Christian morality" has been so successful on this continent (conspicuously more so than in those European countries where Christianity is established de jure) because it is not at all foreign to the rudimentary aims of the society at large.[35]

To ask whether Christianity can help to provide a perspective from which North Americans could expose themselves to their own contradictory state is to ask whether Christianity can in any sense free itself from this real establishment. Although Søren Kierkegaard was raising that question at the same time that Ryerson and Strachan were quarreling over establishment in Upper Canada, Kierkegaard's question has never been raised seriously on our continent. Even now it is raised only by a few critics, mostly within the churches, and is understood only by a few. Yet it is for us today a more pertinent form of the question of establishment than it is for Europe, where the *de jure* establishments do not involve as great a subordination *of the gospel* to the culture as occurs in North America. Only if Christianity can extricate itself from its marriage to the North American dominant culture can it hope to offer itself to that culture as a renewing and redeeming possibility.

This is not easily imaginable, however, for the roots of this marriage are deep. For the Western world in general, this alliance is embedded in sixteen centuries of Christendom. Hardly anyone can overcome at least the emotional, if not also the intellectual, implications of this relationship.

For North Americans, however, there are particular difficulties. These difficulties can be examined at two different levels. At one level there are difficulties introduced by our historical and geographic separation from the roots and remnants of the older cultures upon which our civilization was based. It is hard for us to imagine a time *before* the Constantinian arrangement. We do not live in the ruins of Roman or Greek civilization with their constant reminder of other epochs. Nor have we until recently lived with any conspicuous alternatives to Christianity, especially the ancient religious alternatives that were directly and indirectly influential in the formation of Christian thought. Indeed, our society has been singularly and almost artificially "Christian" in a way that European society never was, with its invasion of Moors, its proximity to Mediterranean Africa and the Near East, and its own indigenous never finally stifled paganism. Christianity entered Europe as a foreign religion. For all its official triumph, it never really succeeded in routing the old gods of the forests and mountains—something that should have been indelibly impressed upon our minds by the ease with which the Nazis reintroduced the myths and rituals of Teutonic religion. Christianity also entered North America as a foreign religion—but no longer a weak one! By mostly dishonorable and often despicable means, it soon disposed of the cults and the cultures that it found on this continent. The religions of our Indian peoples have played virtually no role at all in the development of Christian thought and life on this continent—something that could not even be said of Christian missions in Africa and Asia.

Beyond these historical and geographic considerations, and at a quite different level, there exists another order of problems for any who attempt to disengage Christianity from its cultural moorings. It has to do with the particular type of Christianity that established itself in North America. It was a Christianity that had already adjusted to the spirit of modernity, a Christianity already dissociated from its essential entanglements with earlier epochs. It was already pretty much at one with the fundamental assumptions of those visionaries who saw in "America" the new world as a habitation for the new man. It is true that this Christianity, in its more conservative forms, retained the language of the Bible and many of the symbols that belonged to earlier epochs. But this linguistic and symbolic continuity was, and still is, extremely superficial. The underlying "positive Christianity" of the fundamentalists is only rhetorically different from the underlying "positive Christianity" of liberals and modernists. Former President Richard Nixon saw this clearly when he named as his two "favorite theologians" Billy Graham and Norman Vincent Peale. Biblical literalism, which fundamentalists regard as their real link with New Testament faith, is quite inexplicable except as a modern phenomenon. What this literalism produces by way of a vision of the good life is different from that of the society at large only in details. It would not be wholly inaccurate to say that it is a version of the North American way of life adapted to the typical values of the lower middle class. Significantly, a representative of this Biblicism is still considered "the second most popular personage" in a nation considered the most secular in the modern world.

Stripped of operative links with earlier epochs and wedded to the spirit of the modern world, the typical Christianity of this continent lacked the resources for both prophetic social criticism and authentic self-criticism. The appeal to older traditions, so important for any attempt to reform the church, has hardly been a plausible or effective tactic for would-be reformers in the North American scene. The "older traditions" to which such appeal could be made were often little more than denominational conventions, most of them strictly homegrown and well on this side of the first Thanksgiving. Instead of opening the churches to the creative scrutiny that might have come from decisive earlier periods of crisis and re-formation, this appeal to denominational past usually served only to harden churches against change. It produced reactionary movements and the endless multiplication of denominations and sects.

An ironic dimension of the religious establishment in North America is that its commitment to the vision of the fathers prevents its credibility to the sons. Long after vastly changed conditions have made it outmoded and questionable, the vision of the fathers is perpetuated in the churches as nowhere else. Long after other institutions have adjusted at least their language to new occasions, it is still possible to hear the original version of "the American dream" in the original language inside the churches. To hear it, to pray it, and to sing it!

It is possible that Christianity has been the primary vehicle for the communication of the positive outlook of the modern epoch. It would be difficult to demonstrate such a thesis. But what needs little demonstration is the extent to which Christianity as we have it has been itself shaped by that vision. The character of the establishment of Christianity on this continent cannot be grasped until it is understood that the attempt to hold on to that vision today expresses the churches' struggle for self-preservation. They not only have embraced the vision as the most conducive political and cultural context for the faith, but they have identified Christianity with the vision. So far as the majority of churchgoing North Americans is concerned, "Christianity" and "our way of life" are inextricably bound up with each other. Hence any attack upon "our way of life" is *ipso facto* an attack upon Christianity.

It is not sufficient, however, to acknowledge that Christianity is "established" among us. The analysis requires that we ask *how:* not only how it *did* come to be so, but how it *could* come to be so. We have reflected briefly on the former; we can only discern how it could have come to be so if we turn from broadly historical to specifically theological considerations. The potentiality for such an occurrence must lie in the faith itself. What were the elements in the faith as such which made it compatible with the modern vision, and how were these elements incorporated into the vision?

In the Image of God

The positive outlook, as we have seen, is the product of a new image of man, the formative concept of which is the idea of mastery. It is doubtful that such an image could have taken root except on "Christian" soil. Yet its emergence represents a decisive overcoming of the Biblical doctrine of man. The establishment of Christianity in the New World is grounded first of all in the identification of the Christian view of man with the modern image of man as technocratic master of his environment.

This identification could have occurred only because the idea of mastery is present in the Biblical view of man. Nevertheless, its occurrence represents an ultimate rejection of the Biblical view. While it took over one of the primary elements of Biblical anthropology—i.e., man's transcendence of nature—it eliminated the Biblical consciousness both of man's involvement in and his tragic distortion of nature. It removed the dialectical tension implicit in all Biblical anthropology in favor of a simple, monistic view of man.

This analysis requires that we consider further the Hebraic-Christian view of the relationship between man and nature, in connection both with the doctrine of creation and with the doctrine of sin.

It is true that in the intention of God, man is granted a certain authority in the creation, and so over his own destiny, according to the Biblical concept of man's creaturely nature. But man's "dominion" is a matter of permanent dialectical tension from the outset in Hebraic thought. The nature of this tension can be expressed in four ways:

1. In the first place, it is to be observed in the ontic and psychic makeup of man himself. He is both united and not united with that nature over which he is given "dominion."

Certainly he is not only "natural" in the manner that other creatures belong to nature. Had he been only a creature of nature, could he possibly have wrought so much in the world that is unnatural? Neither apes nor elephants have brought about a technological society that is about to overwhelm the earth! Man stands above nature: he thinks, he remembers, he hopes, he speaks. His "dominion" presupposes that. He is a historical creature, not only a natural one.

But at the same time the Bible places him unmistakably *within* nature. No other world religion, and perhaps not even the most secular of men's philosophies, have presented mankind with such a fundamentally *natural* view of itself as has the Judeo-Christian faith. When the Scriptures of Jews and Christians affirm man's "creaturehood," they affirm that he is of the earth, body and soul. The Christian religion has constantly betrayed that insistence by making the human soul immortal. But that is a distortion of Biblical thought—part of a greater distortion which is the subject of our present inquiries. Nothing could be more explicit concerning man's earthiness than the second (and older) of the two creation sagas, in which the man is shaped from the dust of the earth. He is *adam* from *adamah:* he bears an innate proximity to the ground. Moreover, this Biblical sense of man's identity with nature is enshrined in the Christian dogma of *creatio ex nihilo*, with its insistence that "nothing" (soul, spirit, or whatever) preexists, except the Creator himself with his will to create. It is confirmed, as well, in the New Testament doctrine of resurrection. That declaration, far from presupposing the immortality of the soul, affirms the real mortality of man: so much so, that it must apply also to the representative man, Jesus, the Christ. Like every beast of the field, every flower and blade of grass, man is proceeding toward nothingness. His "dominion" over the beasts, birds, and other creatures can only be rightly understood so far as it is recognized that man himself *participates* in that same biological-psychological life which sustains those whose existences are his special charge. Apart from an utter distortion of creaturehood, his dominion can never become a matter of sheer superiority, nor of two distinct orders of existence. In his dealings with *adamah, adam* is obliged to recognize that he is entering into a dialogue with himself.

2. In the second place, the dialectical tension at the heart of the Biblical concept of man's relation to nature is to be seen in connection with the multiplicity and complexity of man's relationships.

We may say that man in the Judeo-Christian understanding is the focus of a threefold relatedness: he stands in relation not only to nature but also to his fellowmen and to the Creator God. His very being is bound up with these relationships. It is peculiar of Biblical anthropology that it does not speak strictly of "being" *(ontos)*, as Greek anthropology does, but only of "being-with." [36] The being of man *is* his being-with. He *receives* his being (he does not possess it!) in his being-with, his being vis-à-vis these others. Moreover, these others are never independent one of the other; they are inseparable. God, the neighbor, and the inarticulate creation all converge in man's consciousness and in historical existence. They are distinguishable and must remain so; yet they become strangely representative one of the other. Messengers of God appear in the form of man: my neighbor is Christ to me, as Luther put it. And the ground cries out, the earth groans, and bushes burn but are not consumed. It is better, then, to speak of a threefold relatedness than to picture three distinct relationships.

For our purposes, man's relationship to nature is neither simple nor immediate, but complex and always somehow indirect. Already as creature in God's intention (we are not yet speaking of man's distortion of what God intends), his relationship to the natural environment is limited by the other two aspects of his creaturely relatedness, from which he can in no wise be separated. The relationship to God and the relationship to the fellowmen (represented, significantly, by the woman in the second creation narrative of Genesis) condition and circumscribe the character of man's relationship to nature. So much so that a violation of nature is at once a violation of the other two relationships (cf. Gen., ch. 3). The relationship to the Creator, which for the Scriptures is the primary focus of man's relatedness, means that man's dominion of nature is set within the context of *God's* dominion over the whole world, including man. Man's mastery is conditioned and circumscribed by the mastery of the One who grants him mastery. It is also *defined* by the divine "dominion"—which according to the entire Biblical story is vastly different from what has been meant by the concept of dominion in the history of Western civilization and in Christendom. Man's relationship to the human partner means that his mastery of the earth and its creatures presuppose the presence and the "equal rights" of the brother, as is expressed in the story of Cain and Abel.

Nature is not divine in Biblical faith. It is not peopled with gods and demons. It is creation, and therefore finite, temporal, secular. Yet it is so bound up with the deepest and most personal and central of man's relationships, so inseparable from that Thou from whom he received his life and those others with whom he shares it, that he can only behave toward the inarticulate creation as though there were also an implicit "Thou" within it. Buber has grasped this in his meditations on the tree.[37]

3. In the third place, the dialectical tension in the Biblical concept of man's relationship to nature becomes visible as soon as one asks about the character of the dominion that man is called to exercise.

Dominion is no doubt a strong word, as many today have rightly perceived. The word could be used to apply to God himself, and later in its Latin form it came to be the primary way of addressing the Christ, *Dominus*. Man is commissioned to a certain "lordship"; he bears some authority in the world. Again one notices that in the Biblical view man is by no means regarded as *simply* a part of nature. He is given a command, singled out for authority. It is assumed that no other creature could bear this responsibility.

But what is the nature of this dominion that man is called to exercise among the creatures? Many persons who feel they can trace the present crisis of nature to these Biblical roots do not wait to ask that question. Hearing only the word "dominion" and related concepts, they immediately associate it with an imperialism of humanity against nature, a crass unconcern for the natural—in short, with the modern concept of mastery. There are good reasons why critics outside the churches should not think it necessary to inquire after the original meanings of words like this. The churches of North America and of all Christendom have not given men cause to think that they *intended* these words to be interpreted differently from their use in the society at large. But even a superficial reading of the creation story in which the word "dominion" appears (Gen., ch. 1) should indicate that there are dimensions here that are conspicuously lacking in a civilization which has made itself triumphant on the basis of the cry, "Nature is the enemy; she must be brought to her knees!" [38]

A more sophisticated Biblical exegesis makes it even less permissible to maintain any real continuity between the Biblical concept of man's dominion over nature and the modern concept of technocratic mastery. For in the total Scriptural story, the word "dominion" has to be defined primarily and ultimately by reference to the dominion of the One who is Lord, *Dominus*. The exact paradigm for the Biblical use of this word is not to be sought in modern political philosophy but in Biblical testimony. For in his dominion of nature, man is required to do nothing more nor less than to "image" God.

What, then, is the essence of this authority which man bears vis-à-vis the other creatures, seen in the perspective of the divine dominion? Certainly it has nothing to do with the arbitrary exercise of power. Nor has it anything in common with the plunder of nature stimulated by the impression that nature exists merely to satisfy human needs. Only if the priority and normative character of the divine dominion were totally ignored would it be possible to consider man's dominion in such terms. God does not exercise his lordship arbitrarily, or for the display of his own power. The Creator and Redeemer of the Biblical story does not indulge in the sort of self-centered relationship to that over which he has dominion, which asks only how it can meet *his* needs. On the contrary, his rule is for the sake of the ruled. His *dominion* is nothing other than his love, expressing itself in order.

Moreover, the expression of this love is determined, not by the One who offers it, but by the conditions and potentialities of the creatures for whom it is intended. It is not love if it takes no thought for the capacities of the beloved to receive love. Hence the *Lordship* of Jesus Christ is his *Servanthood;* his dominion is his friendship for those who call him "Lord." He is the Lord because he is the healer of the sick, the seeker of the lost, the one who forgives and seeks the restoration of the sinner. That even Christians could hear the word "dominion" without a thought about the manner in which that word has been defined by the One called *Dominus* indicates the extent to which Christendom has lost touch with essential Christological reasoning.

Whoever returns to the Christological foundations of Christian thought realizes that the dominion of man over nature could only mean what the Genesis story also maintains: man's loving care of the natural world. Loving care does not mean something merely sentimental. There *is* authority in this concept. We do not want to destroy the dialectical tension by suggesting that man is asked to behave merely as a sentimental worshiper of nature, who makes no attempt to order but simply allows whatever will be to be. He does not go about with a watering can showering blessings on weeds and flowers alike! On the contrary, there is a command to "have dominion." Only those who have never really encountered nature's own violence, as is true of many contemporary city dwellers who take up ecological causes today, could imagine that nature "left to itself" would be altogether wonderful. But the command is not a license to *impose* order. Rather, it is the permission and command to assist the order that is *in* nature to realize itself, to the end that the "good" which is in it can be brought forth. The need that exercises jurisdiction over the orderer is not his own need to display or vindicate his authority, but the needs of the creatures of the garden-wilderness. That includes, paradoxically, his own needs as well, for he is himself one of those creatures. He too seeks his meat from God. But let us say that it "includes" his needs, rather than that it is in order to meet his needs that all the others exist in the first place. The other creatures also have their needs. Even the ground—*adamah*—requires a special kind of care; it will not settle for something less (witness the dust storms of the 1930's). If man selfishly attempts to superimpose his own arbitrary schemes on the natural environment, nature is not slow to retaliate.

4. The fourth way in which the dialectical tension in the relationship of man to nature expresses itself in Biblical thought is contained in the concept of stewardship.

The modern idea of mastery presupposes the ownership of what is mastered. Man is no longer accountable for what he does to nature. In reality such a vision of man and nature could have taken shape only in a world that no longer took seriously the fundamental tenets not only of Biblical faith but of all religious belief. It was possible in a world that had banished the gods to the far reaches of heaven, as the Deists did. For it is basic to the beliefs of all the great religious traditions of man that the world belongs to Another. Biblical faith expresses this succinctly in the affirmation: "The earth is the LORD's and the fulness thereof." (Ps. 24:1; see also Ps. 50:12; 89:11.) Man is a tenant.

On the other hand, the tension must not be overcome or ignored. Unlike many of the so-called higher religions of man, Biblical faith does not permit man only to play the role of a poor tenant, perhaps even an intruder, in the world. What has given Judeo-Christian belief its impetus is just its unique courage to offer man not only a place in the sun but the right to consider the earth his home, his very dwelling place. He is almost permitted to speak and act as though he owned it! Almost—but never unambiguously, undialectically. Without the possibility of "almost" considering it his own, he could not feel at home in it. Contrary to the murmurings of the pious who long for heaven, every article of Christian faith drives toward the goal that man *should* feel at home in the earth, should feel his affinity with the ground, and not be fearful or ashamed.

So there is a rationale for the Biblical affirmation that the earth, which is the Lord's, also in some sense belongs to man. It is bound up with *his* sense of belonging to the earth. On the other hand, there can be no question of out-and-out ownership. How could he own it, since he is clearly a part of it himself? He is unable to contain it; he is himself contained by it. It is perhaps a great wisdom on the part of the Biblical authors that they realize men will *not* feel at home in the world just when they imagine that they own it. The critique of the prophets against the people of Israel in their "settled" situation in Palestine—in their cities!—always centered around that awareness. Ownership, far from producing the sense of "belonging," produces anxiety, the anxiety of which Jesus often spoke: the anxiety of those who worry about tomorrow, who hoard up treasures on earth, who build greater barns and lose their souls. Anxiety of ownership—a thing that Marxism also recognizes in its way—leads inevitably to distortion. The home becomes a fortress, a defense, a false attempt to achieve permanence and security. The tents of the wilderness, say the prophets, are more truly home than the palaces of Solomon.

The earth is the Lord's! If it is given to man—and according to Biblical thought it is—it is given "with strings attached." The conditions of the gift are man's *responsible* treatment of the earth, and his *gratitude* to the Giver. The two things are, in the last analysis, one and the same. Gratitude is not a religious rite or a pious attitude, observed in prayers at table and on Thanksgiving Day (though it could also sometimes be that). It refers, rather, to a certain kind of deportment in relation to the earth and all its creatures. Let us say straightforwardly, it is exactly the antithesis of the attitude we have described as "technocratic": i.e., the attitude that produces pigs or turkeys (scientifically, of course) in order to market them, and never sheds a tear over their beauty or their fate; the attitude that processes and consumes living creatures, as if they had no other function beyond that of feeding the human race and, more significantly, lining the pockets of a few men. Gratitude, in the Biblical sense, is entirely extraneous to the modern concept of technocratic mastery.

The Bible turns more frequently to the term "steward" than to any other when it wants to express this state of tension between owning and not owning the earth and its fullness. According to the doctrine of creation, man is called to be caretaker and dispenser of that which belongs finally to another. He is a tenant, as in Jesus' parable; yet not "merely" a tenant—at least not in the modern sense. He is given rights and responsibilities that do not normally belong to tenants today. A better image would be that of keeper or squire, but they belong to another time. The central idea is that man may and must engage in original thought and planning with respect to that for which he has charge. But he is accountable for what he does. Moreover, his decisions and actions in relation to the "vineyard" must be compatible with the needs and laws inherent in its plants and animals, which "have their own seeds in them."

For finally the earth is not quite inarticulate. It does not speak only through the one who has learned a language and may converse with God himself. It has its own access to the Owner; and its groans will be heard by him. When man is silent, the very stones of the ground will cry out. Yet, in the order of creation it is man who is called to speak for the others. Not merely to name them, but to answer for them. That is at last the essence of his stewardship: to be articulate for the others. Man is the locus where creation gathers itself together into words, where the whole creation delights in God and in itself, and translates its delight into song. Man takes the rejoicing of the trees and the applause of the little hills and translates it all into words. His responsibility as steward is representational. He stands before the Creator in behalf of all the others—they find their voice in him—and praises him for the gift of life. Man's *authority* in the midst of the creatures is nothing but the other side of this representational existence. He stands before the creatures as the one who has spoken with their Creator and desires now to translate the Creator's love into an ordering of their profusion.

THE DESTRUCTION OF THE DIALECTIC

The image of man that has informed the modern epoch came at that point in time when Christianity no longer recognized, or no longer cared to defend, the dialectical tension which runs throughout the Biblical anthropology and expresses itself in these four ways.

It is not within the power of the church to prevent worldly winds from blowing, to stem the tide of movements, to ward off the development of new images. But it *is* within the power of the church to recognize its own divergence from these movements and images of man, and to bear witness to what it considers false in them. And that is what the churches of North America—and of that Europe which dreamed the American dream in the beginning—did not do. Instead, they allowed the new image of man to clothe itself in Christian and even Biblical garb. Many of the greatest Christian thinkers and preachers were themselves happy to contribute to this transition. They could regard their work as an "updating" of the faith and a necessary apologetic—extricating Christianity from the entanglements of feudal thought. That Christian belief required such a rescue from cultural moorings is not at all in doubt. But what has to be confessed as an error is the wholesale manner in which, borrowing from one side of the Biblical dialectic, the "fathers" of modern Christianity made it possible to confuse the Christian and the modern images of man.

The one side from which they borrowed was, needless to say, the "positive" side: positive, as seen from the perspective of the new *imago hominis* to which they wished to adjust the faith.

Specifically that meant: (1) disregarding the affirmation of man's involvement in nature in favor of his transcendence of it; (2) divorcing the relationship with nature from personal relationship (and, conversely, removing the natural from the personal); (3) concentrating on man's "right" to exercise authority over nature, to the exclusion of nature's "rights" for a responsible authority directed by its own needs; (4) finally, abandoning the idea of stewardship in favor of something closer to ownership. In each instance it was possible to find a religious rationale; and it is still altogether possible to hear that rationale from some who are at the forefront of Christian theology today.

1. In the first instance, the removal of man from nature in modern thought took the form of a positive operation. It was not so much a matter of denying man's natural affiliation as it was of emphasizing his *supra*-natural capacities. Specifically, that meant propounding an extravagant view of human rationality. Man became the possessor of mind. The "rational animal" of Aristotle became more "rational" than "animal." He was the measurer of nature; how could he be nature's child? The Romantic movement of the nineteenth century attempted to reintroduce something of the tension—to put man back into nature. Not only was it hardly heard of in North America, but as a countercultural movement it was too obsessed with its objection to rationalism to offer a real alternative.

There was a basic readiness on the part of Christians at the outset of the modern period to accept this transcendent view of man. It expressed itself in such "Christian" rationalists as the English Deists. But the more influential religious expression, so far as North America is concerned, is to be found in that pietism which regarded man not so much as mind but as spirit or soul. From the earliest days of Christianity there was a temptation to cast off the soul/body unity characteristic of Hebraic thought in favor of a dualistic version of man's nature. This age-old temptation of the Christians found a new outlet in the modern insistence upon man's essential differentiation from nature. On the basis of the new insight, it became possible to speak of man's "higher" and "lower" nature, and by the latter to mean quite unambiguously man's biological identity.[39] Salvation could be spelled out in terms of freeing man from bondage to the necessities of the "lower nature," freeing him to be pure spirit, governed by the instincts of the soul, not those of the body.

This spiritualizing of essential manhood expressed itself finally and most succinctly in the doctrine of the "immortality of the soul." That concept, borrowed more from Athens than from Jerusalem, had to do with more than life after death. It pinpoints an entire anthropology, and offers a complete soteriology. It means not only that man's essential being utterly transcends nature but that salvation is salvation *from* nature. Thus the pietistic version of overcoming this aspect of the dialectical tension in the relationship between man and nature outdoes the secular version. Even more than rationalism, spiritualism not only divorces man from nature but regards nature as evil. The influence of this spiritualism on the entire religious scene in North America cannot be overestimated. Certainly it is not limited to sectarian groups that have given it an exclusive position in their beliefs. It lingers in all our expressions of Christianity and has informed the culture in many subtle ways.

2. Secondly, the new image of man that came to be in the modern epoch removed the category of the personal from nature. Medieval thought had hardly separated itself from the pagan past in this respect. Nature was peopled with otherworldly beings. In the new understanding of man vis-à-vis nature, not only was man removed from nature but, in a complementary sense, nature became devoid of personality.

Biblical thought, as we have seen, refuses to think of nature as either divine or demonic. But it does not regard it as merely impersonal. This is because, for the Biblical writers, nature becomes again and again the scene—even the medium—of the divine presence. And nature is strangely interwoven with the most personal of man's relationships. In the new understanding of the modern world view nature became impersonal, quantitative, raw material for man's use, a backdrop against which he plays his clever games and carries on his clever conversations. He may "humanize" nature; but by that he does not recognize the interwovenness of history with nature. Rather, he means the superimposition onto nature of his own rational design. Thus the eighteenth-century gardens become models of symmetry and order, reflecting the mind of their creators. Nature is acceptable only as a garden.

Christians did not object to this depersonalization of nature. In fact, they heralded it and still do so as a doctrinally sound and necessary "secularization" of nature. There was no awareness that it meant the removal of mystery from the natural environment; that it would open the earth to technological manipulation and rape; that it would make possible a war against nature that the ancients would have found as horrifying as our modern wars against one another. Nothing like this occurred to the Christians who joined their voices to the chorus that sang the praises of the new era. Those who objected were regarded as reactionaries and romantics.[40] The majority found and still find the depersonalizing of nature liberating. They blessed the industrialists who under the aegis of this new mood went to work on the "raw material." [41] And they saddled their cart to the new social class—the middle class—which formed around the economic potential of the new freedom to move about in the world.[42] From now on, the love and defense of nature for the most part passed to those who no longer identified with the mainstream of Christianity, or were cryptopagans in the churches—singing the praises of Jesus but picturing him in the garb of St. Francis. Increasingly, this segment of our culture has had to find its identity, significantly enough, in opposition to the church.[43]

3. Thirdly, the modern world view represents a final overcoming of the dialectical tension between the two Biblical answers to the question of the rationale of man's dominion. It is for the sake both of nature itself and, in a particular sense, of man, that he must exercise authority in the earth. In a world characterized by the discovery of man's centrality and autonomy, on the one hand, and nature's objectification on the other, there was no longer any meaningful way of speaking of the needs of *nature*. It is quite another thing to speak of the *laws* of nature. An entirely different attitude toward nature is produced when the eyes of the beholder regard it in terms of laws. To be sure, to think of laws and measurements is still to maintain a certain respect for nature, but it is a respect born of the egoism of the measurer, who reckons nature's worth or threat to himself.

In the contemporary world it is almost impossible to grasp the difference to which I am attempting to point. It is difficult to discover instances of that attitude which beholds nature in terms of nature's own needs. Even those who live "close to the soil," the farmers, have learned the technocratic attitude, the attitude that contemplates natural laws and does so more and more expertly, but does not love what it contemplates. Here and there, however—often in the backwaters of civilization—one encounters relics of this other attitude. My maternal grandfather was such a man. He wept over the pain of his animals. He was a modern man and not unaware of nature's laws, but his farm was operated for the most part on another principle. He asked, always, not only what was necessary for him to do in order that he might reap the best benefits from his land and his animals, but what he must do for the land and the animals. His decisions were made, not only in relation to the needs of his own family but in relation to the needs of the families of sheep and cows and horses for which he had responsibility. It was not altogether efficient. He was never poor, but he might have been much wealthier. The trouble was that he could never treat his animals, or even the ground itself, as though they were strictly objects, behaving according to certain patterns, existing to be used. He kept sheep at a time when it was not profitable to keep sheep,

because he found them beautiful. It is not incidental in this connection
that my grandfather read the Bible a great deal. Nor is it incidental to our
whole discussion that today his farm, together with all the other farms of
his former neighbors, is owned by a large cement company.

"Dominion" means something quite different as soon as this sense of
nature's need is lost. The "husbandry" of animals, plants, and land gives
place to the "development" mentality. Between the man and the earth to
which the man also belongs there comes to be an intensity of alienation
quite different from what has been known in ages past. Men have always
experienced nature's strangeness and enmity. The Scriptures attribute
that to man's own act and state of estrangement. But never before in
history has man been able to reduce nature to forces so totally devoid of
spirit, so completely material, so incapable of "need," that he recognizes in
it no real affinity with himself. He no longer finds it necessary to refer to
animate or inanimate things by use of the masculine or feminine personal
pronoun; everything is "it." Nature is an enemy so impersonal that man
cannot even think of it, in terms of the ancient metaphor, as "Enemy."

Christianity in the modern world not only did not object to the
overcoming of this aspect of the dialectical tension in man's relationship to
nature, but it aligned itself with the modern world view also at this point.
That is particularly obvious in the experience of the New World, where
the new man began to eke out his livelihood. The celebrated "pioneer
spirit" is in many ways noble, but who can estimate the damage done to
nature on this continent by men who were determined to take advantage
of nature's bounty. Not only the damage that was perpetrated in the
initial stages of the settlement of this continent, which may indeed be
negligible, but the lasting damage set in motion by an attitude toward
nature which was inculcated into the spirit of our peoples in these very
woods and plains.

The Christians of the New World might have learned something
important from the people they found here—the people they "European-
ized" in the name of "Christianizing" them. That people had a very
different attitude toward the trees and the animals. Our decision
was—and still is—that their attitude was "primitive," "pagan," "supersti-
tious." But may it not in fact have been more Christian, more Biblical,
than we were willing to grant? The Bible also is a book of a people whom
we regard for the most part as primitive!

But the technocratic attitude toward nature was already too strong, and
Christianity was too thoroughly identified with it to be able to recognize,
in the strange religious rites and customs of the Indian peoples, any

possible affinities with their own better traditions. Already by the time our ancestors were moving into the central and western parts of this continent, Biblical scholars had discerned "progressive" stages of development and maturity in the Biblical material. The desire to eschew the "primitive" was strong in them. Naturally, among the material adjudged "primitive" was all that strange data of the Old Testament which smacked of nature gods and holy locations. (Did not the Bible itself provide the greatest judgment against these things?) Progressive Christianity, in the name of the purer monotheism, blessed man's right to look upon nature as devoid not only of deity but, in the bargain, of spirit and whatever could be expected to have needs. Henceforth "dominion" could only imply man's right to satisfy *his own needs* from the presumably bountiful supply.

4. Fourthly, modern cultural Christianity took from Biblical Christianity the concept of the earth as man's home, but it excluded the paradoxical corollary that it is a home which man himself does not own.

After all, the entire direction of modern thought has been to exclude God from the human horizon. That is obvious enough. What is not so obvious is that this exclusion of God has been the corollary of man's vision of himself as the god of the planet—and it is not possible with accuracy to say which principle was primarily causative. Only when God is "edged out of the world" is it possible for man to regard himself as possessor and lord of nature. With the elimination of the Deity from interference in the universe, man is no longer accountable for what he does within and to the world.

We have learned, as was noticed earlier, to regard this possibility with mixed feelings, verging increasingly on despair. For the twentieth-century man, the absence of God has come to mean something more negative than it did for our predecessors: that man is alone in the world; that no one cares what becomes of him; that no one will come to the rescue of his fatal mistakes in nature, least of all nature itself, which he has reduced to an uncaring objectivity. Still, for those who first thought these thoughts, it was exhilarating to dare to think in terms of ownership. The concept of mastery could not have been devised apart from this daring. Only with God utterly remote and disinterested—not necessarily nonexistent or dead—could man assume mastery in the world. But in a strange sense, the Promethean dimensions of the image of mastery presuppose a divinity from which man wrests the earth.

Obviously Christianity did not openly condone such a belief. Throughout these three or four centuries there have been Christian thinkers and others peripherally connected with Christianity who were willing to go far in this direction. But not even the most modernistic Christianity as it was found in the nineteenth and early twentieth centuries in North America could be accused of openly encouraging men to think in such terms.

The capitulation of Christianity to the new world view has at this point to be understood more subtly. No Christian intentionally preaches that man owns the world outright and is not accountable to anyone. But Christianity is never only a matter of words. Deeds, associations, and silences speak, often more clearly than words; they may even drown out the words altogether. From the outset, the Christianity of this continent associated with those who owned property and who made the ownership of property their way of life. It blessed capitalism and carried its approval of property so far as to condone the institution of slavery. Not only did the church accept property as a legitimate concept, but it aligned itself with property, land ownership, industry, capital *over against* the classes that did not and could not participate in this exploitation of the earth. It became in effect—and its major denominations still remain so to a large extent—an institution of the capitalistic elements of the society (a fact often not understood by Christians in connection with the Marxist struggle against the churches).

This may be regarded as a spurious argument. In reality it is the most pertinent reasoning that could be brought to bear in this matter. It matters very little that in the churches throughout these centuries sermons could be heard on stewardship, and men referred to as tenants in God's world. Those who heard such sermons (and who preached them!) were themselves thoroughly enthralled in the business of ownership, possession, and all that goes with it in terms of the manipulation of nature—including human beings. The words were betrayed by the realities of Christian identification. The real tenants in the world, who in very truth could not lay hold of the ground they tilled or the products they molded, were never directly influential *in the churches* any more than they were influential in the world. They had nothing to do in fact with the image of the church in the world, though they were sometimes fodder for its membership rolls or its Christmas bales! The concept and machinery of ownership was and is so thoroughly bound up with Christianity in our culture that it is practically unthinkable to convey the Biblical idea of man's stewardship to our typical middle-class congregations.

Man Estranged from Nature

The new image of man built, then, on one side of the Biblical dialectic, while eliminating the other. And the churches both blessed and facilitated this translation. Christians were pleased to permit the doctrine of creation to yield such an image.

But the image of man as technocratic master of nature could only have developed as a positive image insofar as the churhces failed totally to convey what was contained in the doctrinal tradition of the fall of man. At its deepest level the doctrine of the Fall could hardly be more accurately stated than as man's prideful attempt to become the master of nature—especially if that is understood to mean, as it always in fact does mean, of human nature as well.

It would not be an exaggeration to say that the new image of man represents a failure of the Christianity of the modern Western world to understand and communicate its own doctrine of sin.[44]

For what the doctrine of sin declares is that precisely man's propensity to ignore and transgress the limits he experiences in his relationship with others—including the inarticulate creation—is his *distortion* of his creature-hood. It is hardly possible in the annals of human history to find a more pervasive condemnation of the vain imagination that man should be master of the earth! Thus it staggers the imagination to attempt to understand how the Christian church, of all human institutions, could have permitted itself to be identified with such an image, and even to champion it. It surely says something judgmental about the church and Christian theology that only at that point in history when the modern image of man began to appear conspicuously exaggerated, questionable and even dangerous—namely, around August 1, 1914—was there any significant attempt on the part of some theologians and Christians to rediscover what the Bible and the older traditions of the church meant by sin![45] The so-called "theology of crisis" was really nothing more than the rediscovery of the doctrine of sin. Kierkegaard anticipated it. But to this very day it is resisted vehemently, because to understand it would mean to dispense altogether with Christianity as we have known it here.

Our present purposes are not to exhaust the meaning of the doctrine of sin. It is far too mysterious and encompassing a reality. But for reasons that have already been established, we shall concentrate on the meaning of the Christian concept of sin for the question of man's relation to nature. It is integral to our understanding of that question that the discussion cannot be separated from other aspects of the doctrine of sin. It is our business here, however, to investigate the origins of the modern image of man in terms of their "Christian" connections. Our primary concern must be to ask, first, what the doctrine of sin contributes to our understanding of the idea that man should master nature. Following that, we shall turn to the question already introduced above: How could the church have permitted its understanding of man to be identified with the modern *imago hominis?*

We shall discuss the first inquiry under four somewhat arbitrary, and certainly interrelated, observations: (1) sin as man's transgression of nature; (2) sin as man's refusal to accept his own nature; (3) sin as man's attempt to construct an alternative environment; (4) sin as a tragic state of alienation from nature.

1. *Sin as man's transgression of nature.* It is not accidental that in the classical Christian myth of man's fall (Gen., ch. 3), the act of disobedience is depicted as a transgression of nature: eating the forbidden fruit. When all sexual and other possible connotations have been exhausted, the "original disobedience" is inextricably bound up with a violation of nature.

The Christian doctrine of sin is not dependent upon Gen., ch. 3, in isolation from its context. As Bonhoeffer and others have pointed out,[46] there are two temptation stories in the Bible: the temptation in the Garden of Eden and the temptation in the wilderness; the temptation of Adam and the temptation of the Second Adam. One can agree with Bonhoeffer, as well, that Christians ought to read the temptation of Adam in the light of the temptation of the Christ. In doing so, however, precisely the same point is upheld: the temptation of Jesus, too, is a temptation to violate nature. It is the demonic suggestion that nature be used, its order set aside, for the purposes of establishing the prestige and authority of man—"the Man." Jesus rejects this temptation and chooses instead the role of the sufferer. His suffering, moreover, is to be understood not only in terms of his subjection to the will of God and, on the other side, to the will of man but also in terms of his subjection to nature. He will not attempt to subjugate nature to himself, even though it is understood throughout the New Testament that he could have such power if he willed to have it. He will not come down from "the tree" upon which, at last, he is hanged. Even this final temptation to violate nature is rejected.[47]

Now obviously neither these stories of temptation nor any other discussion of sin in the Bible is intended to present the idea that sin is primarily man's violation of nature. Classical Christian theology has rightly identified sin in the Biblical tradition as disobedience—violation of the divine command. The limit that man transgresses in his sinning is not in itself a merely natural limit, it is a limit imposed by the Creator. God makes himself the limit of our humanity, not for the sake of belittling us, but in order that we may discern our own glory as men. We *are* men; we are not gods. When we try to be gods, we can only be "unhappy" (Camus). We are able to participate only in the *doxa* for which we are intended only by discovering our essential *humanity*. But we can only discover that humanity as we discover our relationship to what is not humanity, only as we discover and are discovered by God. To be a man is to encounter again and again, in our search for authentic being, this limit. To be a man is to come time after time to the discovery, "I am not God." In itself, this divine *limit* to our humanity contains no necessary humiliation. It is just another way of speaking of human definition, of the possibilities of manhood. We are defined by our limits. Without limits we are indefinite, lacking an identity. But while there is no *necessary* humiliation in the discovery of this limit, the testimony of the Scriptures is that man invariably—perhaps inevitably—experiences this limit as humiliating. He is driven to overcome it—to become "like God." Encountering God, he finds his own glory unsatisfactory. He tries, pathetically, to extend the limits, to define himself more gloriously. That, in the first instance, is what sin means.

Sin is thus sin against God: "Against thee, thee only, have I sinned." [48] But it is not incidental in the Genesis story of the Fall, which classical Christianity has regarded as somehow normative for its understanding of sin, that the divine prohibition is bound up with nature. Man's abrogation of the divine command involves at the same time a violation of nature. Not only is the Bible unwilling to segregate the "vertical" from the "horizontal" dimensions of man's threefold relatedness, but it will speak of the "vertical" only in the context of the "horizontal." That is the only context man understands. Man's attempt to extend himself beyond the limit represented by God is expressed, therefore, not in unearthly mystical or religious terms, but in the quite concrete terms of his attempt to leap beyond the limits inherent in his relationship to nature. For in nature, too, he experiences a whole series of limits to his humanity. He is limited both in terms of his own involvement in nature and in terms of his authority within it. His humanity is possible within these limits, and it is "good." But instead of experiencing nature's limit as "possibility"—the boundaries by which his own peculiar glory is defined—man experiences it as limitation. He is driven to overcome his involvement in nature and extend his limited authority within it. This is not a second step in sin; it is part of the "original" sin. The violation of the divine commandment *is* a violation of nature. The attempt to usurp the power of God *is* the attempt to become limitless in his dominion of nature.[49]

2. *Sin as man's refusal to accept his own nature.* Not only is sin a violation of nature, but it is also a refusal of man to accept his own identity as a biological creature. The human creature belongs unmistakably to the biosphere; he participates in the same necessities and possibilities as the

other creatures. It is his rejection of this identity and participation that is sin.

The rejection takes this form: man identifies as his *essence* that which he believes to have least in common with nature. Clearly that means one thing—and although modern thought refined that one thing and made it the center of an apotheosis undreamed of by the ancient Hebrews, the latter knew well enough what the one thing was. Modernity called it rationality, or sometimes freedom. The ancients recognized it from the outset as a matter of "knowing": "You will be like God, knowing . . ."

Knowing becomes man's weapon against nature and against his own involvement in it. It becomes the lever by which he attempts to extricate himself from the slimy pit of participation in the bodily functions, the blood, tears, and grime of nature. Knowing, under the conditions of the Fall, becomes equated with technique; and all technique is geared, finally, to the transcendence of nature. Man regards himself as a knowing being, in distinction from the others. But in the last analysis this knowing is primarily a defensiveness. It prevents him from attaining true knowledge, the knowledge proper to man.

True knowledge, as the Hebrew ancients knew, is profoundly also the function of the body: "Adam knew his wife, and she conceived." The knowing that seeks to transcend the body is at last a participation in falsehood. It appears to provide freedom. Universities have written over their gates other Scriptural words, which they think pertain to their enterprise: "The truth shall make you free." They mean that knowing is that process by which man rises above nature. That is not what Jesus meant. True knowing would be that which enables a man to live within nature, without resenting it, "content and glad to be a creature." [50] The Jesus who promised his hearers the freeing truth spoke about lilies of the field and birds of the air, and proposed that man's knowing should enable him to live, like them, without anxiety! Free, not in the sense of having escaped from nature and the fate of all things natural, but free in the sense of *willing* to be what one is.

3. *Sin as man's attempt to construct an alternative environment.* Sin in the Biblical understanding is not only man's transgression of nature and his pathetic attempt to extricate himself from his own involvement in nature; it is also his prideful and perennial endeavor to create an alternative environment. The environment that God has provided is rejected. The new god, who has risen above nature in his vanity of imagination and will, sets out to create an environment more suitable to his vision of himself.

The essence of this better environment is the exclusion of nature. From the outset, the habitat man wills to make for himself is inspired by the desire to exclude. The city is the symbol of this desire—and more than a symbol. As Jacques Ellul has shown in his provocative Biblical study of the city, it is from the outset man's endeavor to construct an environment from which all reminders of his own nature, and of nature as such, have been banished. The Biblical city, from Babylon onward, is the testimony to man's sin. Not that the city is wholly rejected by the Biblical authors; for God, too, is at work building a city. He is constructing his redemptive city, the new Jerusalem, in the midst of the other, unnatural city of man. From man's side, however, the city is his bid for power and permanence, and his defense.

It is instructive to remember in these days of walls and boundaries that the first city, according to Biblical testimony, was defensive. But it was not a defense against other human enemies in the first instance; it was a fortress against nature. "Come, let us build ourselves a city, and a tower with its top in the heavens, . . . lest we be scattered abroad." [51] The purpose of Babylon is to preserve its inhabitants from nature. We who have contrived wondrous machinery for controlling nature may laugh at the belief—essentially a religious one—that thinks that walls will keep nature out, or that towers guarantee transcendence of the earth. But we should only have to examine our own cities to recognize that our laughter may be premature. Do our complex machines finally keep out nature? The weeds and grass break through our thickest concrete; death enters through the sterile walls of our apartments and hospitals. "Of these cities, all that will remain is that which blew through them, the wind." [52] It is conceivable that the walls which human civilizations have built to keep time and nature out have in reality only confined within them the worst elements of *human* nature.

4. *Sin as a state of alienation from nature.* The Christian concept of sin in its classical expressions includes the belief not only that sin is an *act* in which, time after time, man declares himself against God, his fellowmen, and his natural environment, but also a *state* in which, even apart from willful acts of apostasy and rejection, human life is lived. It is not only that we will our own estrangement from the others; we inherit a condition of estrangement that is centuries old, a labyrinth of distorted relationships, old greed, revenge upon revenge. Like the young lovers of Shakespeare's *Romeo and Juliet*, we find ourselves prevented from consummating our best ideals by our tragic involvement in the struggles of our clan. Existence has this tragic dimension, and every account of existence is shallow if it does not acknowledge it.

It is this tragic dimension that the traditional dogma of original sin was intended to preserve. Unfortunately that dogma became associated with such theories as the biological transmission of Adam's sin through the act of procreation, which render it questionable for our present purposes. But when modern thought dispensed altogether with this ancient teaching of the faith, it dispensed with one of the best insights of Christianity for understanding the world as many have experienced it in the twentieth century.

Included in the concept of original sin is the recognition that there is a deep enmity between man and nature which cannot be readily set aside. The condition into which each new generation is born is a condition not only of complex alienations between men, families, nations, races but of an estrangement between man and the ground. Man's rejection of the biosphere as a suitable environment is no new phenomenon. Even though it is always expressing itself in new ways (e.g., in the thinly cloaked attempt to find a better environment that lies behind the vaunted space programs of Russia and the United States), it is an old endeavor. The doctrine of original sin recognizes that the whole of man's *history* is in some profound sense a struggle to escape *nature*.[53]

The saga of the Fall expresses this struggle symbolically in the expulsion of the man and the woman from the Garden of Eden and the curse of work. These symbols uphold the Biblical insistence that sin alters irrevocably the essential harmony between man and earth, *adam* and *adamah*. There can be no simple return to Eden. One cannot just will it one fine day, or develop a new ideology on whose basis man might enter into friendship with earth. We are not born into a garden; we are born into a wilderness. Significantly, the temptation of the Second Adam occurs in the wilderness. However sincere our desires for a new relationship with the earth may be, we are the children of the fathers who ate bitter grapes. The soil has been poisoned and many species of birds and beasts made extinct. Lake Erie cannot be refreshed overnight by our good intentions. It will take hundreds of years to restore basic ecological balances in nature, even if we could rid ourselves of the factors that promote the imbalance. New possibilities there may and must be. But they are not simple, they are complex and tenuous. And always there is in them, if they are real possibilities, the recognition of the impossibility through which they must pass. Always there is in them some sense of the miraculous.[54]

THE DOMESTICATION OF SIN

If modern Christianity embraced only the "positive" elements of the traditional doctrine of creation, it applied this principle even more ruthlessly to the traditional doctrine of sin. It is rather difficult to eliminate altogether the negative connotations of this doctrine, let alone discover "positive" elements in it. Sin is sin. Even in the most secular world of today it retains a certain "bad" or at least "naughty" connotation—which to be sure can frequently be turned to the advantage of those who profit from the exploitation of man's fascination with whatever he regards as dangerous and immoral.

Since it is impossible to make sin "positive," the whole intention of modern Christianity as witnessed in the theological literature of the period is to rid itself altogether of the doctrine of sin.[55] It is an embarrassment. It is infinitely more embarrassing than the outmoded cosmology with which Christianity early recognized that it had been associated.[56]

The doctrine of sin touches upon something more fundamental than cosmology. It was and is in radical opposition to the modern vision, for it insists that man neither is nor could be fit to be master of the world. It insists, moreover, that man's *attempt* to do so is the quintessence of his distortion of humanity. In short, it enters into deadly combat with the whole image of man on which the modern experiment was based: the image of man as technocratic master of nature, with history going his way.

But this opposition was not permitted to come into an open combat. The inheritor of the doctrine of sin, modern Christianity, recognized more intuitively than consciously that doctrine's basic opposition to modernity. Quietly, without fanfare, and certainly without the attention achieved by the great disputes between science and religion, Christians adjusted their doctrine of sin to the times. To follow the history of this adjustment is very difficult, because it is such a noiseless affair. But that it actually occurred cannot be doubted. How, otherwise, could the strong doctrine of sin rediscovered by the Protestant Reformers—in a real sense the cornerstone of the Reformation—have given way within the space of two centuries to something entirely different? So different, indeed, as to have more in common with the popular medieval Catholic version of sin upon which the sale of indulgences was based than with Luther's which challenged the *distorted* doctrine behind the sale of indulgences!

The Biblical concept of sin has hardly ever been understood in the church. Except in rare instances—an Augustine or a Luther, a Pascal or a Kierkegaard—there has always been a tendency in organized Christianity to reduce sin to something less than the original sense of rebellion against God—against nature, against life itself. Few men have the courage (it is perhaps more a matter of courage than of wisdom) to face the truth that their condition could be a rejection so pervasive and deep. This is the real explanation of the church's unceasing abhorrence of the concept of "total depravity." It is not surprising therefore that throughout these twenty centuries—and in the centuries of Israel to which they are bound—a consistent attempt on the part of the "faithful" to reduce the meaning of sin to something less drastic can be documented. Even in the Bible itself there is evidence of this tendency.

In the modern period, however, the tendency took on the proportions of a movement. Never before had it occurred to mankind to think of itself in terms of mastery, and to have such brave goals for the species. Never before was it conceivable that man was strong enough or good enough to take his destiny into his own hands. Now at least it seemed that he had the power to do so. Whenever power is believable, it is never difficult to demonstrate the plausibility of a thing's wisdom and rightness as well.

On the strength of its tradition, its Scriptures, its confessions, the church was obliged at this point to raise the question about man's goodness. At least about goodness! [57] Is man *good* enough to master the earth? The question was not raised. If that question had been raised with sufficient seriousness by Christians at the outset of the modern epoch, it is possible that we should not today have come to the conclusion that nature's greatest problem is man-the-master.

Instead, the doctrine of sin was dispensed with as quickly and quietly as possible. Naturally it could not be eliminated altogether; it is integral to the language, liturgy, and—at a certain level—the appeal of Christianity. Where would the churches be without their reputation for providing comfort and rehabilitation for "the sinner"? But sin was reduced to something domestic. It became synonymous with immorality. "Sin" became "sins." Thus the churches could continue in their role as "curer of souls" without entering into the social and political fabric of life as questioner of basic cultural assumptions.

Another side of the process of sin's domestication could be called its spiritualization. Sin became a religious matter, the specialty of certain pietistic groups. Although the Biblical concept of sin makes it in the first instance rebellion against God, this rejection of God is never isolated from the other counterparts of man's threefold relatedness. What is from one perspective a rejection of God is from another the rejection of the fellowman, and from yet another the rejection of the natural environment. The definition of sin as a *religious* misdeed or failing is part of its domestication. It removes this insight from the arena of human life and brings it into the sanctuary; it becomes a matter "between a man and his God." It is a question of individual "rightness" or "wrongness" vis-à-vis "the Lord." Finally, this pietistic interpretation of sin, while in some respects more profound than the more secular Christian reduction of sin to immorality, is even less accessible for prophetic critique of the society than is the latter. At least when sin is defined as immorality it can be interpreted still as *social* immorality. In that way it can serve as the basis for potentially significant inquiry into and criticism of cultures—a possibility demonstrated prominently enough by the so-called social gospel in North America.

But neither pietism with its religious domestication of sin nor liberalism with its secular reduction of sin to immorality was able to raise the question that Christianity ought to have raised for the modern age from the start: the question whether man was good enough to master the earth. To put that question to modern man, it would have been necessary for the churches, precisely in the moment of man's most positive estimation of himself, to take up the posture of an Amos in the world and to become witnesses to the evil that lurks behind every human claim to greatness and goodness. Instead of searching the tradition for "more light," to corre- spond with man's sense of sloughing off the uncertainties and bondages of the "dark ages," the churches would have had to explore—in that moment—the gospel's witness to the darkness of the human situation. "The day of the Lord is darkness and not light."

At bottom the doctrine of sin is no doctrine at all—nothing so ineffectual as that—but a decision at the very heart of the faith. It is the decision that man's situation is one of darkness, sorrow, and profound need. Like all the central doctrines of Christianity, sin is never quite definable. It is a mystery. For it occurs at the deepest level of our relationships. Its reality has always evoked from men the propensity to reduce it to its consequences: to make sin "sins." For the mystery beneath the deeds is too deep for us to understand and too devastating for us to face. It is comforting for us to think of sin as evil, whether religious or moral evil, and so to posit goodness as its antithesis. But the antithesis of sin is not goodness, it is love.

Accordingly, when it is said that the one pertinent question that Christians ought to have raised was whether man was *good* enough to master the earth, this is not a simple question about human morality. Nor is it a religious question in the sense of pietism; it is not a question of man's "righteousness." At the most rudimentary level, *it is the question whether man, who would be master of the earth, is capable of loving that which he wants to master.* Is his will to mastery born of love for his fellow creatures, or is there in it a discernible contempt, even hatred? Is it because he wants to bring them to the fullness of their own potential—for such is always *love's* desire—or is it rather more a matter of their potential for aggrandizing his own existence? Will he sacrifice his own comfort, his own convenience, his own pleasure, his own wealth, for the object of his attentions; or will he allow rivers to run with corruption, forests to expire, species to die out, and his own body to be poisoned, because he does not love what he masters? Is it love that impels him—or perhaps the spirit of revenge?

Nietzsche, who pondered these things at a time when the Christians were at their most "positive" pursuits, knew at least that only those who are no longer driven by the spirit of revenge deserve to be masters of the earth.[58] Christianity is even more radical: it makes the prerequisite of mastery the love of what is mastered. It defines love as a spendthrift who gives everything for the sake of the beloved.[59] It is not enough to have lost the spirit of revenge, although that in itself is a wonder beyond our experience. But mastery—"dominion"!—according to Christian faith requires that the spirit of revenge, hatred, alienation, utilization, be replaced by love. A love that lays down its life for—the sheep!

The Christian doctrine of sin declares that man cannot meet this prerequisite for mastery. It dares to say this not only of degenerate, "natural" man but also of "the saints." Not even the apostles of Christ are acceptable for this mastery! It is somehow promised them: they are to become judges at last, to stand above the creatures. But it is at best an eschatological reality: it is "not yet." Those who through suffering are perfected in love may one day inherit the earth. Meantime, though they are learning love, they still bear the sin of Adam. They too still aim at a mastery whose motivation is more nearly revenge than love. It is never so obvious as in their attempts to master one another.[60]

The eschatological vision of the prophet Isaiah does indeed promise a "new creation" in which man is at last master. It confirms precisely the whole Biblical insistence that mastery is given only to those who love. In contrast to the mighty of the ancient or modern worlds, the one who masters in this vision of the consummation of things is a little child: "A little child shall lead them." [61] It is the most graphic symbol, not of power but of weakness, and of tenderest affection for the creatures who share his lot. But between this possibility and our time—the time of the church— there is a deep gulf which can be bridged only by the final judgment of the loving Creator. The vision of love's mastery may sometimes be antici- pated; but it is never realized, except by the One who rode without honor into Jerusalem on a beast.

Neither this doctrine of radical sin nor this eschatological vision of salvation influenced the dominant mood of Christianity during the period when Christians might have raised with insight the question of man's right to master the earth. Both in terms of its analysis of the human condition and its word to that condition, modern Christianity has been a pale shadow of Biblical faith. Having lost touch with the depths of the human predicament expressed in the doctrine of sin, Christianity lost touch also with the high vision of human destiny to which both the doctrine of creation and the doctrine of redemption speak. With neither heights nor depths, mainstream Christianity has functioned in the modern world chiefly as the religious expression of that cultural mediocrity which has become synonymous with the bourgeoisie. One might have said that it functioned as an ethic. But even as an ethic it is uninteresting, for it has been demonstrated again and again that the most influential movements respecting personal and social morality have been inspired by other sources. An imaginative ethic must exist in a state of tension with the culture. Christianity in the modern epoch was so industriously bent on claiming the modern outlook for itself that it minimized all tension. In the service of that claim, the Biblical concept of sin had to be rendered innocuous. With the disappearance of the doctrine of sin, any possibility of a truly prophetic critique was forfeited.

CHRISTIAN INCOMPETENCE IN THE FACE OF THE NIHIL

Behind its eagerness to be rid of a radical doctrine of sin and its exaggeration of "positive" elements in the doctrine of creation lay a complex quest for power on the part of the church in the modern era. We cannot analyze that quest adequately in the present context.[62] Suffice it to say that the effective cause of the wholesale theological surgery that has typified Christianity from the eighteenth century had to do with the ecclesiastical thrust for prominence. It was necessary for the church to position itself favorably in relation to the new power in the modern world, i.e., that social stratum which had most fully absorbed the possibilities of the new *imago hominis*—the middle class. After more than a thousand years of proximity to power, Christianity in the modern epoch was not about to relinquish this mode of relating to the kingdoms of this world.

But proximity to something as amorphous as a class is not easily acquired. It is one thing to achieve such proximity in the imperial civilization (convert the Emperor!), and to maintain it in the feudal situation (stay friends with the princes!). But what can be done when power moves from palaces to houses of merchants and civil servants and becomes diffuse throughout an entire social segment? There was only one way: the church in the modern world had to align itself *with the world view* of that class. It did not do so consciously, with Machiavellian craft; but quietly, automatically, following the dictates of a well-established instinct for proximity to power. To survive in the form to which it had become accustomed, Christianity had to adjust to the new, intensely positive estimate of the human condition upheld by this new power.[63]

At the theological level, what occurred in this process of realignment can be summarized in a single phrase: *the elimination of the negative.* As we have seen, this entailed a virtual overhauling of the faith. It meant adjusting the doctrine of divine providence to the doctrine of progress—and for that purpose the concept of radical evil in history had to be forfeited. It meant removing from the doctrine of creation those "primitive" elements offensive to modern rationalism—and for that purpose Christianity had to relinquish what it knew of man's immersion in nature. It meant, above all, the elimination of the Biblical understanding of man as sinner.

It would be inaccurate to say that the Christianity typical of the modern epoch, exemplified in its purest form on this continent, has merely *disregarded* the negative. From one point of view it could be legitimately claimed that the negative has been its preoccupation. Nothing so occupied its energy as the transformation of the negative. Whether liberal or conservative, individualistic or communal, the gospel by which the churches on this continent have lived is one that performs the same basic service. It transforms life's negatives into positives.

This practice should not be associated only with its more obvious forms, such as the cult of "positive thinking." What this cult has always offered to the American public is not an aberration, something altogether different, but the distillation of a more complicated but essentially identical gospel which has informed our entire continental experience. Norman Vincent Peale chooses different forms of the negative from those entertained by Christian conservatives such as Billy Graham. He has a different language and technique for exorcising it. But the basic thrust of Peale's "modernism" is the same as Graham's "Biblicism." It is to alleviate and remove the experience of negation. That is what salvation means for both. While it is certainly possible to find more sophisticated interpretations of this, it is extremely difficult to discover instances of Christian proclamation which do not assume that this transforming and eliminating of the negative is the function and task of true Christianity.

Inimical to this Christianity is not the negative as such, but the sustained experience of negation. It is unable to entertain an *unresolved* negative.

The practice of resolving the negative, however, contains an implicit pitfall. Given certain circumstances, this pitfall becomes obvious. Such circumstances have come upon the churches today.

To elaborate: Almost everyone who sets about to provide answers regularly defines problems by the capacity of his answers to satisfy them. This is, for instance, the whole basis of the technological salvation to which secular hope clings today. A problem is defined by the technological solution required to amend it. Problems defying technical solution are regularly ruled out as non-problems. They cannot summon the necessary empirical data to give them the status of problems. There are parallels to this process in the positive Christianity about which we have been reflecting.

Human beings manifest a certain willingness to accept this approach at most times. During *critical* times this willingness amounts to a psychic necessity. People need to hear that their problems are understood, and to believe that they are soluble. They will listen gladly to any who can offer credible applications of this method of problem-solving.

There comes a point, however, where reality overwhelms this process. Problems refuse to be silenced by answers. The problem that is beneath the problem surfaces. The conquering positive becomes impressive only in theory, or when carefully sheltered from the winds that blow. Life itself throws up too many negatives. Men cease to lend credence to the system, with its well-known techniques for coping with every predicament, for it has become all too obvious that these techniques are only stopgaps.

Christianity on this continent has never been known for its readiness to take on overwhelming human problems. It has usually shied away from them, especially at the theological level. An example is the problem of evil. This has been partly because we did not have the grand historical and natural exhibitions of evil and suffering that have been visited on other peoples. (The blacks are an exception, but they had another theology, too!) It has also been due, however, to an *a priori* theological decision. North American Christianity has been committed to a version of historical existence that denied in principle the possibility of the tragic; and it found that denial supported especially in its naturalistic interpretations of the doctrine of resurrection.

But we have seen our world moving daily toward the brink of tragedy. This is felt by more and more of our people today. Because it has been an "answering" religion, the Christianity of this continent has enjoyed a certain longevity, beyond that of the mother churches of Europe, which were more interested in announcing than in answering. But the very habit of answering has become the downfall of the churches in North America in these days. What has been happening increasingly in our midst is that the negative experiences to which we are subjected are so numerous, so various, and so complex that they overwhelm every attempt at resolution. More and more persons, even among the Middle American segment for

whom the churches have been sanctuaries against the darkness, find
Christian answering simplistic and unconvincing. There is a recurrent
and irrepressible sense that the problem has not been taken seriously
enough.

The search for an alternative theology can begin at the point where this
sense of dissatisfaction with Christian answers is permitted to grow; where
one faces that the problematic of contemporary man is unresolvable
within the terms of reference of positive religion.

Many who have reached that point already have found no alternative
posture *within* the Christian churches—or even within the Christian faith
less ecclesiastically defined. Some have given up faith of every kind,
finding that they could only be honest about their experience of the dark
by relinquishing altogether the religious quest for light. Others, perhaps a
greater number, have turned away from earth to the realm of pure spirit:
they seek the answers to problematic historical experience beyond history.
In reality that is not a genuine alternative, but a well-known variation on
the theme. It merely transfers the negating of the negation to another
world, thus providing a convenient rationale for the abandonment of this
one.

Anyone who refuses to adopt the solution of a flight from history, on the
one hand, or the abandonment of hope on the other, can only ask: Is there
a gospel which, without offering unbelievable earthly answers or unacceptable heavenly ones, will nevertheless help me to live in this world without
ultimate despair? Is it possible to discover a faith that does not require me
to repress the unbelief that rises up in me as I contemplate the present and
future darkness of this world? Is it possible to hope without embracing the
official optimism of this society and of its religion?

Christianity gave away all of its greatest insights for understanding the
contemporary world in order to make itself acceptable to the *modern* world
view. The task of theology in North America today is to ask whether the
characteristic experience of contemporary man can be met, explored, and
illuminated by an expectation that is recognizably "Christian," though it
may be a far cry from the Christianity to which the modern church
introduced us.

PART TWO

IN SEARCH
OF A LOST TRADITION

THE ARGUMENT

THE PHILOSOPHER Nietzsche registered this complaint about Jesus: He promises more than he can deliver.[1] In this, as in many other things, Nietzsche spoke for an epoch. Not for his own, which was still making Jesus synonymous with its new man, but for ours.

Humanly speaking, religion is always a matter of promise. Its chief function seems to be to keep expectancy alive. To preserve us from the death of spirits that have ceased looking for anything new under the sun. Religion feeds the human need to hope: to hope that old patterns and cycles can be broken; to hope that new possibilities may be introduced even when experience denies the prospect; to hope that the unheard of may occur even at the edge of the Red Sea. Whoever has sympathy for man and some understanding of human culture does not despise religion, even in its humblest forms. Apart from the hope that men's religions have provided and sustained, human civilization would long ago have become extinct. Perhaps that is why there is today a new quest for religion, precisely on the part of the young, in whom the instincts for survival are strongest. It is at the level of this basic need to hope that culture depends on cult.

But there is an obvious danger in all religion. Religious belief, preoccupied with the human need to hope, too easily ends by creating a secondary world—a world that is conformed to its hope; a world that no longer touches upon the world in which we really live, where to live is "to be sad" (Keats). The pain of *this* world is "answered" (but not really answered) by the creation of another, better world, where hope is possible and realizable. Thus the very world that has given rise to the need that religion seeks to fulfill is bypassed by the religious zeal for the perfecting of hope. In the service of expectancy, experience is set aside.

109

Consequently, religion becomes unbelievable to the most sensitive, honest, and earthbound. Their commitment to *this* world, with its inherent possibilities and promises, prevents them from accepting solutions to its *im*possibilities and anguish which in reality substitute for it some other world. The danger of such a religion, however, is not merely that those most committed to earth are excluded almost *a priori,* but that it carries off from the daily concern for earth many who might otherwise serve the causes of humanity more usefully. From the standpoint of worldly responsibility, such religion becomes a destructive and even demonic force.

Something of this kind happened to Christianity in the modern epoch. There was, however, an important nuance in it. Whereas heretofore the tendency of Christianity was to produce secondary worlds which transcended this one spatially and temporally, modern Christianity gave itself over to a vision that promised the imminent emergence of the better world *within history.*

From the perspective of the Biblical affirmation of this world's goodness and reality, this was in a certain respect commendable, for it was the declaration, especially eloquent in its best representatives, that Christian faith has after all to do with *this* world and that the abandonment of creation in favor of some heavenly secondary creation is the very essence of disobedience. But in its final effect, this version of Christian expectancy was not different from the earlier versions. For in order to embrace the this-worldly expression of the heavenly Kingdom, it had to minimize the character of evil and maximize the good to the point of exaggeration. Thus the modern religious vision became the preoccupation with a secondary world at least as dangerous as its precursors.

Was it not in fact more dangerous? At least the earlier versions of expectancy identified the Christian hope with visions of beatitude from the perspective of which its adherents were able to recognize evil in *this* world. The modern form of expectancy adopted by Christianity, and by the culture at large, was committed to a secondary world which had to manifest itself in daily demonstrations of progress. It no longer transcended "this vale of tears," a mystery somehow real although invisible and contradicted at every point. The world entertained by the hope of modern Christianity was visible, and daily becoming more so. Its visibility in theory required confirmation in practice, for it was a theory of *historical* existence. Thus the nonrecognition, minimization, and resolution of evil formed an integral part of the new world view from its inception.

So long as the ideology of progress could seem to be sustained by experience, it did not require so great an effort to close one's eyes to the evils that were present, always, even at the height of the age of progress. The secondary world of expectation could seem a veritable primary world, the world of experience, or at least the reasonable end toward which the experienced world was inevitably moving. But in these latter decades, the world dreamed of by our pious and impious forefathers alike has been contradicted continuously and devastatingly by experience. It can be maintained as an expression of hope only at the expense of shutting one's eyes to experience altogether. The nonrecognition and minimization of evil, which was part of this enterprise from the outset, has assumed the proportions of a way of life: the way of the repressive society. To cling to this secondary world of expectation today is to abandon the world of daily suffering and responsible stewardship.

Modern Christianity let its hope be tied to the secondary world of the expectations of modern industrial optimism. Thus it has become unbelievable to those most committed to the primary world of experience, who during the past decades have learned that modern optimism is premature. Identifying itself with the day that seemed to be dawning for man after so many "dark ages," Christianity too hurriedly discarded what it knew about the night. So thoroughly did it banish the children of darkness from its house that it has been unable to recognize them in their later return, seven times more deadly. In the age of light, Christianity was naturally ashamed of its long association with the dark. It seemed to be suffocated by trafficking with sin, death, and the devil. Its pertinence, its very survival in such an age, seemed to require ridding itself of these dismal associations. In that zeal for identification with the expectations of the most expectant epoch in the history of mankind, the dominant Christianity of the West—especially highlighted in North America—became a stranger to the age-old experiences of mankind: the experiences of guilt and judgment; of tragedy, chaos, failure; of despair and death; of the whole range of negation.

It is still so. Notwithstanding the Christian sages who have appeared in these decades to interpret, in the light of faith, our own awful darkness, North American Christians still insist on being strangers to the night. The typical Christianity of our cities and villages even today, after nearly a century of war, after Auschwitz and Hiroshima, and in anticipation of devastations still more terrible, is speechless in the face of the experience of evil. This Christianity has neither awareness of nor the wherewithal to reflect upon the contemporary darkness. In reality it functions primarily as insulation against the darkness. It leaves the detailing of the night to sociologists, novelists, and others, whose estimate of the human condition it regularly pronounces to be exaggerated—the pessimism of unbelievers!

The great works of art, literature, drama, and music of our epoch, which are overwhelmingly concerned with the experience of negation, are as hateful to most avowed Christians as to the middle class at large—and for identical reasons.

On the other hand, this Christian incapacity for the negative is evidenced by the great willingness of Christian pastors and others to refer to "the experts" every real encounter with that which negates. Having no active remembrance of its own theological, liturgical, or pastoral traditions for the encounter with the darkness, such Christianity can only turn with helpless gestures to psychiatry, medicine, or some other branch of science when it senses the preserve of the "Prince of Darkness." In the face of the "last enemy," death, this Christianity would be totally incapacitated were it not for the well-ordered ministrations of the funeral establishment and the elaborate secondary world of which it is part.

Beyond that, it is even possible that official Christianity is more deeply committed to the positive modern outlook than most other institutions of society, even the educational establishment. Being more conservative than most other institutions, the churches are proving to be almost the only places left in the "free" Western world where one can still hear the great affirmatives of modern man proclaimed with something like enthusiasm.

But for those who cannot repress experienced evil, the world testified to by these Christians has become a secondary world quite beyond reach. The Christians, mistaking this for the modern rejection of God and the prescientific world view of the Bible, busy themselves with new apologies for God and updating their universe. But the most characteristically contemporary men in the world today are not those who reject God and the tripartite universe of early and medieval theology. What is offensive to the sensitive is Christian naïvety—not about science, but about evil. What they reject in the first instance (they do not get so far as God!) is Christian bourgeois optimism about man and his world. It is the *expectations* of the churches that they find incredible and naïve. For these expectations are still put forward as though nothing had happened since August, 1914, to call them into question. In short, it is the very world view that Christians learned from modernity that makes Christianity inaccessible, in a primary sense, to contemporary men who have entered most deeply into the spirit of our times. The Jesus testified to by this Christianity—who is in reality the embodiment of the new image of man produced by the modern epoch—promises more than he can deliver.

What can be learned from all of this? Evidently that the crucial thing about any religion is the character of its expectancy. Just what does it offer by way of hope? That it will be in a basic way an expression of the human need to hope is a matter of definition. But today it has been precisely the need and right to hope that has been called into question. As Camus put it, we must now learn to think soberly and hope no more. Just that is the most succinct expression of experience in our time. If therefore there is any possibility of religious faith beyond this experience (and it is not axiomatic that there is), it will depend even more than in the past upon the care with which religion defines its expectancy for man and his world.

Concretely and for us, the test of authenticity where hope is concerned today is its awareness of hopelessness. What has to be asked of any system in which human hope embodies itself is whether its expectations have emerged from the crucible of honest encounter with human experience in its present, especially in its most denigrating, forms. That an ideology of hope, whether secular or sacred, will find adherents today cannot be doubted. Precisely on account of the darkness, many run with willing feet after anything that announces itself in positive terms. Witness the fate of the European and South American "theology of hope" on this continent. Popularity is therefore no test of authenticity, and may even indicate that something is amiss. The test of hope is whether it can be entertained, even for a moment, by those who "think clearly and hope no more." What is offered by way of hope today can be taken seriously only insofar as it is continually being distilled from the conflict with that manifold hopelessness which permeates the contemporary world. Nothing is more impertinent than the parading of expectations of the past, or of some other culture, as if they were accessible now and here.

Is Christianity capable of articulating a theology of expectation which is not in essence and *a priori* a denial of contemporary experience? Can Christian faith really enter into the darkness of the world today without succumbing to it, on the one hand, or on the other without carrying with it all sorts of ersatz light—light that may have been real for past generations—that has nothing to do with the light of the world, our world? Can Christian faith become a meeting place for the creative conflict of experience and expectation today? Or is it the nature of Christianity, and perhaps of all religion, to produce secondary worlds, and so to be accessible only to those who desire openly or secretly to have done with this one?

What follows is written in the conviction that at least there has been in Christian history a thin tradition which tried to proclaim the possibility of hope without shutting its eyes to the data of despair, a tradition which indeed insisted that authentic hope comes into view only in the midst of

apparent hopelessness and probably over against what announces itself as
hope in a given society. This is, we must emphasize, a *thin* tradition. It has
appeared only here and there, now and then—it never really belonged to
Christendom. It was altogether lost to the modern mind. Certainly it has
never been part of the experience of that Christianity whose establishment
we have traced on this continent. In itself, it is by no means beyond
reproach. Like every theology, it has its own inherent dangers. But it is
eminently worthy of our attention today, for it offers itself to those—and
only those—who have failed, and who suspect that whatever future
remains to them can be entered only through a profound exploration of
the meaning of their failure. It steadfastly refuses, in any case, the demand
for a new beginning that does not pass straight through the center of what
is ending. For it rejects, above all, the creation of secondary worlds. It is
grounded in this world, like the cross of Calvary, and it will not abandon
this world for all the hope of heaven. If it offers new expectations, it does
so only for those who pass through the experience of darkness and death
with open eyes.

We shall begin our search for this thin and lost tradition by examining
some of its exemplars. This journey into the past (and the near-present)
will not in itself suffice to acquaint us with the tradition in question.
Perhaps the most significant thing that this tradition has to teach us is that
the authentic expression of Christian hope depends upon the encounter
with the despair that is native to our own time and situation. But we are
obliged to relate to expressions of this tradition in the past, to learn its
elements there. In the final section of the study, we shall attempt to apply
these elements indigenously to the situation that has been described in
Part One. It would thus be possible to think of this portion of our research
as an endeavor to obtain help from the past for the sake of understanding
the present and the future. That in itself is a practice inimical to
modernity, for it involves reaching behind the age of progress for wisdom
that was lost to that age. Our scouring of the past, however, ought in no
way to suggest the desire for a romantic return to an earlier period. That
would be a betrayal of the whole enterprise. We have no more desire to
find a better, secondary world in the past, as a way out of present trouble,
than to court the transcendent world of spirit or to savor the otherworldliness of some current this-worldly ideologies! We look to the past for help
only—not for refuge.

IV

EXEMPLARS
OF A THIN TRADITION

The "Other" Gospel

"I am astonished," wrote the apostle Paul to the Christians at Galatia, "that you are so quickly deserting him who called you in the grace of Christ and turning to a different gospel—not that there is another gospel, but there are some who trouble you and want to pervert the gospel of Christ. But even if we, or an angel from heaven, should preach to you a gospel contrary to that which we preached to you, let him be accursed." (Gal. 1:6–8.)

The "other" gospel against which Paul wrote in such strenuous language was a religion of law, of moralistic and liturgical observations, of distinctions between persons, of pretension to possess righteousness. For hope it substituted immediate realization of the goal; for faith it substituted vision; for love it substituted obedience to laws. It was, above all, a religion that offered men clear-cut paths to the attainment of a glory in keeping with their human expectations. As such it was the very antithesis of the gospel that Paul preached, which found the only authentic glory in the cross of Christ, at the point where human possibilities and hopes were canceled. "Far be it from me to glory except in the cross of our Lord Jesus Christ, by which the world has been crucified to me, and I to the world. For neither circumcision counts for anything, nor uncircumcision, but a new creation." (Gal. 6:14–15.)

Perhaps the most ironic fact of the history of Western civilization is that the "other" gospel against which Paul spoke in the name of the crucified Christ became, in a very short time, the dominant religion of the West, bearing the name and emblems of the Christ, including his cross! So

normative did this "other" gospel become that from the standpoint of
quantitative comparison, it is the gospel of Paul, and not the Galatian aberration, that must be regarded as the exception—the "other"
gospel.

What makes Paul's gospel "other"—i.e., different from the gospel that
has dominated Christendom—is the kind of attention it pays to the cross of
Jesus Christ. The dominant gospel of Christendom—the one that the
Galatians and others discovered very early in the game—is by no means
unaware of the cross. It could hardly be left out of account. It is said that
Constantine, through whom Christianity first became the official religion
of the West, conquered in the sign of the cross. The world of official
Christianity has been full of crosses and crucifixes, and remains so until
this very day. But there is an infinite difference between the ways in which
the cross is regarded in these two traditions. The dominant, Galatian
tradition looks at the cross from the standpoint of its overcoming. It exists
as the symbol of that which stood in the way of human expectations, and
which has been set aside. Thus, "In this sign, *conquer!*" the emphasis is
upon the last word. Modern Protestantism, especially as it was expressed
in our New World, was a legitimate extension of this dominant tradition
when it eliminated the cross altogether from its centers of worship, which
was the case in Protestant churches until three or four decades ago. At
least it eliminated the *crucifixus.* The cross-without-the-Christ became the
symbol of victory, triumph in the face of all difficulties, unlimited horizons.
In the gospel of Paul, where the thin tradition for which we are looking
has its New Testament origins,[2] the cross is regarded as the permanent
standing ground of the Christian. It is a symbol of the reality in which he
participates and into which he must again and again be initiated. It is a
place of waiting for the hope that is against all human hope. It insists that
possibilities are given only through the experience of limits; that the way
to victory lies through exposure to death and defeat. It calls into question
everything that commends itself to men as heroic.

Luther, who gained most of his best insights from Paul, gave the thin
tradition a name. He called it "the theology of the cross": *theologia crucis.*
He also named the other, dominant tradition: *theologia gloriae*—"theology
of glory." In our search for the lost tradition we shall turn first to this one
who classified it. Although the tradition is much older than Luther, it
achieved a certain clarity in him—largely, perhaps, because by his time
the questionable elements in the other, dominant tradition were manifested openly and without bothering to disguise their basically crass
intentions.

The Theology of Beggars

In a fragment of a sermon prepared for St. Martin's Day, Nov. 11, 1515, we read one of Luther's first allusions to the theme that became the heart of his theology: *"Unum praedica: sapientiam crucis"* ("Preach one thing: the wisdom of the cross").[3] Luther's last written words, thirty-one years later, were: *"Wir sind Bettler; das ist wahr"* ("We are beggars, that's true").[4] Between the memorandum of the young preacher and the moving summation of the dying Reformer, there is an essential unity: To confess "the wisdom of the cross" means, at the most existential level, to know oneself devoid of wisdom. It means being a beggar where understanding is concerned—where life itself is concerned. The gospel of the cross condemns every pretension to possession. It divests man of all he has attempted to use to cover up his essential nakedness. It reduces him to the status of a beggar, robbed, beaten, and naked at the side of the road. Only a beggar can receive the gift of grace. Moreover, he must become a beggar again and again. His natural tendency is to regard himself as self-sufficient, autonomous, master of the situation. Even the man of faith—he especially—falls into this habit. He turns faith itself into the stuff that will elevate him above the beggarly condition. He regards himself as growing progressively beyond his beggarly condition. Luther made sanctification and justification almost synonymous, precisely to avoid this implication. At the end as at the beginning, "we are beggars."

Theology itself is not excluded from the beggarly condition. "The theology of the cross" is not only a way of speaking about existence, it is also a way of speaking about theology. It was in fact in response to his recognition of his beggarly condition *as a theologian* that Luther penned his final words. The theology of the cross can never be a brilliant statement about the brokenness of life; it has to be a broken statement about life's brokenness, because it participates in what it seeks to describe. Apart from that participation, it would be empty chatter. Hence, for Luther "a man becomes a theologian by living, by dying and being damned, not by understanding, reading and speculating."[5] The anti-intellectuals of modern Christianity should not find in this any support for their cause.

What exactly is the theology of the cross, according to Luther? Although it is at the very heart of the Reformation, the *theologia crucis* is hardly understood today among Protestants. As Ernst Käsemann has pointed out, "In English-speaking circles especially it represents a confessional narrowness or even a gross misinterpretation, and these opinions have had unfortunate effects in ecumenical conversations."[6] Many Anglo-Saxon Christians have never even encountered the term, and others are bound to hear it as if it were a rather technical reference to the doctrine of atonement.

It is therefore necessary at once to clarify that for Luther "the theology of the cross" is a way of speaking about the entire enterprise of Christian theology. It is sometimes argued that the theology of the cross was Luther's emphasis only in his early career as a Reformer. This is, however, based largely on a failure to understand what Luther means by *theologia crucis*. It is true that he seldom uses the term in his later writings. And it certainly must be asked whether he ever learned to translate this theology into ethical terms, especially the terms of a social ethic. Nevertheless from beginning to end his whole approach is consistent with what he wants to say in this category, *theologia crucis*. For him, it is not a special theological theme or an emphasis adopted for polemical purposes. Nor does it connote merely a particular doctrine—the doctrine of the cross or the doctrine of atonement. Obviously it is polemical. From the first it was defined in opposition to another theological approach, the *theologia gloriae*. Obviously also it does have something to do with the cross and the atoning work of the Christ. As Aulén and others have pointed out,[7] Luther created a turning point in the history of the doctrine of atonement because of his special theological approach. But its being polemical and integrally related to the theology of atonement should not obscure the fact that it is far more inclusive than these applications. The truth is, *theologia crucis* in Luther refers to a spirit and a method, a way of conceiving of *the whole* content of the faith and the task of theology. It is, in short, Luther's appropriation of the Pauline decision "to know nothing among you except Jesus Christ and him crucified" (I Cor. 2:2). To this Scripture, Luther returns again and again. It is the *locus classicus* of the theology of the cross.[8]

The term as such, *theologia crucis,* was first employed by Luther in 1518. In that year he prepared the theses known as the Heidelberg Disputation for delivery before the brothers of the Augustinian monastery. In this document, Luther introduces the two slogans, *theologia crucis* and *theologia gloriae,* to distinguish two different, antithetical ways of regarding the faith. The theology of glory is Luther's way of designating that against which he is conducting his search for a true theology. It refers to the whole endeavor of Scholasticism and the triumphalism of papal Christendom. It stands for the attempt of man to have direct access to the power and glory of God. In terms of knowledge this has meant the identification of faith and reason; in terms of salvation it has meant the confusion of faith with works. Over against the theology of glory Luther writes the following theses:

(16) The person who believes that he can obtain grace by doing what is in him adds sin to sin so that he becomes doubly guilty. (17) Nor does speaking in this manner give cause for despair, but for arousing the desire to humble oneself and seek the grace of Christ. (18) It is certain that man must utterly despair of his own ability before he is prepared to receive the grace of Christ. (19) That person does not deserve to be called a theologian who looks upon the invisible things of God as though they were clearly perceptible in those things which have actually happened (Rom. 1:20). (20) He deserves to be called a theologian, however, who comprehends the visible and manifest things of God seen through suffering and the cross. (21) A theology of glory calls evil good and good evil. A theology of the cross calls the thing what it actually is.[9]

It is hard to exaggerate the radicalism of what was being propounded here. The older monks of the Heidelberg monastery could only shake their heads in dismay at what they heard. We who have been reared in the linear Protestantism of North America, which not only never knew the *theologia crucis* as such but also followed the general tradition of empiricism in having no traffic with paradox, are just as dumbfounded.

The true *theology,* we are told, is one that discerns the presence of the omnipotent God, not in manifestations of power and glory, whether in nature or history, but on the contrary in the midst of peril and uncertainty and suffering. In short, where he seems altogether absent.

The true *God,* we are told, is not in fact the omnipotent monarch whose glory the religious attempt to reflect, but One who divests himself of power, who hides himself under the opposite of what the world recognizes as omnipotence. Luther does not even hesitate to employ the term (shocking to every theology of glory) *Deus crucifixus* ("the crucified God"). His doctrine of God, like every other aspect of his theology, is determined by the decision to know only "Christ crucified." God is therefore no other than the One who manifests himself on the cross. "He who has seen me has seen the Father."

The true *Christian life* is not a life of *securitas,* lived out in the midst of a world in which the triumph of the good is assured. On the contrary, to enter upon such a life is to be denied every form of security. For Luther sees man, too, under the form of the Crucified *(sub specie Christi)*. The only real security is the security of the beggar. It entails being stripped of everything men call security and safety. "A theologian of the cross," says Luther, "(that is, one who speaks of the crucified and hidden God) teaches that punishments, crosses, and death are the most precious treasury of all and the most sacred relics which the Lord of his theology himself has consecrated and blessed." [10]

Therefore true *faith* is the antithesis of a triumphant confidence. To be sure, there is a certitude of faith. But it is not at all what men usually mean by it. The certitude of faith is not a matter of demonstration or success, but a matter of trust: trust in the promise of a God who gives life to the dead and calls into existence the things that are not (Rom., ch. 4), a God who creates *ex nihilo*, who according to the Scriptures raised his Son from the dead. This certitude of faith is not available for possession. In fact, it is experienced only here and there, now and then; and it lives in constant tension with its antithesis. As Paul Althaus has written of Luther's *theologia crucis:*

> The theology of the cross is the theology of faith: the theology of faith is and remains, however, the theology of temptation *(Theologia der Anfechtung)*. Theological thinking and speaking does not occur apart from doubt and temptation, and faith's overcoming of temptation; rather it is and remains a thinking within this process, that is, thinking within the framework of *Anfechtung.*[11]

True faith, then, is "not sight." It is a possibility only as that which awakens the antithesis, radical disbelief. It persists, if at all, only in the midst of "attacks of utter despair" (Tillich's translation of the German word *Anfechtung,* one of Luther's favorite terms).[12] In Luther's own words:

> Faith has to do with things not seen (Heb. 11:1). Hence in order that there may be room for faith, it is necessary that everything which is believed should be hidden. It cannot, however, be more deeply hidden than under an object, perception, or experience which is contrary to it. Thus when God makes alive he does it by killing, when he justifies he does it by making men guilty, when he exalts to heaven he does it by bringing down to hell. . . . Thus God hides his eternal goodness and mercy under eternal wrath, his righteousness under iniquity.[13]

Most significant for our present concerns is that the theology of the cross as Luther elaborates it takes its stand *within* the experience of negation. It neither minimizes nor seeks to absorb the evil and impossibility of human existence into a finally triumphant goodness. The negative is not annulled by an overwhelming positive. Evil remains evil, and the theology of the cross does not have to lie about it: it can "call the thing what it actually is" (Heidelberg Disputation, Thesis 21).

Expectation, if it is authentic, only comes out of the experience that cancels the right to expect anything. The Christian, no less than the "natural man," and in a real sense even more than he, lives and must live with this canceling out—this overwhelming sense of failure and negation. For Luther, the child of his times, that experience amounted at times to absolute certainty that he was eternally guilty and had been abandoned to the fury of hell. He had to live not only with a vague and indefinite sense of nothingness but with one that expressed itself in the lurid and specific terms of his own world of experience. Expectation—i.e., the hope of forgiveness and redemption—could become real only as it emerged from the grim recognition that such expectations are after all without foundation in the data of one's own daily experience. What experience puts forward as the prospect of the future is, on the contrary, a hell of abandonment.

Protestant piety on this continent has prided itself in the declaration that the cross is "empty." In the Reformation theology of Martin Luther, the cross is by no means empty. It is, to be sure, the cross of the Christ. If with the religious one is able to regard it as Christ's *alone,* it is not difficult to think of it as having given up its victim long ago. It is not difficult to get such a Christ off his cross. But Luther is no docetist. The cross belongs first to us—to mankind, to every man. It becomes the cross of Jesus the Christ because only so can he identify with us and so break the power of what destroys us. The cross is the logical, "necessary" point to which the incarnation moves: to be "made flesh" is to become "being-towards-death" (Heidegger). He was "crucified, dead and buried," because that is *our* destiny—and for the same reason the creeds affirm that he "descended into hell." The theology of the incarnation is and remains a theology of the cross, for it proclaims a God whose will is to be with us, where we are (Emmanuel). To get the Christ, the Son of God, off the cross has never been a difficult problem for the theology of glory. But to get *us* off the cross—which is, after all, Christ's own work—is another matter. Least of all can it be achieved by reiterating the confession that Jesus has risen. When that is done, as it is so often done, with a certain fanfare and Easter Sunday gusto which behaves as if now everything were entirely put to rights, it is ironic and sometimes repulsive. The cross of the world and of man remains after all the Easter sermons have been preached and all the Hallelujahs sung. "Vietnam" has not disappeared. Nor have our own deepest personal involvements in the night. We cannot indulge in expectations of release which are only credible to those who are prepared "to call evil good." The test of expectation is whether it articulates itself from the cross, from the grave, from hell—and knows it!

   This is not to say that Luther's theology of the cross constitutes a denial
of the resurrection triumph. The question of the relationship between
cross and resurrection is the most difficult one in Christian theology. We
shall return to it specifically in the subsequent chapter. For the present,
let us notice merely that Luther's conception of the resurrection is framed
within the *theologia crucis*. That is, he avoids speaking about the resurrection
in such a way as to imply that the human condition of forsakenness, into
which Jesus as the Christ entered unreservedly, has been surpassed. "Even
the exalted Christ is not the last word; his sovereignty is still being
disputed by the power of death, and is therefore contested till the end of
time, and is therefore questionable." [14] Christ has traversed the infinite
abyss between cross and resurrection. Decisively—and yet not finally.
Were it final, we should have been left behind, nailed to our crosses,
doubly forsaken. So Luther's Christ forever returns to his cross, to his
grave, to hell, in order to be "with us." He can be "for us" only insofar as
he is "with us." Hence, in distinction from the Calvinistic tradition, which
was much more attracted to the resurrection triumph as its basic
statement, the crucifix was retained in the Lutheran tradition as the
normative liturgical symbol.
   There can be no simple statement of this. It lies within the heart of the
eschatological mystery which Christian theology tries—in vain—to articulate: what has been called the paradox of the "already/not yet." Still,
what Luther was trying to do is clear enough, even humanly speaking. He
wanted to offer salvation that was not cheap, that did not simply bypass
the real damnation of the human condition. He was nauseated by a
system which, with all its academic excellence and religious seriousness,
had boiled down to heaven-for-money at the level of common life.

>   Wenn das Geld im Kasten klingt,
>   die Seele in den Himmel springt.

What made this religion cheap was not its crudeness, its vulgarity. Luther
himself was not above vulgarity. What made it cheap was that it
offered—and finally offered for sale!—what could not be offered: viz.,
immediate release, deliverance, glory. That could not be offered because
it was simply not available. It could not be offered because life in this
world is and remains participation in evil, sin, death, and temptation; it is
and remains exposure to nothingness. A salvation which promises
deliverance from all that is simply a lie: "A theology of glory calls evil
good and good evil." It *must* contradict experience. It can function only as
a false comfort. Marx was standing within the line of Luther when he said
that religion was the opiate of the people. The attempt of Luther was to

make Christian faith something different from that. He wanted a gospel that drove men into the world, not away from it; that opened their eyes to what was there, rather than assisting them to look past what was there. "The theology of the cross calls the thing what it really is."

Luther's theology of resurrection is—to borrow Käsemann's excellent phrase in describing the Pauline theology of the cross—"a chapter in the theology of the cross." [15] Certainly he proclaimed the *victory* of the Crucified—and as Aulén has proposed, Luther even rediscovered the concept of "victory" as the central concept in the early church's doctrine of atonement. But however boldly Luther announced this victory of the third day, he never did so in such a way as to suggest that now, after Easter, the cross is no longer an authentic representation of the human situation. On the contrary, what makes Luther's theology a theology *of the cross* and not, in a roundabout manner, a theology of glory, is that the gospel is for him not the good news of *deliverance from* the experience of negation so much as it is the permission and command to enter into that experience with hope. "The glory of Jesus consists in the fact that he makes his disciples on earth willing and capable to bear the cross after him." [16] The grounds for the hope are not found in natural or historical experience generally; they are not openly accessible to human reason, or available to the religious. They are visible only to beggars, who in their own forsakenness and suffering find themselves in the company of One forsaken as they are; One who leads them ever more deeply into the night, with the promise that the day is at hand.

FAITH SEES BEST IN THE DARK

Søren Kierkegaard was a Lutheran, but not in the usual sense. He was not interested in perpetuating the thing that has inspired so much Lutheranism and has made it finally a repudiation of Luther. Luther's theology of the cross was soon dissipated. It was either turned into a frankly triumphalistic emphasis which never had much difficulty relating to Nordic aggressiveness—"from cross to crown" *(durch Kreuz zum Licht)*. Or else it found its way into the popular pietism which fed that Nordic melancholy of which Karl Barth later complained. No doubt the seeds of this dissolution are already to be found in Luther himself. He was hardly a consistent theologian, and there were elements in his thought which did militate against his main theological emphasis, the *theologia crucis*. Of these, two have particular importance for our study of the thin tradition: his identification of sin with guilt, and his failure to apply the theology of the cross to social structures and to the church itself. It was Kierkegaard,

more than any other in the tradition of Luther, who made the theology of
the cross speak to these areas which were still inaccessible to the medieval
man in Martin Luther.

Few theologians ever explored the concept of sin more imaginatively
than Luther. In spite of that, his is a vision of human pathos and
degradation that is bound to seem dated to modern men. It belongs to
another epoch—a time in which God and righteousness, Satan and the
smell of sulfur were much closer to earth than they are today. It goes with
a world in which sickness could be attributed to immorality, witches were
burned, and lightning meant the wrath of God. That world, as we have
already had occasion to observe, began to wane very soon after Luther's
time. It was already on its way out during his lifetime. Some, like
Erasmus of Rotterdam, and even Philip Melanchthon, were better
representatives than Luther of the new *imago hominis* that was coming to
be. Within a century the world had been demythologized by the learned,
and the measuring and mastering of it had commenced. Within a
century, too, another man who explored the human condition at depth
was writing about life's negation in terms very different from those of
Luther:

> To-morrow, and to-morrow, and to-morrow,
> Creeps in this petty pace from day to day
> To the last syllable of recorded time;
> And all our yesterdays have lighted fools
> The way to dusty death. Out, out, brief
>   candle!
> Life's but a walking shadow, a poor player
> That struts and frets his hour upon the stage
> And then is heard no more. It is a tale
> Told by an idiot, full of sound and fury,
> Signifying nothing.[17]

While the scientists, full of boyish enthusiasm, set about measuring the
earth, the poets had already begun to measure the souls of the measurers.
They found them wanting. But the new sense of negation of which
Shakespeare is an early explorer is not so much associated with guilt,
damnation, and enslavement to principalities and powers—nothing so
dramatic. It is, rather, this petty pace, this meaningless round, this endless
playing of parts.

Luther's understanding of sin and the abyss had more in common with
Anselm's than with Shakespeare's. He looked for a loving God, and could
find such a God only by exploring in depth his own unloveliness and

sordidness. The new explorers began to look for any kind of God at all. The condition they had to chart was one that gave little evidence of such a being. It was called, later, the condition of the absurd. It did not wait for Auschwitz; it laid the foundations for Auschwitz. The early explorers of the absurd were at work long before Camus and Sartre. Some of them, like Shakespeare, were contemporaries of those explorers and developers of that new world in which the new man had determined to create a new society.

The association of Christianity with guilt is in itself not wrong. The gospel is a word of forgiveness; and guilt, as Kafka, Freud, and numerous other impeccably modern men have demonstrated anew, belongs to the human condition. But in the context of Christian conservatism, the association of Christianity and guilt becomes regressive. What it has meant is that instead of permitting itself to enter into the experience of negation characteristic of the age, Christianity by and large has been content to receive its analysis of the misery of man from those who explored it deeply in previous ages. Thus Paul, Augustine, Anselm, Calvin, and Luther—all of course drastically codified and domesticated— became the definers of the human condition for all time. It was not necessary for orthodoxy to go into the marketplace to find out what sin meant at the moment; it was all there in the confessions, in creeds and catechisms and volumes of dogmatics. So even today the churches continue to address a world oppressed by the sense of guilt, when the most devastating manifestation of sin today is the pervasive sense of purposelessness.

Kierkegaard knew he was living in a world that begged this question of meaning. From the perspective of the twentieth century it could be said that the fullness of the experience of the absurd was not to break through in Kierkegaard; nevertheless he provided many of the categories in which the late explorers of man's emptiness could express themselves. The fact that not all of these have been able to follow Kierkegaard in his confession of faith that "sees best in the dark" [18] does not disqualify his analysis. On the contrary, it means that he was struggling with the reality of sin in our own epoch. He *had* gone out into the marketplace. Although he spent much time in solitary confinement at his writing desk, he lived in the marketplace too. This Socrates of nineteenth-century Copenhagen took his daily constitutional at evening and listened to the common people. He could not mistake the fact that the reconciliation of the world offered by Lutheran orthodoxy and, in another version, Hegelian philosophy, was conspicuously absent from daily existence. He encountered contradiction in the square outside the house of his rich father and in his own soul. He was perhaps the first articulate Christian to sense the experience of nothingness, and to realize that the Christian gospel could only dare to announce itself in the world henceforth if it permitted encounter by this most devasting form of negation.

For Kierkegaard, the characteristic definition of sin is not guilt, but despair. The medieval man could speak also of despair. He despaired of the prospect of forgiveness and salvation from the judgment. He despaired because of his guilt. Despair in Kierkegaard's thought is something else, for it has no object. It is not despair over death, but over not being able to die.[19] It is an "inexplicable" dread.[20] Despair that can trace its object can be dealt with; indulgences can be found and cures offered. But such is not despair in Kierkegaard's terms: "To despair over something is not yet properly despair." [21]

So unnerving is the despair beneath despair that most men can maintain the semblance of health only by repressing it; hence the "unconsciousness" of despair is the commonest form of despair.[22] The price of this repression is, however, the loss of the soul.

> But in spite of the fact that a man has become fantastic in this fashion, he may nevertheless . . . be perfectly well able to live on, to be a man, as it seems, to occupy himself with temporal things, get married, beget children, win honour and esteem— and perhaps no one notices that in a deeper sense he lacks a self. About such a thing as that not much fuss is made in the world.[23]

Before Nietzsche and before Ortega y Gasset, Kierkegaard analyzed the pathos of the "last man"/"mass man." He understood that this phenomenon was a direct response to the universality of despair, the loss of hope in a world that gave no evidence of meaning. Repression in such a world becomes the way of life of the majority. The despair of the mass man is such that he

> forgets himself, forgets what his name is . . . , does not dare to believe in himself, finds it too venturesome a thing to be himself, far easier and safer to be like the others, to become an imitation, a number, a cipher in the crowd. . . .
> . . . So far from being considered in despair, he is just what a man ought to be.[24]

The end of the process of the repression of despair is a state so innocuous that it can hardly be called a state of sin:

> The lives of most men, being determined by a dialectic of

indifference, are so remote from the good (faith) that they are
. . . almost too spiritless to be called despair.

. . . How on earth can one expect to find an essential
consciousness of sin . . . in a life which is so retarded by
triviality, by a chattering imitation of "the others," that one
hardly can call it sin, that it is too spiritless to be so called.[25]

So entrenched are the men about whom Kierkegaard speaks in the
"dialectic of indifference" that their true condition—that of despair, of
sin—has to be revealed to them.

Precisely the concept by which Christianity distinguishes itself
qualitatively and most decisively from paganism is the concept of
sin, . . . and therefore Christianity also assumes quite consistently that neither paganism nor the natural man knows what sin
is; yea, it assumes that there must be a revelation from God to
make manifest what sin is. For it is not true, as a superficial view
assumes, that the doctrine of the atonement is the qualitative
difference between paganism and Christianity. No, the beginning must be made far deeper, with sin, . . . as Christianity also
does.[26]

The point is, Christianity as Kierkegaard understands it is a catalyst
which awakens man to the real despair, danger, and ignominy of his
existence. It begins with the exposure of a human being to the abyss over
which his life is suspended—and though it does not end there, it causes
him to live always with the consciousness of that abyss. Christianity "takes
a prodigious giant-stride . . . into the absurd." [27] It confronts one with the
impossibility of his situation and offends him with the offer of forgiveness!

Only in the darkness does the faith that sees beyond darkness become a
possibility:

The decisive thing is, that for God all things are possible. This is
eternally true, and true therefore every instant. This is commonly enough recognized in a way, and in a way it is commonly
affirmed; but the decisive affirmation comes only when a man is
brought to the utmost extremity, so that humanly speaking no
possibility exists. Then the question is whether he will believe
that for God all things are possible—that is to say, whether he
will *believe*. . . .

So then, salvation is humanly speaking the most impossible
thing of all; but for God all things are possible! This is the fight

of *faith,* which fights madly (if one would so express it) for possibility.[28]

Kierkegaard's theology was a theology of the cross because he could find no direct route from man to God, no direct route to glory. Reasoning from an ordered universe had exhausted itself, for him, in the folly of the Hegelian synthesis. The feeling after the divine which moved Schleiermacher and others to posit a whole theological superstructure on the human sense of dependency did not constitute for him an alternative to Thomistic reason. What he found within his own consciousness was such that it moved him to flee from God, not to be drawn toward him.

> When Christianity requires us to love our enemies, one might say in a certain sense that it had good reason to require this, for God would be loved, and (speaking merely in a human way) God is man's most redoubtable enemy, thy mortal enemy.[29]

Existence for Kierkegaard was participation in despair and contradiction; and the only route to God, across the "yawning qualitative abyss" [30] separating us from him, was the one that exists as God's possibility; namely, his own willing entry into the impossibility and absurdity of our condition. So remote is this from the counsel of human wisdom that it can only appear to us the height of absurdity itself.

> What now is the absurd? The absurd is—that the eternal truth has come into being in time, that God has come into being, has been born, has grown up, and so forth, has come into being precisely like any other individual human being, quite indistinguishable from other individuals.[31]

The absurd is: that the glory of God must not be visible.

> If the glory had been directly visible, so that everybody as a matter of course could see it, then it is false that Christ humbled Himself and took upon Him the form of a servant; it is superfluous to give warning against being offended, for how in the world could anybody be offended by glory attired in glory! And how in the world can it be explained that with Christ it fared as it did, that not everybody rushed up to see what was directly to be seen! No, there was "nothing about Him for the eye, no glamour that we should look upon Him, no outward appearance that we should desire Him"; directly there was nothing to be seen but a lowly man, who, by signs and wonders

and by affirming that He was God, *continually posited the possibility of offence.*[32]

For modern Christianity, faith is light. In reality, it is religion's word for what other modern men meant by reason. Even Schleiermacher, whose Christian Romanticism represented a staunch criticism of the Enlightenment's view of reason, assumes this. He simply redefined reason in more Platonic-Augustinian terms. Almost alone, Kierkegaard challenges this modern equation of faith and light. For him faith belongs to the dark: it can only be given in the dark; it is only useful in the dark. The darkness is faith's habitat. On a Christmas Day, Kierkegaard wrote in his journal:

> Unto you is born this day a Saviour—and yet it was night when he was born.
> That is an eternal illustration: it must be night—and becomes day in the middle of the night when the Saviour is born.[33]

A faith that is accessible only in the night is not the religion that the world wants. But if the darkness is indeed man's real situation, then a religion that leads him away from it into realms of light is nothing but a deception. The only light worth having is one that sometimes illuminates the darkness.

Kierkegaard's rendering of sin as despair, and faith as the courage to dialogue with despair, is undoubtedly his most important contribution to the thin tradition that we are exploring. At the same time, that tradition is equally indebted to him for another insight, one that is of increasing importance to Christianity as it faces the future as a finally nonestablished faith. He applied "the wisdom of the cross" to the doctrine of the church.

It is true that Kierkegaard did not carry this to the point of a "constructive" doctrine of the church. With him it remained a critique, indeed "an attack upon Christendom." But it nevertheless established for subsequent analysts a frame of reference for a new understanding of the church under the cross. It meant that the criticism of the church, which has become the mark of all the major architects of contemporary civilization, was brought inside the church very soon. As Tillich has observed, "Kierkegaard . . . as a critic of the church . . . was perhaps even more radical than Marx and Nietzsche put together." [34]

The most disappointing aspect of Luther's thought and life is his failure to apply his *theologia crucis,* the antithesis of the *theologia gloriae,* to social structures in general and in particular to the church. He not only accepted the institutions and forms of society native to his own period, but gave them new doctrinal justification. He defended them strongly against those who found in the gospel the stuff of social criticism and even revolution. The consequences of this failure are enormous and even terrible to contemplate. Certainly one should not exclude from such reflections what transpired under Adolf Hitler. When the theology of the cross does not lead to a social ethic it leads, if only by default, to social quietism. It leaves the world open to the principalities and powers that are always willing to take over. Moreover, when it is combined with the affirmation that these principalities and powers are ordained by God himself, and must be obeyed largely without question, this theology becomes a fearful thing. Yet even today, after the fearful thing ought to have made itself obvious to all concerned, many of those most committed to the way of Luther are suspicious of any attempt to draw radical social consequences from the gospel.

Kierkegaard hardly altered the situation in that respect. His preoccupation with the individual was by no means apolitical, as has sometimes been alleged. Indeed, it may have been the most pertinent political reflection conceivable, given the emergence of the mass culture that was already in his time moving toward the suffocation of the person. Yet it was not an antidote to the lack of social conscience and criticism in Protestantism, especially Lutheran Protestantism.

In the case of one institution of society, however, Kierkegaard could not have been more rigorous in his denunciation. The church as an ecclesiastical institution, while purporting to preach a very Lutheran gospel of the cross, paraded itself in the world as a power to be reckoned with. His "attack" constitutes a criticism, from the vantage point of a highly articulate theology of the cross, of the whole experience of Christendom. His indignation at triumphalistic Christianity knows no bounds. Nothing that has been said since about the pretensions of our cultural religion has been so damning—and so instructive!

Christendom, Kierkegaard accused, is "a criminal case, corresponding to what ordinarily is known as forgery, imposture." [35] It is indeed "the betrayal of Christianity," [36] which depends upon an enormous hoax, namely, "the maxim that one becomes a Christian as a child, that if one is rightly to become a Christian, one must be such from infancy." [37] Thus "Christendom is from generation to generation a society of non-Christians." [38] The question is: Does Christianity exist at all?

> The religious situation in our country is: Christianity (that is, the Christianity of the New Testament—and everything else is not Christianity, least of all by calling itself such), Christianity does not exist.

What exists, asserts Kierkegaard, is a "prodigious castle in the air: Christian states, kingdoms, lands; this playing with millions of Christians who reciprocally recognize one another in their mediocrity." [39]

True Christianity, according to Kierkegaard, is spirit; and therefore

> inasmuch as Christianity is spirit, . . . there is of course nothing which to its detective eye is so suspicious as are all fantastic entities: Christian states, Christian lands, a Christian people, and (how marvelous!) a Christian world. [40]

The fact is, in Kierkegaard's view, that the very willingness of such "entities" to embrace the Christian religion in itself demonstrates that the religious offspring of that embrace is an impostor and a betrayal of Christianity. Real faith is not amenable to states, nations, "the world"; it is a scandal to man and repugnant to worldly powers.

> Christianity is situated so high that what it understands by grace is what the profane would of all things most heartily decline with thanks. [41]

The real acceptance of grace means a real rejection of the power that man and the kingdoms of man covet and strive for; it is a case of "either/or." Kierkegaard does not deny the universality of the divine offer of grace—but at a cost!

> Everyone, absolutely everyone, if he absolutely wills it, if he will absolutely hate himself, will absolutely put up with everything, suffer everything (and this every man can if he will)—then is this infinite height attainable to him. [42]

But under existing conditions such an offer will not be taken up by many: "At no time are there more than a few who attain it." [43] And as for entities—states, nations, the world—it is unthinkable that they could embrace such a gift; for it calls into question the very basis of their power and glory. In relation to the kingdoms of this world, the Kingdom of Heaven can be apprehended only as a threat. Like Bishop Mynster, who for Kierkegaard so embodied the spirit of Christendom, man's kingdoms manifest such "infinite dread of everything radical" [44] that Christian faith must appear to them a veritable case of "incendiarism." [45]

We can hardly envisage the indignation caused in nineteenth-century Denmark by Kierkegaard's self-financed pamphlets attacking the Christian Establishment. It is said that no one in Copenhagen named his child Søren for decades afterward! All the same, the essence of the angry response of Christendom to Kierkegaard's attack is not altogether foreign to us, one hundred years later. The identical response can still be experienced by anyone who calls into question Christian privilege, tax exemption, the practices of infant or other indiscriminate baptism, the use of Christian symbolism in the life of nations, etc. There is still today a sense that all such criticism is spurious, undignified, and—most of all—simply exaggerated. To speak of "Christendom" as a criminal case—surely that can be nothing more than poetic license!

But Kierkegaard was deadly in earnest. What was at stake for him was Christian faith itself. Because he took with utter seriousness the Biblical picture of the Christian, he could not accept a Christian "society" that received the solution without exposure to the problem. To be a Christian in the Biblical sense is to be taken out of the spiritless, problemless world of the bourgeois and thrust into the dark night of suffering under and with the Christ. Christendom, on the contrary, is Christianity without the cross:

> In the case of Christianity the situation is this: the gift and the obligation correspond to one another in an exact proportion. In the same degree that Christianity is a gift it is also an obligation.
>
> The knavish trick of "Christendom" is to take the gift and say goodday to the obligation, to want to be heir to the gift, but without assuming the obligation, to want to make it appear that mankind is indeed the heir, whereas the truth is that only by performing the obligation is mankind, or rather . . . I would say that every single individual of mankind is the heir.
>
> However, hypocritical as everything is with "Christendom," they have made it appear as if Christendom too did maintain that Christianity is an obligation—one has to be baptized. Ah! That is making confoundedly short work of obligation! A drop of water on the head of an infant, in the name of the Trinity—that is obligation!
>
> No, the obligation is: the imitation of Jesus Christ.[46]

In this insistence that Christian existence is an *imitatio Christi*, Søren Kierkegaard not only applied the lesson of grace that he had learned from the tradition of Luther but he applied the corrective that has to be introduced whenever the lesson of grace has been learned too well—i.e., learned as a "lesson"! Dietrich Bonhoeffer later, in the same spirit, applied the same corrective: grace is not "cheap," but "costly." The cost is "discipleship." [47] The theological roots of this *imitatio Christi*, however, are not to be found in medieval piety and the religion of law. It is not at all connected with the treasury of merits or with "good works." It is based on a way of conceiving the gospel, Christology, eschatology, and all aspects of the faith, which is inimical to every form of Christian triumphalism. It is based on a theology of the cross. It insists that Christian existence is a matter of being set down in what Karl Barth, especially in earlier volumes of his *Dogmatics,* called "the environs of Golgotha." Light is there, or the dark is light enough. But it is not the light in which there is no shadow or turning, and from the standpoint of worldly men it is for the most part particularly dark. There is glory there, but it is not the glory we crave. It is manifested in suffering. It is hidden beneath its opposite. It is by no means visible. Well, it must simply not be visible!

> If the glory had been directly visible, so that everybody as a matter of course could see it, then it is false that Christ humbled Himself and took upon Him the form of a servant; . . . directly there was nothing to be seen but a lowly man, who, by signs and wonders and by affirming that He was God, continually posited the possibility of offence.[48]

A Broken Theology

As a final exemplar of the *theologia crucis* we shall turn to Karl Barth. Other contemporary theologians (Bonhoeffer, for example, and in important respects both Paul Tillich and Reinhold Niebuhr) may be more *consistent* theologians of the cross than Barth. But we shall consider Barth because, in him, there is both a powerful statement of this thin tradition and an entree into its particular problematic.

The "theology of crisis" understood itself from the outset as a theology of the cross. "They desired," writes Berkouwer of the young theologians initially grouped around this banner, "to construct a theology which would call men back from finding to seeking, from having to praying, from triumph to 'honourable and complete spiritual poverty.' "[49]

"Dogmatics," Barth declared, "only exists as the *theologia crucis.*"[50] His commentary on Romans, particularly the earlier editions, is throughout a documentation and elaboration of that affirmation. In order to see this theology at work in Barth as concretely as possible, we turn to a more manageable instance, an early essay entitled "The Problem of Ethics Today."[51] It is an excellent example of what the younger Barth intended by *theologia crucis.*

This paper was delivered in 1922 before a conference of ministers in Wiesbaden. Barth begins by depicting the contemporary scene in the language of "crisis":

> There was a time when the ethical problem . . . was the kind
> ordinarily called academic. . . . Fundamentally, it was a matter
> not of asking *what* to do, . . . for it was obvious that what to do
> was to further this infinitely imperfect but infinitely perfectible
> culture. [But now] whoever wishes seriously to ask and to answer
> the question, What ought we to do? . . . must have remarked
> something of the difference. . . . The era of the *old* ethics is *gone*
> forever. Whoever now desires certainty must first of all become
> uncertain. . . . For something has happened. . . . It is simply
> that over against man's confidence and belief in himself, there
> has been written . . . a *mene, mene tekel.*[52]

But having described the situation in these critical terms, Barth hastens
to warn his hearers that they are not to jump to the conclusion that he is
merely preparing the way for "the answer" to the question of ethics today.
He is well aware of the procedure, so predictable in the world of Christian
theology and preaching, of moving from question to answer, from cross to
crown! But the current situation, he says, is "a crisis of man" which
"points us *away* from all . . . comfortable conceptions." Therefore,

> I would beg that this peculiarity be not neutralized by a
> *theological* and *philosophical* process with which indeed I am
> familiar. . . . I have heard that crisis is a dialectical conception
> which not only allows but calls for its opposite—that this
> negation, which removes from human conduct all false value,
> may *restore* to it its original value. . . . I simply warn you against
> taking refuge in dialectic. . . . I simply ask whether the process
> actually corresponds with *reality*. Who can transform the *No* of
> the ethical problem in which we find ourselves today into a *Yes?*
> . . . That such a thing may ultimately be done (but not by us!)
> is a possibility which has its definite and appointed place among
> other possibilities; but so far as we are concerned, it lies "deeper"
> in the No than in the Yes. The problem of ethics may sometimes
> paradoxically resolve itself into justification and new possibility,
> but to *us* it reveals more clearly the negative of life, the judgment
> upon humanity—for we cannot be blind to the facts of our own
> day.[53]

Like Luther and Kierkegaard, Barth wishes to avoid theological
solutions to life's questions which could only be received at the expense of
truth about the world. The theology of the cross is committed to calling
the thing what it really is. It must correspond with reality. It is better to

lose something of the positive Christian message than to lose touch with
the negative in which we really participate. A gospel that can be believed
only at the cost of oblivion to human experience is no gospel, but the
betrayal of the gospel. In this vein Barth continues, issuing the most
insistent warning against incorporating the experienced negative into an
overwhelming theological positive:

> The first demand is that we stand firm to the negative insight
> . . . and avoid it neither by making light of the basic seriousness
> of our question, *nor* by discounting something of the transcendent
> quality of the origin and end of truly moral conduct, *nor* by
> giving ourselves any illusion, when confronted by Scylla and
> Charybdis, as to our own ability to escape them. We are to
> understand the whole unbearable human situation, espouse it,
> take it upon ourselves. We are to bend before the doom revealed
> in the problem of ethics.[54]

It is no wonder that the Barth of such pronouncements was rejected by
the official theology of the period. He was heard in the English-speaking
world only rarely, but almost invariably as a kind of theological monster
flung up from the abyss of the Dark Ages onto the shining shores of
enlightened religion. Even observers as sympathetic as H. R. Mackintosh
had "grave misgivings" about Barth's failure to give *positive* content to the
gospel. "The idea of the *Deus absconditus*—the hidden God—filled a place
in his argument that at times seemed to overshadow the *Deus revelatus*,"
wrote Mackintosh of the early Barth.[55] Phrases such as "the whole
unbearable human situation," "bend before the doom," and "God is pure
negation," [56] in which Barth's earlier works abound, deeply disturbed
those, even, who were steeped in the Presbyterian tradition of total
depravity. It was not until Barth had, by his own confession, divested his
work of existentialist influence ("existentialist screaming," as he called it
later)[57] that they were able to give full approval to his program.
Mackintosh reports his considerable relief in discovering at last that his
"misgivings, excusable as they may have been, turned out to be based on
misapprehension":[58] Barth had a gospel after all!

There was a suspicion on the part of many in the Anglo-Saxon world
that Barth's whole theological program was reactionary: a return to
Biblicism, to the Reformers, to pre-modern orthodoxy (neo-orthodoxy).
On the other hand, a few more astute commentators thought him
post-modern. "Barth is an atheist!" declared one of my well-known
teachers of theology. That criticism is profound in its own way because it
is the honest reaction of a representative of the positive, pragmatic

Christian of modern Anglo-Saxon convention to a theology in which the day of the Lord is darkness and not light. Certainly the Barth of the *Römerbrief* was no atheist in the usual sense. But he was a modern man, living on this side of August 1, 1914. He knew himself to be addressing men who were a-theistic—men who were "without God in the world," and whose experience of existence "lies more deeply in the No than in the Yes." What the charge of atheism does not understand (and therefore it is not truly profound) is that such atheism may be required of any who would appear even initially credible as witnesses to "Jesus Christ crucified" in the world today. Bishop Robinson discovered this same atheism rather later. Theism of the sort presupposed in most Anglo-Saxon Christianity—this pervasive, somehow natural and overall comfortable sense of the Divine—has never had difficulty overcoming the cross: the cross of Jesus or the cross of man. But such theism, however nostalgic one may be for it, belongs now forever to the musty libraries of sheltered theological institutions. It will no longer help to remove Christ from the cross or the cross from human existence. It belongs to the sunny Sunday mornings of yesteryear, when children wore white and the local Church of England smelled of God and Easter. "The abyss between Cross and Resurrection can be bridged only by God," wrote one who lives more nearly in the *late* twentieth century. "All human architectural attempts are bound to collapse into it. This is a fact more obvious to atheists than to believers." [59] If Barth were an "atheist," it was in this sense: he knew much about the abyss between cross and resurrection.

At any event, Barth offers no alternative in his essay but that of entering into the "doom": "Espouse it, take it upon ourselves." Georges Bernanos, the French Catholic writer, put it this way in his *The Diary of a Country Priest*—a work that could be understood as an artistic expression of the *theologia crucis:* we must take the night into ourselves.[60] It may be that in the darkness, God will light our way. "*Through* our doom we see . . . what is beyond our doom, God's love." [61] This possibility is by no means automatic. There is no necessary transition from doom to love, sin to forgiveness, death and the omega to a new alpha. It is no "process," bound to work. It is purely a matter of promise, of faith, of revelation. And, says Barth, in order to make it quite clear that he has altogether repudiated the realm of necessity:

> For a definition of *faith* I go to that place in the gospel where the words are found, "Lord, I believe, help Thou mine unbelief"; and for a definition of revelation to a sentence of Luther, "I do not know it and do not understand it, but sounding from above

and ringing in my ears I hear what is beyond the thought of man." [62]

The faith in which the Christian stands is thus a "*desperatio fiducialis,* the confident despair to which man joyfully gives himself up for lost—joyfully, because he knows what it is to be lost in this way." But this faith and joy "has *absolutely* nothing to do with so-called 'religious certainty'; for it is not our certainty but *God's.*" [63]

Significantly, Barth brings his paper for the ministers in Wiesbaden to a close by reading them the story of Lazarus. The gulf between our situation and its overcoming is so great that it amounts to nothing less than a resurrection *of the dead.*

V

THE PROBLEMATIC
OF THE THEOLOGY OF THE CROSS

EVERY THEOLOGY contains within itself the possibilities of distortion and danger peculiar to it. This is true also of the theology of the cross. Indeed, the problematic of the theology of the cross may be greater than most. It cannot be appreciated fully until the analyst is driven to ask whether a theology of the cross is in fact possible under the aegis of *Christian* faith.

There are two different but related perspectives from which this problematic must be viewed. First, from the perspective of theological analysis it must be asked whether, within the full context of the Christian story, the theology of the cross does not inevitably resolve into a theology of glory. Second, from the perspective of Christian ethics it must be asked whether the theology of the cross is capable of producing an ethic, particularly a social ethic. The present chapter will treat these two questions.

IS A THEOLOGY OF THE CROSS POSSIBLE?

The theological problem implicit in the *theologia crucis* can be stated in the following way: In view of the obvious insistence of the Christian gospel upon the *triumph* of God in Christ, how is it possible to prevent the Bible's equally indisputable acknowledgment of the reality of evil, death, and decay from being swallowed up? Or if the theology of salvation is taken seriously, how is it possible to avoid the dialectic which posits a theology of the cross only as the negative thesis presupposed by the decisive positive? Or: If the resurrection of the Christ defines what is really real, can the cross be anything more than an appearance of reality? In its most basic sense, the problem is simply this: Is a theology of the cross possible or permissible under the banner of *Christian* theology?

The case of Barth is instructive.

According to the well-known thesis of Berkouwer, Karl Barth was finally unable to sustain his *theologia crucis*. In fact, Berkouwer believes that the "triumph of grace" informed Barth's thinking from the outset:

> Barth's theology must from its inception be characterized as triumphant theology which aims to testify to the overcoming power of grace. We do not find in it a transition from crisis to grace, or from disjunction between God and man to fellowship between these polarities which Barth was concerned to set forth in varying emphasis and accents.[64]

This thesis has been welcomed both by the official Barthians, who, like Mackintosh, never did approve of the negativism of the early Barth, and by the critics, who from the outset suspected Barth of merely *using* the existentialist analysis for blatantly conservative Christian purposes. It is certainly an exaggerated thesis. There can be no doubt that it is possible to distinguish between Barth's earlier writings, where the *theologia crucis* is the dominant theme, and his later works, in which the divine Yes is stressed and Barth fears the association of the theology of the cross with pessimism and "Nordic morbidity." But Berkouwer's thesis points, all the same, to an evident truth: Barth moved more and more away from the theology of the cross and toward something that must be called a theology of glory, even if it is not identical with the *theologia gloriae* that Luther attacked. It is this movement which Bonhoeffer deplores when in the *Letters and Papers from Prison* he refers to Barth's "positivism." [65]

If and insofar as this is the case, it must be taken with utmost seriousness. If a thinker of Barth's depth—depth not only of theological insight but of involvement in the age—had to move away from a theology of the cross, it underscores the relevance of the question: Is a theology of the cross possible for Christians? Is it even desirable? Should we not perhaps take our cue from some of the later pronouncements of this "only universal doctor of the modern Church," as Barth was called by an admiring editor,[66] and recognize that, as the old Barth himself said, "we have to do with the Crucified only as the Resurrected. . . . There is no going back behind Easter morning!" [67]

The problem cannot be answered in strictly theological terms; it ought not to be treated as a matter of doctrine alone. Doctrinally, Barth's statement that "we have to do with the Crucified only as the Resurrected" is correct enough. But it is a truth which in certain contexts could serve only to alienate men altogether from Jesus Christ, who is "the Truth"! How and where and under what guise the Christ meets men is determined not by doctrine but by life. And as the preacher, Koheleth, has said, "There is . . . a time, . . . and a time . . . " (Eccl., ch. 3.)

There are, no doubt, times and places where the proclamation of the "Yes" of Easter must be definitive and unconditional—although the danger is always implicit of a false triumphalism. Evidently Karl Barth interpreted the situation of war-torn, defeated Europe as such a time and place. So did Jürgen Moltmann, who linked his earlier work on the "theology of hope" specifically to the situation of defeat and hopelessness that followed upon the war for countless Germans of his generation.[68] Even today in Europe, in those nations which no longer give external or material evidence of defeat and ennui, it is possible to detect a deep-seated and sometimes degenerate fatalism, which assumes that nothing can be achieved in such a world as this. In this situation it is reasonable to think that the truth of Jesus Christ should meet men with the possibility and demand of an Easter faith that penetrates walls and overcomes death itself!

But there are also times and places when the preaching of the Easter triumph can only be received by the frightened—by those who cannot bear to face the cross of their experience. That is more nearly the North American situation. The timid, desperate to cling to the positive outlook, are glad enough to hear of a crucified one with whom we have to do only as resurrected! At the superficial level the theology of hope has had no more lasting appeal anywhere than in North America. It could have been predicted that this would be so, given the desperate need of our dominant culture to find support for its expectancy. In this way, however, the Christ—the Resurrected!—is not encountered as the truth. On the contrary, he is only another prop for the lie that has worked out in devious ways—in Vietnam, in Watergate. Middle America has all along been meeting "the Resurrected"—not, certainly, in Karl Barth's version, nor yet in the version of the theology of hope; but still, a risen, triumphant, and eminently positive Jesus. It is time now that North Americans in their churches and on their billboards and television screens should meet the Crucified. He is not the pre-crucified Jesus of Hofmann's *Christ in Gethsemane,* nor the post-crucified Christ-with-halo who stands at the door and knocks. Rather, he is the horrid, mutilated Christ of Grünewald and the man of sorrows depicted so many times by Rouault. Until such a mutilated, sorrowful, forsaken Christ can be met in the churches of suburbia, there will be no facing up to the mutilation, sorrow, and forsakenness that this continent and its European satellites visit upon millions of the poor, including our own poor. Nor will there be any confrontation with the sickness within the soul of this society which causes it to seek the enemy outside its own soul. It is nothing short of blasphemy and sacrilege that the Christ encountered by Middle Americans in their sanctuaries is a bland, sweetly Aryan Jesus who can never be dissociated now from that picture by Sallman, Christ-of-the-chestnut-hair, which can be found in literally every town, village, and city on this continent. Not only does such a Christ perpetuate the lie, but he prevents men from encountering the truth which could deliver them from their need to perpetuate the lie!

The significant thing, surely, is not that men should be met by "the Crucified" or "the Resurrected," but that they should be met, wherever they are, by the living Lord. The devil, as Luther knew, can be encountered under the guise of "Christ crucified." But he can also be encountered as the Risen One! Dionysus with stigmata! There is no easier way to perpetuate the rejection of Christianity today by those who could be its greatest advocates than by continuing to present to men the Jesus of Easter triumph. Such a triumph can only be received by the sensitive as a *superficial* "Yes" in the face of a pervasive and thundering "No." There can be no doubt that what comes through today to the great majority both of intellectuals and of the poor is that what they hear from the churches is a positiveness that is phony and even ridiculous; a bright and happy message that has all the depth of a singing commercial. Many men and women are open to genuine declarations of hope, but only if those declarations emanate from persons who give evidence in their words and deeds of knowing the extent of the degradation to which it is possible for human life to sink. As Camus wrote in what could be regarded as a "Letter to the Churches":

> If the epoch has suffered from nihilism, we cannot remain ignorant of this nihilism and still achieve the moral code we need. No, everything is not summed up in negation and absurdity. We know this. But we must first posit negation and absurdity because they are what our generation has encountered and what we must take into account.[69]

There is a kind of triumphalism in the Christian faith we have inherited that renders it inaccessible to an age when triumph is hardly the characteristic experience of man; when, on the contrary, the strongest and most sensitive men experience an inextinguishable sense of melancholy and apprehension that is no longer susceptible to the cures of the

Enlightenment. To such men, the very triumphalism of the faith constitutes its offense. We ought not to mistake it: it is just such men who must be the measuring stick—the canon—for the authenticity of our gospel. Only such men have the courage to reflect in their words and deeds the characteristic experience of the age. To base the Christian apologetic and mission on the needs of other kinds of men—for example, on the expressed needs and experiences of those who are seeking, consciously or in spontaneous desperation, to maintain the expectations of official optimism—is to falsify the gospel. It is to make the gospel the servant of the most obvious struggle of little men for preservation and permanence, to regard it as a shield against the experience of despair, to offer it as artificial light. It is no sign of the relevance of the gospel that our churches are full (where they are full) of the same people who raise no questions about the critical moral and political issues of our time, and who trust authority implicitly. The test of authenticity is, rather, the reponse of those whose vigilance for man has made them anxious—those real "citizens" [70] whose sense of truth and justice has driven them to question every principle, every institution of our society.

It is quite obvious that such "citizens" are rarely if ever found at the center of official Christian existence. With respect to the churches, as in relation to other institutions of our culture, they are if anything "underground." They find in the confident triumphalism of our resurrection faith, even in its liberal and insipidly demythologized versions, a scandal. And we should not immediately assume that it is the scandal of the gospel about which Paul spoke in I Corinthians. It is more likely a false *skandalon,* perpetrated by a frightened and mediocre church which has identified the transcendent victory of God in Christ with "bourgeois transcendence." [71] The triumph of light to which we have been bearing witness in our churches is offensive to these strongest and most honest spirits. To entertain such a triumph, they would have to eschew everything that had impressed itself upon them as men who are open to the spirit of the times. They would simply have to abandon what they had experienced, in order to become expectant in the sense of this positive Christianity. They could only then become believers, in a parody on Paul's struggle against the Jerusalem disciples, by first becoming Middle Americans!

Surely the point of theology of the cross is that a man does not have to falsify what he finds in life by way of darkness and failure. He does not have to become an optimist in order to hope. He does not have to gloss over death in order to hear of the possibility of life. He does not have to repress his whole life's experience in order to expect a conclusion—a verdict, so to speak—other than the one to which his life's experience seems logically to point.

Theologically, the last word of the gospel *is* one of triumph. There is that in man which wants to hear such a word, and will even demand it and manufacture it *ex nihilo.* It is therefore almost inevitable that the word of the cross be transformed—naturally, regularly, and with much theological and experiential testimonial—into a triumphal word of victory over the cross. In that moment, it will become accessible to some and totally inaccessible to others.

It is the latter about whom true theology must always be concerned. For they are those who, of all mankind, are most committed to this earth. They find a faith incomprehensible that heals the wounds of man lightly. So does God himself, if we can believe the Scriptures.

The only thing that could prevent the transformation of the word of the cross into religious triumphalism would be the discovery, constantly renewed, of a radical difference between the gospel's account of triumph and the triumphalism that has informed the Christian church as well as the whole of Western civilization that was nurtured by the Christian church. In particular, it would mean having to discover ever and again the distinction between the Biblical account of God's conquest of evil in Christ and the imperialism that informs the image of man by which the modern epoch has been impelled.

As Ernst Käsemann has written in his profound response to the resurrectionism of the "No Other Gospel" movement, "everything depends on the manner in which we speak of glory." [72]

> For Paul the glory of Jesus consists in the fact that he makes his disciples on earth willing and capable to bear the cross after him, and the glory of the Church and the Christian life consists in the fact that they have the honour of glorifying the crucified Christ as the wisdom and power of God, to seek salvation in him alone, and to let their lives become a service to God under the sign of Golgotha. The theology of the resurrection is at this point a chapter in the theology of the cross, not its supersession. Since the time of Paul all theological controversy proceeds ultimately from one center and is therefore decided only in terms of this center: *Crux sola nostra theologia.* [73]

Triumph *is* of the essence of the story. That cannot and should not be denied. But what kind of triumph? Could it be that no one in the world of Western Christianity has quite adequately or authentically understood that thus far? Not even Luther? Not even Kierkegaard or Barth? Is it possible that we are all so emotionally bound to Christendom concepts that we are in no position as yet to contemplate, let alone expound or exemplify, what sort of triumph is truly of the essence of the gospel?

For Luther, who may have come very close to it, especially in the earlier part of his career, there was still the model of the triumphal church and the triumphal state. He could hardly be expected to free himself altogether from this paradigm.

For Kierkegaard, there was the model of the courageous individual—a model that reflected certain pretensions of grandeur peculiar to his own period.

And for those of us who live in the present time there is still, apparently, the model of a triumphant technology. This model does not fail to fire the imagination of many Christians who regard technology as a merely neutral power that could be directed toward human and even Christian goals.

It is possible that only the "little flocks" of the future church (Rahner)[74] will be able to discover what triumph means in the gospel's sense. Perhaps only they will have been distinguished sufficiently from "the kingdoms of this world and the glory of them" to proclaim a *theologia gloriae* that does not from the outset absorb and annihilate the Christian confession of "Jesus Christ and him crucified."

Still, it is necessary for the sake of those "little flocks"—necessary for their very formation—that already we attempt to glimpse what such a theology would look like. It is likely that very few of us presently concerned with theology and the church can rid ourselves sufficiently of the models of triumph that have characterized both our society and our religion. Our emotional and psychic ties to Christendom's conceptualizing are grounded in sixteen hundred years of triumphalism. Perhaps with our minds we can at least envisage a different way, even if our hearts are bound to turn again and always to "the fleshpots of Egypt." In any case, this is our mission and responsibility for the sake of the immediate future.

Above all, we have to endeavor to learn that the real triumph can only be an object of faith, not of sight. Confusion with Western cultural and religious triumphalism has made this Biblical insistence particularly obscure. Western man's delusions of grandeur, especially the flowering of those imaginings that has characterized the modern epoch, have always demanded visible and immediate confirmation. The glory accessible to those who adhere to the cross is perceived by faith, not by sight. To quote Luther, it is always hidden under its opposite.

What that may mean concretely is not predictable. But it will certainly imply such things as these: the necessity of witnessing enormous quantitative reductions in church membership, finances, and influence, without regarding this as defeat; the prospect of experiencing lower standards of living, restrictions of personal and communal freedom, and even hunger, famine, and catastrophe, without despair. In short, the loss of those expectations which we have been taught to have, and have imagined are *God's own* promises, without losing hope.

We shall have to learn to live with doubt. The false triumphalism of the *theologia gloriae* will not be driven from us until we have realized that the hope which belongs to faith and is not confirmed by sight always lives with the prospect that it never will be confirmed. We have been accustomed to finding metaphors for Christian hope in nature: the flowers that bloom in the spring, the dark clouds that have their silver lining, etc. We now have to realize that in history, unlike nature, nothing is "necessary." There is not necessarily a new beginning in every ending, an alpha in every omega. We must live as Christians under the cross without assuming a *necessary* resurrection. It is neither logically nor existentially necessary.

But the alternative to the necessary resurrection that has informed our cultural Christianity is not the acceptance of doom and gloom. The antithesis of necessity is possibility. It is *grace!* The alternative to the security of a theology that guarantees in advance a happy issue out of all our troubles is not insecurity and anxiety but—hope! The ultimate purpose of the theology of the cross is to establish the grounds of Christian hope.[75] The theology of glory deals in the necessary triumph of the good. In the last analysis, it eliminates not only hope, for which it substitutes (or tries to substitute) security, but also human freedom. For it is deterministic. It can only offer security, in fact, by ruling out human freedom— which is precisely what every form of determinism does. The theology of the cross deals not in the necessary but in the *possible* triumph of the good. It cannot offer security, but it does offer freedom and the basis for hope.

Only a theology of the cross does not end by eliminating man, because only it is courageous enough to describe man's condition "as it really is."

CAN THERE BE AN ETHIC OF THE CROSS?

It is important to be utterly frank. The danger of a consistent theology of the cross is that it apparently ends, too easily, in resignation. At least, certain aspects of the history of this "thin tradition" could lead one to that conclusion. The theology of glory, it would appear, fans the fires of expectation. Kingdoms are built; clergy become princes; the church moves "like a mighty army." There are excesses, to be sure, but it inspires confidence and boldness. The theology of the cross, on the contrary, while it keeps men focused on the reality of their human situation and teaches them to hope within history, seems to prevent their hopes from taking wings. They resign themselves to the evils of existence: Is not life, after all, "a cross"? War, poverty, inequality, the abuse of power and wealth, crime, human greed: Should not one expect them, since this life is from beginning to end an exposure to that which negates it?

Does the theology of the cross lead to ethical quietism, or to the reduction of Christian ethics to personal morality?

If the experience of Barth exemplifies the need to raise the theological question about the theology of the cross, the example of Luther and Lutheranism can be cited in connection with the ethical question.

Luther seemed incapable of developing a social ethic that could reflect in the structures of society the reforming power of his gospel. Not only did he fail to explore the potential of his theology for reforming society, he actually used it *against* social reform and against those who would have carried it into the political realm. In the Lutheran world, the theology of the cross became a way of justifying the powers that be, together with their evils. Nor was Luther himself slow to discover grounds for such an attitude in the Biblical theologian from whom he had learned so much. Paul's thirteenth chapter of Romans became the companion piece of the chapters in which Luther found his doctrine of grace and the theology of the cross.

The criticism that the theology of the cross stops short of an ethic is serious. If this theology is not capable of expressing itself in a social and political ethic, it is absurd to pursue it in the way we are doing. Our aim, after all, is not merely the discovery of a basis for individuals in our society to confront the nothingness they sense in the world today but dare not face. It is not merely a pastoral theology that we are looking for, although there is no reason why a theology should not be pastoral and political at the same time. In such a world as ours it is necessary to ask serious questions about theological systems that have no interest in pastoral questions. However, it is obvious that the fate of individuals in our world is bound up with the aims of political and societal movements. If our earlier analysis is right, the problem is one that applies to society at large, to the technological society which is at the same time officially optimistic. In company with others who sense the futility and danger of the obsolete *imago hominis* that has motivated life in the modern epoch we are searching for a new image of man, an image that is a social and cultural reality.

To reiterate our purpose: If the old *imago hominis,* which is as much behind the Marxist ideology as behind capitalism, is no longer adequate and is indeed threatening, is it still possible to discover in the tradition of Jerusalem the stuff out of which a new image could be shaped? To speak more modestly, it is possible to discover in that tradition certain elements that could give form and direction to the new *imago hominis* that may already be coming to be.

Our question, then, is a political one in the most fundamental sense. It asks about the vision, the aims, the sort of world that would be desirable today, given the quite definite conditions that we have to work within. It asks about expectations that mankind might entertain and build into institutions, which would not deny experience. Specifically we are trying to discover whether the tradition called *theologia crucis* can yield any insight for such expectations.

It is altogether necessary, in that case, to ascertain whether past tendencies of the theology of the cross to lead to social and political resignation belong to this theology as such, or whether this is attributable to extraneous factors.

Certainly in the case of Luther it is possible to discern nontheological reasons for his reluctance to pursue the gospel of unmerited grace into the political realm. As a reformer he was personally dependent upon the protection of the princes. He had good reasons to fear the revolutionary left wing of the Reformation. It carried with it excesses of zeal through which the lot of common men was by no means unambiguously furthered. He was by class, as well as disposition, a conservative man. In theology and matters of the ecclesia, he was daring; but in his response to "enthusiasm" he demonstrated that sense of order for which the Germans have fought as other peoples do for liberty. Luther was by no means ready to think that the gospel he championed should become the cornerstone of a new society. That was Calvin's dream, and it is not without its own problems! The suspicion that something drastic happens to the purity of the gospel when it is taken into the arena of public life was strong in Luther, and became even stronger in Lutheranism. The result was a vacuum in the area of social ethics regularly filled, in Lutheran contexts, by other forces in society.

But does this attitude belong to the *theologia crucis* as such? Granted these personal preferences of Luther, is there an intrinsic relation between the theology of the cross and ethical quietism?

There can be no doubt that the *theologia crucis* can become the expression of such an attitude. It attracts the ethically hesitant, perhaps, because it suggests a basis for resignation. The cross can be regarded as a final statement about life in this world. It can signify that in this world human expectations are always futile, a belief that has never been far from the consciousness of man. Combined with individualism and otherworldly pietism, as it has been frequently enough, the theology of the cross can breed that posture of knowing pity which shakes its head mournfully at every attempt of man to better his condition, and scorns all dreamers. It is never surprised by evil. It even takes a certain delight in pain, because suffering, while it hurts, has this gleaming benefit for the bearers of this attitude: it proves them right. Similarly, such a posture is predictably skeptical about every report of goodness. So many reports of that sort have been premature, after all! Does it not come to the same thing in the end? A cross? Do not all paths lead to the cemetery? Can the Christian do more than hope that beyond the impossibilities of this world his life will be granted a reward of meaning that it could never assume here? Shall he not simply await that reward, doing in the meantime whatever he can to mortify himself to every other prospect of meaning, happiness, satisfaction?

Nevertheless, it is by no means obvious that this attitude belongs to the *theologia crucis*. It is not somehow *inherent* in the theology of the cross. What is obvious is that this attitude belongs to man. It is inherent in human experience. To be sure, there are relatively few men in whom it achieves the depths of a consistent and articulate philosophy. Classical pessimism is, after all, not the sort of stance conducive to the various responsibilities that most men are called upon to assume in their lives, such as scholarship, parenthood, and social concern. It is no basis for a society, certainly. But what classical pessimism crystallizes into a world view is not something extraordinary and rare, but an experience that comes to every man: the experience of thwarted expectations, the experience of failure. Only a programmed and naïve optimism denies knowledge of this experience. For the majority of men, today and throughout the aeons that are past, it has been the characteristic experience of life. The wonder is that it has not killed in man altogether the habit of expectancy. As it is, men have continued to hope, and therefore there are still men. But underneath their hoping, as a defense against its excesses, there has always been the awareness that more human hopes are denied than are granted. That is an axiom which belongs to the wisdom of the race. It can be discerned in the most lasting legends and folk tales. It is found in that folk wisdom passed on from generation to generation in the form of proverbs and practical advice—a wisdom that mercifully transcends ideologies and the official philosophies of the times. It is implicit in most systems of government and jurisprudence and in social customs. It is built into the very structures of our psychic and biological makeup. Only modernity has tried to erase it. Only modernity attempted to construct a world in which expectation would always be confirmed by experience. One can admire the attempt when it is expressed in the words and deeds of its greatest exponents. But in the long run it is naïve. Perhaps it is more than naïve;

perhaps it is perverse. For to eliminate failure and the disillusionment of failure is to attempt to create an alternative, not merely an alternative world view but an alternative world. Failure and disillusionment are facts of daily human experience. There is no controverting or overlooking that without dire results. Plans and dreams, ideologies and faiths that do not reckon with failure and negation end in giving us the lie. Today that lie has become visible, a fiction that tries to maintain itself in the form of public figures spouting an ever-cheaper and more official optimism. Pessimism at least does not have to shut its eyes to such disgusting things.

There is, all the same, no immediate connection between pessimism and the theology of the cross. Every theological posture has its danger, and no doubt the danger peculiar to the theology of the cross is that it readily lends itself to religious pessimism, melancholia, and despair. But something altogether disruptive must happen to this theology before it can become the vehicle of a religious pessimism, i.e., *it must cease to be a Christology.*

It must not be overlooked that the whole intention of this theology is to bear witness *to the incarnation.* The theology of the cross is first of all a way of speaking about the character of God's entry into the sphere of human history. It is not merely a statement about the death of Jesus, but about his life and the meaning of his life for our lives. It is not merely a statement about the human condition; it is testimony to the *assumption* of the human condition by the One who created and creates out of nothing. The basic point of this theology is not to reveal that our condition is one of darkness and death; it is to reveal to us the One who meets us in our darkness and death. It is a theology *of the cross,* not because it wants to put forward this ghastly spectacle as a final statement about life in this world, but because it insists that God, who wills to meet us, love us, redeem us, meets, loves, and redeems us precisely where we are: in the valley of the shadow of death. It is the repudiation of a theology of glory, not because it is fundamentally masochistic and mistrusts or despises man's search for happiness, but because it insists that authentic happiness can only be found as we confront and enter into that which under the conditions of existence negates and dispels happiness. "Blessed are the poor . . . those who mourn . . . the hungry . . . the persecuted . . ."

The theology of the cross declares *God* is with you—Emmanuel. *He* is alongside you in your suffering. *He* is in the darkest place of your dark night. You do not have to look for him in the sky, beyond the stars, in infinite light, in glory unimaginable. He is incarnate. That means he has been *crucified.* For to become flesh, to become one of us, means not only to be born but also to die, to fail. But it means that *he* has been crucified; and therefore that the way of the cross, which is in any case our way, need not be regarded any longer as producing only negative results. There may be after all a kind of expectancy that is not extinguished, but actually springs into life through the experience of negation.

What should be said about the relationship between the theology of the cross and the human disposition that is called pessimism is not that the theology of the cross is pessimism in religious form, but that it has a certain basic sympathy with the pessimistic experience of existence. Certainly it is unsympathetic to what most "moderns" mean by optimism, which is nothing more nor less than the buoyant assumption that man is basically good and will take the right course of action in important matters. It is difficult to think that *any* religious faith, apart from humanism raised to a religion, could accept such an evaluation. Certainly Christianity, which in the most rudimentary sense is a religion of grace, of redemption from beyond the sphere of human possibilities, could only be optimistic in the sense of modernity by stretching itself beyond recognition. This is in fact what happened to our Christianity. The search for a theology of the cross is simply a search for what is fundamental to Christian belief. Perhaps it is even misleading to call it by this special nomenclature. Christianity at its roots assumes that man's situation is such that he cannot "save" himself. It is therefore obviously closer to the pessimistic than the optimistic disposition in terms of its analysis of the human condition.

Finally, however, it surpasses the "childish categories" (Heidegger) of pessimism and optimism. At any rate, it renders them unusable in describing its own account of reality.

Unlike the pessimistic disposition toward existence, Christianity does not end in withdrawal or resignation. Withdrawal is the only reasonable prospect in classical pessimism; and it is not without a kind of courage that one should respect, as in Stoicism. If there can be no hope for man, finally, then the responsible thing to do is to "think clearly and hope no longer." (Camus). If, having entered the darkness, one can see no light there, but only darkness, then the honest thing to do is to say that it is dark. If, having entertained expectations, one finds nothing in experience to confirm them, then the courageous thing to do is to withdraw from activities that assume the validity of those expectations!

But the theology of the cross is not the discovery that there is no hope for man. It is, rather, the confession that the hope there is, is a judgment against the hopes that men conjure up. It does not fix its sights on the darkness, but on the light that can only be seen in the darkness—and that makes the darkness very dark. It does not counsel withdrawal or resignation, but honesty. What is undertaken must be purged of the false hope that is maintained only by keeping itself from exposure to the data of despair.

Pessimism, in its most poignant expressions, as in the early Camus, is the entrance into the nihil which finds there nothing but nothing and says, rightly enough, *ex nihilo nihil fit*. The theology of the cross is the detailing of an entrance into the nihil, an abandonment just as negating, which nonetheless meets in that void the creative Word, the Word which creates *ex nihilo*.

Because it is a theology of the *creatio ex nihilo*, the theology of the cross will produce an ethic that is different from theologies that assume an uninterrupted, continuous relationship between creator and creation—for example, theologies that proceed on the assumptions of natural law. But that the theology of the cross can, or at any rate should, produce an ethic, in particular a social ethic, is evident.

What could be more pregnant with *ethical* implications than to affirm that the God of the gospel is one who incarnates himself in human suffering and degradation; that the God who creates *ex nihilo* is present in the midst of that which negates? Paul Lehmann says that the task of the Christian, ethically speaking, is to ask: "Where is God acting in the world to make and to keep human life human?" [76] The ethic of the cross begins with the supposition that the Christian search for God's presence in the world should always be guided by an awareness of this primordial fact of God's self-manifestation in Jesus Christ: that he incarnates himself in a humanity that *must* suffer. The predisposition of the ethic of the cross is thus to seek the prevenient action of God, the *a priori* of all Christian ethics, in those places especially where the God of glory and power seems absent. In human suffering and degradation, in poverty and hunger, among the two thirds who starve, in races that are brought low, in the experience of failure, in exposure to the icy winds of the nihil, in the midst of hell—there it looks for the God whose acting is the precondition of Christian obedience.

The ethic of the cross, however, is no mere *imitatio Christi*. Nor is it just a reversal of the ethic based on a theology of glory, which assumes that God's act is to be identified with manifestations of power and glory in the world. Such an ethic, which in contrast looked for God and the neighbor only in the midst of an easily recognized social stratum, would be just as much an ideology as many others that have been put forward under the aegis of Christianity. The point of departure for the ethic of the cross is not merely an axiom, a lesson, an insight; it is not merely the concept that God's work in the world always reflects creation out of nothing, the resurrection of the dead, the justification of the unrighteous. The point of departure is rather the subjection of the Christian and the Christian koinonia to the experience of the cross. Not once only, but in a "continuous baptism." The beginning of the *ethic* of the cross is the identification of this people with the Crucified One. It is the reduction of this people to nothing, beggarliness, and brokenness. Only through that reduction, continuously accomplished, is it possible for this people to be truly identified with God's work in the world.

Thus the point of departure for *this* social ethic may be the only one that is finally legitimate, even in terms that secular men, such as Marxists, can recognize: namely, *a real solidarity with those who suffer*. Only as the Christian community permits itself to undergo a continuous crucifixion to the world can it be *in* the world as the friend of those who are crucified. Apart from that, it always ends in a theology and an ethic of glory. For it imagines that it has something to bring, something to give, something that will enable *it* to master the situation. Real solidarity with those who suffer recognizes that their condition is our own: we are all beggars together. The possibility of *community,* which is the aim of Christian social ethics, is given at that point of recognition, and nowhere else. True community exists only at the foot of the cross. It is in the image of man as one deprived of mastery, deprived of possibilities and possessing only a capacity to receive, and to share what he receives, that we must look for the basis of a social ethic that is pertinent to our situation today.

PART THREE

AN INDIGENOUS THEOLOGY
OF THE CROSS

THE ARGUMENT

IT IS NECESSARY to be quite clear about our intentions in this final section of the study. We have analyzed the positive Christianity that accompanied, adjusted itself to, and fanned the flames of modernity; and we have criticized it as incapable of coping with the contemporary experience of negation and failure. We have searched in the tradition for a gospel that might be better equipped to relate to the human condition today. Logic and the time-honored practices of Christian apologetics would suggest that now, in conclusion, we should put forward this other gospel as the solution to the human predicament as it is manifest in the present time.

But the time is over when Christianity could imagine itself the provider of conclusive solutions to the human problematic. That is an aspect of the lesson that God has been attempting to impart to the churches, albeit without much success, in these latter days of the Christendom experiment. Besides, the theology to which we have turned for insight is a theology of the cross which is by definition skeptical of triumphs, especially theological ones. It would be highly ironic if, having denounced the triumphalism that fostered such delusions of grandeur in Christian and Western man, we were now to put forward a *theologia crucis* that quietly indulged in the same pretensions from another angle.

Our purpose therefore in this final section is necessarily more modest. We are not asking whether Christianity has "the answer" to the officially optimistic society, but merely whether it is capable of contributing anything to an answer. Such an answer may be emerging in spite of the church as we know it, without direct reference to it, and even in conscious opposition to its dominant institutional manifestations.

One more preliminary word: The most vulgar motive for such an inquiry as this is the preservation of Christianity. Christians who are still impelled by such a motive have simply not yet understood what time it is. It is by now abundantly clear that the survival of Christianity depends upon its willingness and ability to relate to the larger work of the Divine Spirit—to that "answer" which is struggling to emerge among us. But apart from that, something more awesome than the survival of Christianity is at stake, namely, the survival of humanity. And it is by no means certain that what is struggling to emerge as answer to our predicament will indeed emerge, or that, if it does, it will be altogether salutary to the survival of *man*. Not everything that makes for survival makes for *human* survival. Just there lies the special task of the Christian community which tries to serve, to be a pinch of salt, a bit of yeast. It is at least possible (one does not have to invoke Christian triumphalism to think so) that the tradition of Jerusalem has still an important part to play in the history of mankind. Perhaps it is only now, when we can no longer realistically entertain visions of power and majesty in the world, that the church of Jesus Christ can perform a service for mankind that is worthy of the power and majesty of its Lord!

VI

THE QUEST
FOR A NEW IMAGE OF MAN

THE REVOLUTION OF IMAGES

We have spoken of the work of the Divine Spirit—of an "answer" that is, or may be, emerging, and of the need for faith and theology to relate to this "answer."

To speak of an "answer" is in the first place misleading language, and it must immediately be replaced by something better. No answer, no doctrine, theory, or ideology can save humanity and human civilization from self-destruction. Only a fundamental *metanoia* of the spirit—an about-face, something that goes far below answers to the places where the very *will to answer* is fashioned—could do that.

That is what is now taking place, or trying to. It is a movement of unimaginable proportions, a revolution whose most characteristic mark may be its inability to codify or reduce its almost chaotic diversity to "answers," let alone "an answer." The only comparison that can suggest the dimensions of this transition is a geological one—for example, the beginning or the end of an ice age.

It has been called "the revolution of hope" (Fromm), and that, finally, may be the most accurate way to designate it. Yet it resists the attempts of analysts and scholars, and those with their own designs upon it, to classify it too easily and too soon. Certainly it transcends those for whom the word "revolution" connotes not only answers but rigid and constricting little dogmas which "revolutionaries," like children in the catechetical classes of yesteryear, memorize and spout with zeal. Those "revolutions" of the right and the left are "little orthodoxies" that "vie with each other for possession of our souls" (Orwell).

The great revolution may find our little revolutions interesting, for it is driven to investigate every outlet for self-expression. Like an immense unformed mass of pure energy, it seeks forms into which to pour itself. It seeks ideas, sounds, and colors through which it can articulate its dissatisfaction and discover the character of its hope. But because it is a real revolution and not merely a rearrangement of old concepts, it finds all the available forms too confining. It can only overwhelm the precious molds into which the "revolutionaries" want to fit the whole of mankind.

As for those "revolutionaries" of right, left, or center, they are utterly dependent upon the atmosphere created by this deeper movement of revolt. They draw most of their paltry hope, their calculated enthusiasm, from the great reservoir of this amorphous revolution of the depths. Without it they would have little influence outside their own well-guarded bastions.

Even so, the wisest "revolutionaries" know that they are courting the whirlwind. The great revolution is always on the verge of swallowing them up. They can protect their own little tempests only by persistently squelching spontaneity. They fear, above all, the intuitive wisdom which recognizes in their supposedly new and brilliant "answers" mere variations of the world view against which the great revolution is set. They strive to accredit themselves with the young, among whom the great revolution is most present. But they are not very successful in disguising their basic pedigree. In the long run far more of the young than is imagined perceive how the "revolutions" to which they are enticed belong to the same *imago hominis* as do the rival ideologies and empires whose enmity seems on the surface to guarantee a fundamental difference.

What the great revolution is about can be stated in the language that was established in the first part of this study: it is a struggle for a new image of man. It is a revolution at the level of human identity and meaning. The question it addresses, at the most rudimentary level, is: Who is man? It is a revolt *against* the most dominant answer to that question given in the modern epoch: that man is master. It is an openness *for* and a struggle toward a quite different answer to that question.

No doubt those in whom this revolt is making its way are for the most part quite unaware of themselves as pioneers of a new image of man. Most of them are not conscious of themselves as persons in whom an epoch has died and another is potentially coming to be. Few are given to that manner of reflection. Few have the tools of reflection. Even in an era when mass psychology has made us all neurotically conscious of the images we project and the roles we play, it remains true that monumental transitions like the demise and birth of epochs take place beneath the surface of consciousness.

Yet in every such time some are given to sense a little of the dimensions of change that is occurring. Indeed by now it is evident to a considerable number of our contemporaries, an articulate minority of persons representative of diverse points of view, that we are participating in a revolution of images. It is not necessary to speak of it any longer as though one would be considered mad, or indulging in sensationalism. Specific theories of what is happening may be extravagant; some, like that of Charles Reich, are obviously too pat, out-Hegeling Hegel! [1] But it can no longer be considered extreme, or even daring, to suggest that we exist today in the midst of changes so sweeping that our children and grandchildren could end up in a civilization utterly different from the one that modernity strains to bequeath them.

What chiefly fires this epochal transformation is the awareness that in the last analysis the civilization the modern era wanted to bequeath is dangerous and destructive. It is no *civilization*, in fact. There is a growing recognition that the image of man elaborated by the greatest minds of the past three or four centuries, man as master, is ultimately annihilating. Increasingly it is understood that the end of the process that seventeenth-century sages began to call "progress," with man at the helm, is the denigration and extinction of man. The mastery of nature must inevitably mean the mastery of human nature, the subjection of man's own being, to the manipulative techniques he has applied to everything else. What is "blowing in the wind" is the terrible premonition that we are being killed by our own vision of our destiny as lords of nature and history.

To speak of this as an "awareness" is to invite criticism of that type of empiricism which assumes that awareness must always be aware of itself. But it ought to be axiomatic to generations reared on Darwin and Freud that there is a response to one's environment which is most certainly an "awareness," which moves us to act, or to react, even though it is not conscious of the significance of what it does. Consciousness may come afterward. First, there is the movement of the body-soul toward or away from something. What determines the direction of the movement is probably quite simple: living organisms move toward that which enhances life, and away from that which threatens it. The body-soul is intensely sensitive to this distinction. It is a biological awareness that belongs to life as such and is shared by all creatures. Not even man, who tries so desperately to camouflage and transform this immediacy into something he imagines more fitting "the thinking animal," can altogether overcome it. If the "sophisticated" elements of a culture insulate themselves against this sensitivity toward survival, the more innocent elements will still feel it.

It is in this primeval, biological awareness of *danger to life* that the great revolution has its point of departure. So it is not accidental that those in whom the revolution becomes especially visible, and acutely painful, are those most in touch with their biological roots.

Naturally it is hard for a civilization governed officially by rationalism to appreciate a revolution that gets its incentive from the gut more than from the head. Even modern science, which at least in some of its emphases ought to have caused us to take the body-soul more seriously, has reinforced modern prejudices about the absolute primacy of the brain. For that reason, we can give credence to a revolution like the Marxist-Leninist one, which is strictly of the head; but we dismiss the nonrational, physical responses to the times as having virtually no intellectual interest. At least that is what we do at the level of consciousness and intellect. At the more rudimentary level, which not even the intellectuals can overcome, the dominant technocratic culture reacts to the bohemian counterculture in such a way that it becomes abundantly clear that the image of the hippie is infinitely more threatening to the technocrat than anything he finds in the militant revolutionaries of the Left. As George Grant has said, "If one listens carefully to the revolt of the noblest young against bourgeois America, one hears deeper notes in it than were ever sounded by Marx." [2]

The Communist confronts Middle America with the challenge of an alternative to the rule of wealth. That is devastating enough, but Middle America understands it. After all, it is still a question about *rule*. The common denominator is the old image of man as master, and those who share images recognize one another. But the hippie, whether in his earlier overt form or in the more subtle and integrated form which at present he has assumed, has stepped out of the rules of the game altogether. He challenges Middle America to adopt a new life-style. He is living out of another image of man—or at least in anticipation of another image of man. Consequently the reaction to the hippie, like the reaction to the beat and the bohemian who preceded him, is shared by conservatives and radicals alike. It is intense and irrational—the surest indication that it represents a real alternative.

Not only is this bohemian wing of the counterculture more radical than the political Left in the externalities of life-style, it is more radical inherently. Activists dismiss it as "romanticism," the tendency to go off into flights of unworldly fantasy, to escape *this* world. It is noted by such critics that the devotees of this culture are fond of the whole concept of fantasy, as evidenced by their devotion to writers such as J. R. R. Tolkien.

As a matter of fact, both Tolkien and those who read him with such admiration are very close to the ground! What they reject is not "this world" but a world view, a mind-set, which they feel has been superimposed by technocratic man. "It is indeed an age of 'improved means to deteriorated ends.' It is part of the essential malady of such days—producing the desire to escape, not indeed from life, but from our present time and self-made misery—that we are acutely conscious both of the ugliness of our works, and of their evil," writes Tolkien. Fantasy is not necessarily escape, but may be in fact the preservation of a saner, more beautiful view of the world, in the midst of the ugly and unacceptable. "Many stories out of the past have only become 'escapist' in their appeal through surviving from a time when men were as a rule delighted with the work of their hands into our time, when many men feel disgust with man-made things."[3] The Scottish psychiatrist R. D. Laing, who is also followed closely by the counterculture, has made a similar point with respect to schizophrenia.[4]

The creation of a "secondary world" can indeed be escapist in the sense that authentic Christiantiy could not tolerate—and no one should understand such a thing so well as the Christian. Christianity has been more diligent than any other force in the Western world in creating such a secondary world. At the same time, anyone who explores a genuine alternative to the dominant world view will be accused, by the representatives of the latter, of creating a secondary world, of being "unrealistic," or "idealistic," or "romantic." Especially will this be said of any real alternative to a world view that is oriented toward hard fact, rationality, technique, and material.

Precisely the question today is whether this latter world view is so "realistic" as it imagines. Surely an image of man is realistic only so long as it is actually supported by the evidence. It is not at all evident that man is master. Quite the contrary. What is evident is that on the vain supposition of mastery he has put himself in a position where he is about to be hoisted with his own petard. The environment, from which he proudly distinguished himself, no longer supports modern man's image of himself.

In this situation there is a strange reversal occurring in our whole concept of the real. It is as often as not the scientist, whose art was supposed to have displaced metaphysics, who notices this and calls for serious reappraisal of the modern identification of the real with the practical. At the end of his careful study of the multiple crises of our environment, ecologist Paul Ehrlich writes:

> Perhaps the major necessary ingredient that has been missing
> from a solution to the problems of both the United States and the

rest of the world is a goal, a vision of the kind of Spaceship Earth that ought to be and the kind of crew that should man her. Society has always had its visionaries who talked of love, beauty, peace and plenty. But somehow the "practical" men have always been there to praise the smog as a sign of progress, to preach "just" wars, and to restrict love while giving hate free rein. It must be one of the greatest ironies of the history of *Homo sapiens* that the only salvation for the practical men now lies in what they think of as the dreams of idealists. The question now is: can the "realists" be persuaded to face reality in time?[5]

An image of man that participates in reality means a vision that corresponds with the data of man's environment. Realistic expectations must manifest a potential correspondence with experience. On the moon it is possible to think of man as one who, properly clothed, is able to take giant steps with ease. On earth to imagine such a possibility is a sign of madness. What if, instead of something so innocent as walking we were to think about populating, producing, developing, or polluting? The image of man as master of his environment may have been real enough, and necessary, when this continent was in the making as a European satellite. But to apply the same image today is utterly unreal. It no longer corresponds to the data of our environment.

Moreover, it flies in the face of our biological makeup. This point has been made for me most acutely, not by a scientist, but by the strange American sage, Kurt Vonnegut, Jr., who is often mistaken for a writer of science fiction. In a radio interview he commented on contemporary mating habits. Why, he asked, are young women showing more interest in the young men with long hair and loving eyes than in the hard hats? (The interview occurred before the trend toward long hair and loving eyes had become universal. The fact that it did subsequently become so, absorbing even the hard hats, only proves the rightness of Vonnegut's observation about the preferences of young women.) He answered his own question thus: They prefer the long hair and loving eyes because they, the females of the species, the prospective mothers of the race, sense at a deep psychic level the greater survival possibilities of these gentler, less masterful and warlike males.

It is doubtful whether any image of man is capable of becoming the basis of an epoch unless it is fundamentally rooted in our biological identity and the drive toward life which inheres in it. Hence Vonnegut's humorous observation is in fact profound. In this sense, too, the cry, "Make love, not war," which heralded the "Great Refusal" (Marcuse), is the most revolutionary motto our era has produced.

The image of man as master has come, with an almost fearsome historical logic, to connote man as *warrior*. Not, in our time, the honorable warrior, the knight, who goes out to battle for the sake of love. But the destroyer, who destroys for purposes that can no longer be identified. He is the destroyer who cannot love. And there is a logic in that, for love was never congruous with mastery.

So the image of man as master has the smell of death upon it. It cannot dissociate itself from the aberrations it has spawned: the "master race"; the spectacle of American soldiers, innocents raised on homespun truths and mottoes in which the concept of mastery was subtly inculcated, slaughtering helpless women and children at My Lai. War, death, and the repression of spontaneity and life are what mastery has come to mean. For it *must* mean, at last, the mastery also of *human* nature.[6]

Because this image is deeply entrenched in our society; because there are vested, institutional interests in keeping it intact; because it is difficult for modern man to see beyond this image of himself without falling into utter despair—for all these and many other reasons there are never-ceasing, subtle, and obvious attempts to redeem it. But the fact remains that the image is not redeemable. For the logic of mastery leads precisely and inevitably just where it has led: to the death of the spirit, the death of man. It can only continue to be the dominant image of our civilization by standing in the most direct opposition to the biological drive to life by which we are *all* conditioned.

That contradiction, considered at the outset of this study, is seen now from another perspective. We stated it then as the contradiction between expectation and experience. We may now recognize that it has even this physical dimension. "Experience" must refer, surely, not only to events and circumstances in which we are involved but also to our biological identity, our experience as body-souls. The contradiction in which we live today is nothing less than a gross incongruity between the expectations we have been bequeathed and our experience as psychosomatic beings. There is a terrible split between what we think we should be and what we are, what we are at the quite rudimentary level of our biological existence. The lie that was always implicit in the concept of mastery applied unambiguously to man has become visible with us and in us.

No doubt there was a time when the image of man as master did not activate this contradiction. Indeed, there must have been such a time, for unless it had been conducive to life, men would never have moved toward such an image. Why should we not admit that in its earlier stages the image of man as master was capable of stirring men to *life*, of eliciting expectation. It was liberating, life-giving. It delivered men from another, still earlier image of themselves, which had been used by the strong to enslave the weak.

All the same, the concept of mastery contained an enormous lie from the outset. We simply are not masters. We are neither wise enough nor good enough to be masters. We are able to understand this better now—the lie is becoming obvious to more of us. Just at the point where human mastery becomes a real possibility the world shows terrible evidence of our lack of wisdom and our lack of goodness. It does not require great powers of observation or insight for anyone today to draw the conclusion that the self-appointed masters of the world have almost ruined it. Moreover, those in whom the concept of mastery was most inculcated, the northern peoples of the western hemisphere, have contributed more than all the others to this ruination.

So, at the point of its most consistent application—and, as we may add with shame, in the place where it was most firmly entrenched and institutionalized: North America—the image of man as master begins to be rejected. Man, who may after all be more magnificent than his own graven images of himself, revolts against the self that has been given him by parents, grandparents, schools, and churches, the collective expectation of the past. It is the only self he knows. But his deepest impulses warn him that it must be cast off.

Whether the Revolutionaries Can Be Identified

Before we turn to the more important question, whether it is possible to perceive specific features of the new image of man that is struggling to be born, we should attempt to speak more directly to the question whether it is possible to associate this transition with specific movements.

This question is significant for theological analysis of culture today, because it can take us to the sources of the search for a new image of man. Without identifying these sources, Christians are unable to arrive at the basis for a political ethic. For it is in company with those in whom the great revolutionary movement manifests itself in various ways that Christians must seek to discover a way into the future. Otherwise, the gospel of the cross remains an esoteric faith, a private response. The indigenous theology of the cross must be forged in the dialogue with many for whom such a theology has no meaning, but whose basic concern for humanity may in many respects be parallel and be served by it.

Two errors should be avoided in the attempt to identify sources of revolt: on the one hand the precise location of the revolution in one particular place, one movement, one ideology; on the other the tendency to define it in such general terms (religious interpretations are always speaking about "change") that it ends by being entirely elusive. No one can be precise when it comes to the analysis of his own period. However, without the courage to pinpoint specific manifestations of the change, analyses remain idle speculation.

Historically speaking, it would be possible to trace the revolution of images to numerous sources. No *imago hominis* is ever successful in capturing the whole of a civilization, and this is true also of the image of man that moved modernity. In the Romantic movement of the nineteenth century; in the social protest of the critics of the industrial revolution; in those whose genuine Christian or other loyalties took them behind the modern vision to earlier periods that appeared to them more definitive—in all such persons and groups there was always a protest against the dominant image of our own epoch.

It would seem reasonable, however, to follow Paul Tillich and identify the most significant intellectual thrust of the revolution of images with existentialism. At least it would be possible to claim that the most important *earlier* protests against the spirit of the age in one way or another contributed to the large movement that developed finally as existentialism. The significance of existentialism lies partly in the fact that it is the chief *reflective* response to the "mature" stage of the society based on the image of man as master, the technological society.

In his profound essay "Aspects of a Religious Analysis of Culture," Tillich wrote:

> Our present culture must be described in terms of one predominant movement and an increasingly powerful protest against this movement. The spirit of the predominant movement is the spirit of industrial society. The spirit of the protest is the spirit of the existentialist analysis of man's actual predicament.[7]

The spirit of the industrial society is described by Tillich in terms similar to those with which we have discussed the image of mastery. He enumerates two primary qualities at work in the industrial society:

> The first . . . is the concentration of man's activities upon the methodical investigation and technical transformation of his world, including himself, and the consequent loss of the dimension of depth in his encounter with reality. Reality has lost its inner transcendence. . . . God has become superfluous and the universe left to man as its master.[8]

The second characteristic of man in the industrial society is that

> in order to fulfill his destiny, man must be in possession of
> creative powers, analogous to those previously attributed to God.
> . . . The conflict between what man essentially is and what he
> actually is, his estrangement, or in traditional terms his fallen
> state, is disregarded. . . . He is pictured in a position of
> progressive fulfillment of his potentialities.[9]

Tillich then notices that the attitude of the churches toward the
predominant movement of thought in the modern epoch was "contradictory." On the one hand they became defensive and orthodox, "retiring to
their traditional past in doctrine, cult, and life." But this could not prove
to be a genuine alternative to the dominant culture of the industrial world,
because the "supernaturalism" in which the churches sought refuge was in
reality defined by the "naturalism" of the culture, in opposition to it.
"Supernaturalism is only the counterpart of naturalism, and vice versa.
They produce each other in never-ending fights against each other.
Neither could live without its opposite." [10]

On the other hand, the churches responded by adapting to the culture.
This, as we have already noticed, has been the typical response of the
churches in North America. It is the essence of liberalism in theology. It
is right, says Tillich, in its attempt to reinterpret Christian belief in the
terms of contemporary society. But the authentic witness of faith was lost
in the process. "Liberal theology paid the price of adjustment by losing
the message of the new reality which was preserved by its supranaturalistic
defenders. Both ways in which the churches dealt with the spirit of
industrial society proved to be inadequate." [11]

In the meantime, Tillich affirms, "historical providence prepared
another way of relating religion to contemporary culture."

> This preparation was done in the depth of industrial civilization,
> sometimes by people who represented it in its most anti-religious
> implications. This is the large movement known as existential-
> ism.[12]

The existentialist protest is a protest against what Tillich calls
"industrialism" (later analysis would have called it technocracy), and in
behalf of man.

> The protest is directed against the position of man in the system
> of production and consumption of our society. Man is supposed
> to be the master of his world and of himself. But actually he has
> become a part of the reality he has created, . . . a cog within a
> universal machine to which he must adapt himself in order not

to be smashed by it. But this adaption makes him a means for
ends which are means themselves, and in which an ultimate end
is lacking. Out of this predicament of man in the industrial
society the experience of emptiness and meaninglessness, of
dehumanization and estrangement have resulted. Man has
ceased to encounter reality as meaningful.[13]

The existentialist analysis explores not only the loss of meaning by man
in the industrial society but also his primary way of coping with this loss:
namely, repression of the *question* of meaning.

Repression is achieved by limiting attention to a small section of reality.
"This is the neurotic way out which becomes psychotic if reality
disappears completely." A few men, on the other hand, are able "to take
anxiety and meaninglessness courageously upon themselves and live
creatively." This latter is "the predicament of the most sensitive people in
our time in cultural production." The greatest artistic and philosophical
works of culture in this century have emerged from the suffering of those in
this predicament. "They are creative expressions of the destructive trends
in contemporary culture . . . and [these works] show in their style both
the encounter with non-being, and the strength which can stand this
encounter and shape it creatively." Tillich finds the "key" to contemporary culture in this ability on the part of the protesting movement to
entertain the experience of negation without being broken by it. "Without
this key, contemporary culture is a closed door. With this key, it can be
understood as the revelation of man's predicament, both in the present
world and in the world universally. This," he concludes, "makes the
protesting element in contemporary culture theologically significant." [14]

Tillich's identification of the protesting movement with existentialism
must now be qualified. It is too restrictive to fit the contemporary
situation. Even though Tillich has rightly broadened the definition of
existentialism to include the arts as well as discursive thought, it must be
said that the revolution of images greatly transcends what could reasonably be included in the term "existentialism." This has become clearer in
the years that have elapsed since the publication of Tillich's essay (1959).
Professor Tillich could not have anticipated the extent to which the protest
movement against the dominant culture would unfold in the past decade.

This observation does not disqualify Tillich's basic thesis. It is
undoubtedly true that existentialism represents the primary intellectual
embodiment of the protest. That is demonstrated in two ways. Much of
the literature and art of protest in our time relies upon the existentialist
analysis. But also, negatively, many popular movements—such as the

peace movement—suffer conspicuously because of their lack of awareness
of the existentialist analysis of the human condition, and of their own
dependence upon that analysis. Such movements are too easily distorted
and used for purposes not entirely consistent with the authentic grounds of
their own protest. Especially are they drawn into the web of the Marxist
analysis, which commends itself because it is both simpler and seems to
offer a more positive basis for protest.

Because the Marxist analysis operates within the confines of the same
fundamental *imago hominis,* it robs the popular protesting movements of
much of their authenticity and creative energy. The force that might have
been directed toward more genuinely revolutionary ends is thus dissipated
and postponed by association with an analysis and program that is
reactionary in the most explicit sense of the word. It tries to perfect and
cling to an *imago hominis* that is obsolete. The existentialist analysis is basic
to genuine protest, and it must become operative at the political level. It
alone has gone deeply enough into the malaise of man today to know that
the crisis cannot be cured by a rearrangement of society that raises no
questions about the basic relationship between man and his world.

In terms of analysis, then, existentialism is the intellectual core of the
revolution of images. As we have already intimated in the first part of this
study, there are reasons to lament that this is so. But this analysis is at least
preferable to the simpler interpretations of our culture, which naturally
abound. It does not offer a way into the future—except for the few who
can live without hope, or claim to; but it is at least rigorous in its
perception of the past which has brought us to this critical juncture. The
only physician who can be trusted to heal is one who has been thorough
and honest in his diagnosis. Perhaps in the absence of healers, existentialism has been put forward by "historical providence" (Tillich) to save us, if
possible, from *false* healers.

Intellectual analysis, however, is only one aspect of a phenomenon as
encompassing as a revolution of images. Its importance cannot be
overestimated, for it is the point at which the revolt becomes most
reflective. Yet it could not emerge unless, behind it, there were multitudes
in which the more original responses to existence which it articulates in
word were being enacted. If, as Heidegger and others have claimed,
existentialism is the philosophy indigenous to our epoch, it is not because
Heidegger and others have worked it out in their studies! It is because the
philosophers, artists, writers, and other intellectuals have sensed something
in themselves and in their total environment which preceded their
reflection. They merely became spokesmen of an anguish of the corporate

body-soul that had been gnawing away at life long before it reached out for words.

And finally the words are not enough. Since Tillich wrote the concise and perceptive study to which we have referred, that anguish has overflowed the narrow confines of intellectual analysis and artistic expression in an abundance that could not have been predicted. Lacking words adequate to express its indignation and fear, its pain and frustration has found other modes of expression. Perhaps it could be called the existentialism of the streets. However, it may not be helpful to name it existentialism at all, especially in North America. Here existentialism has been successfully downgraded by the representatives of the official optimism, including those empiricists who occupy most of the official chairs of philosophy in our universities. A wrong impression of the size and scope of this revolution is given if one associates it too restrictively with that intellectual movement. The revolution of the word has become a revolution of acts. In the transition, it has undoubtedly lost something of its earlier clarity. But in the first place, that clarity was more literary than real; and in the second place, the clouding of the word which has resulted from the activities of protest groups in the past decade may bring with it the possibility of saving the emergent *imago hominis* from some of the features of existentialism that are of dubious benefit to humanity.

END OF MASTERY AND SEARCH FOR AN ALTERNATIVE POSTURE

The idea of man's mastery of his world, the central concept of the *imago hominis* that inspired the modern epoch, has everywhere unfolded to the point where its fundamental contradiction is a glaring one. Its demise was already made graphic in the *reductio ad absurdum* of this concept by Nazism, with its guiding principle of the "master race." It is perpetuated in the contemporary scene only on the foundation of widespread self-deception, and because it is so deeply entrenched. In the Communist world the pretense of having overcome the contradiction by attributing mastery to "the people" (dictatorship of the proletariat) is constantly betrayed by bureaucratic fascism. In the "free" world, the democratic ideal provides an effective cover under which an enormously complex capitalistic elite exploits nature and humanity with license. In both great empires, the most decisive events of everyday existence are determined by factors that elude the control of the majority. Even the chief bureaucrats and technocrats bow to powers and principalities increasingly difficult to identify. Thus in a new and much revised version of Rousseau's famous statement, we may say that man, who imagined himself capable of mastery of the earth, has everywhere become enslaved.

While the end of this process of enslavement has not fully arrived, it is close enough that many can envisage it with horror and bewilderment. Man has indeed invented the tools of mastery; but lacking both the wisdom and the goodness necessary for mastery, and no longer convinced that history has destined him for greatness, he commits himself and his progeny to the "necessities" of the very processes he initiated. The alternative to this commitment seems to him to be utter despair.

Revolution in all its forms today first of all rebels against the fatalism inherent in this failure of the image of man as master. It is a revolution of hope: that is, it is an expression of human expectancy, which refuses to abide in experience, but looks for possibilities not bequeathed to it by history.

The point at which revolution divides into two distinct and perhaps incompatible wings is the recognition of the crisis of our period as a crisis of failure: the failure of an image of man. The revolutionary elements that come forward with distinct alternatives and well-considered programs have *not* interpreted the crisis of humanity in such terms. They still, in all likelihood, operate within the confines of that *imago hominis:* man the master, the doer, the organizer, developer, planner. Their point is not that the *image* has failed, but that men have failed to apply it rightly. Their own programs are alternative ways to apply the image which they believe will avoid its contradictions.

But the deeper revolutionary element recognizes that the contradictions are inherent in the image as such. These contradictions are grimly manifest in contemporary life, and there is no turning back from their desolation if they are pursued any further.

This is the great gulf that separates revolutionary from revolutionary, the search for new political forms from the search for a new *imago hominis.* Because the revolutionaries who are presenting alternative schemes for the implementation of human mastery are usually more vociferous, and certainly more active, than the others, it can seem that they are the more radical. But radicality—going to the very roots—belongs in reality to the others. For what they question is not merely the implementation of mastery, but the concept of human mastery as such.

Once the decision has been entertained that the whole idea of mastery over nature is wrong, however, there occurs a hiatus: those in whom this has been a matter of conscious reflection are often appalled at their decision. The majority, who are led away from the world of mastery more by their hearts than by their heads, seem to drift to and fro in a sea of indecision. Where can one go beyond that in the world? What can one *do?* The whole ethos of mastery has begotten a compulsive need to be "doing." To immerse oneself forthwith in some alternative "doing" would be to contradict the decision one had made in the most evident manner. Even thought that has been reduced by modern rationalism to a form of "doing" can seem a betrayal to those who have renounced mastery. Hence we have seen many persons in our time, in whom this most decisive, radical step has been taken, apparently dissipating their lives in a morass of inactivity, frustration, and escapist diversions that are served by the sex culture and the drug culture. Are they really wasted for the revolution? Do they contribute nothing to the revolution of images?

According to activist estimates of revolution, these questions must be answered in the affirmative. Complex treatises are put forward proving that the hippies and others who "drift" and "opt out" are doing precisely what the class in power wants them to do. There is a great deal of truth in it. But surely every transition to a new image of man has involved a good deal of hesitation, uncertainty, and seeming wastage. More significantly, there are aspects of the particular transition through which our own period is passing which pose special difficulties. They may not be surmountable.

How does a people, or even a single individual, move *beyond* the concept of mastery? This *imago hominis,* in a way that has not been true of other images of man by which human civilizations have been informed, is inherently capable of clinging to the human imagination long after the circumstances that generated and sustained it have been dissipated. Defeated, even broken, men accustomed to regarding themselves as kings will, as failures, find some way still of asserting their mastery. What other way of picturing themselves could compare with the seeming dignity of this concept? There is glory in it, and can man live, can civilization endure, without glory?[15] What glory could be substituted for this glory? Besides, what alternatives to this image of man are there in a world that seems to have "nothing behind it"? To those reared on the fantasies of mastery—and that applies to all but some minorities in the North Atlantic nations—the transition to any other *imago hominis* could only seem capitulation, failure on top of failure.

The alternative to transition, however, is to remain within the contradictory state. Within such a state civilization is finally impossible.

An image of man is a product of corporate human expectancy. And while expectancy needs to exceed and conflict with experience, it can contradict experience only for a limited duration. Only a quite unforeseen alteration in the course of contemporary human *experience* could revive the credibility of this *imago hominis*. The very fact that so many have become aware of it—have even named it—is indication enough of its obsolescence. For when an image of man is really functioning, few are given to speak about it, though there may be much talk about its effects. Already many of the conventions and values directly dependent upon this *imago* have been deprived of their power to convince the majority of men. It can only be invoked rhetorically on account of the public conspiracy to silence. Among large segments of our people, notably the young, the most sacrosanct precepts have been rendered ineffectual, or even ludicrous, such as the pursuit of education as the key to success, the whole idea of success, the necessity of order and industriousness, wealth and property as the basis of security, the institutions of family, marriage, and government, the entire concept of authority wielded by men or public trust. Beyond this social erosion of the image of man as master, there is the great threat of the omega factor, whose constituents are directly attributable to the spirit that moves and has moved our society. Under such circumstances, the search for a new spirit is greatly expedited. It becomes a matter of life and death.

Why should one not entertain the possibility of life! Are there not prospects of repentance and renewal for societies in decay, in a state of failure? Reinhold Niebuhr has said:

> In their glory, when the disintegration of evil is already apparent in their life and yet ultimate destruction is so long postponed, . . . [the fate of societies] reveals the "longsuffering" of the divine mercy. For God's judgments are never precipitate and the possibilities of repentance and turning from the evil way are many. According to the degree with which civilizations and cultures accept these possibilities of renewal, they may extend their life indeterminately.[16]

ASPECTS OF THE EMERGENT IMAGE OF MAN

I believe it absurd to think that the new spirit has already set in, that repentance and renewal have issued in a new style of life, a new image of man. That notion betrays not only a naïvety about the entrenched character of the image of mastery but also a typical optimism that has not yet come to terms with the most significant discoveries of our times, the discoveries of death and darkness. It has not yet explored with sufficient rigor the meaning of our failure. There is no way into the new that does not pass through the old. And no passing through the old is to be trusted which announces itself as a *fait accompli,* or which expects to get through unscathed!

We must fear, above all, the solutions of those who do not know what the problem is. The only authentic light for *our* darkness is one that has been granted *in* that darkness. To find human salvation in a new spirit, a fourth consciousness, a fifth man, or what-have-you, which has somehow mysteriously descended upon us, is to announce only one thing: the extent to which one belongs to the dominant culture, the officially optimistic society, which one is supposedly denouncing and supplanting. *Not to know how, or even whether,* we can "make it" as a civilization, species, or planet is much better criterion of authenticity. To see the omega which is there for us, and to see it without an implicit, a "necessary," alpha: that is the test of honesty.

The truth of our situation surely is neither that we are already possessed of a new spirit nor that we are wholly without an alternative to the old one. We can see, as from a distance, certain features of the men that we might become—or that our children's children might become. Here and there are persons and "little flocks" who in some limited way anticipate the new *imago hominis,* though often in too self-conscious a way for it to be real. But between us and that new way of being in the world there is a great gulf. It is by no means certain that it can be overcome. Indeed, the whole idea of "overcoming" becomes somehow confusing as soon as one has stepped outside the milieu of mastering.[17] It is possible for societies in decay, as Niebuhr says, to be renewed by new expectations; but it is also possible for them to turn away from the possibilities of repentance and renewal that are offered them. "At some point or other they make the fatal mistake, or a whole series of fatal mistakes. Then they perish; and the divine majesty is vindicated in that destruction." [18]

Contemplation of the possibilities of repentance and renewal means contemplation of the *imago hominis* that is struggling to be born in our midst. It is not a present force so much as it is a future pull. It may nonetheless be regarded as "real," even if it is not "realized" among us. Insofar as it is reflected upon, sought for, anticipated—even if only by a minority at the conscious level—it is already introducing into our environment an atmosphere in which important provisional changes can be implemented. Even if it has not reached the status of an indicative, it can exercise already the force of an imperative. For example, much of the recent legislation concerning highway traffic, the preservation of cities for people, and the protection of natural parks has been made possible only by the "imperative" presence of this new *imago hominis.*[19]

In briefest outline, the new *imago* can be discussed in the following four dimensions: (1) the search for a new relationship between man and nature; (2) the search for a new human identity; (3) the search for an alternative to rationality; and (4) the search for community.

1. Much to the fore in the emergent image of man, especially in North America, is *the search for a new relationship between man and nature.* In part, this is no doubt a result of a negative reaction to the evils of the old image of man, and it is not without its own pitfalls. But it is inevitable that the emergent *imago* could only be new and viable if it presented an alternative on this issue. For the most conspicuous, the most *visible* aspect of the failure of the image of man as master lies in its despoliation of nature.

The essence of the new relationship between man and nature can be stated simply: it is to put man back into nature. He has regarded himself as above nature, as lord of the natural world. Now he must be "naturalized." He must take his place with the other creatures, recognizing that he shares their limitations of strength and wisdom, their dependency upon earth, their mortality. In short, he must become again an animal. Undoubtedly he is different from other animals, perhaps still "rational" but not therefore superior. He must recognize that there are needs besides his own, needs of the other creatures, needs of the earth itself. Moreover, he must recognize that all these needs are knit together in a complex ecological bundle. In this way the meeting of *human* needs cannot be separated from meeting others' needs. The others do not exist merely for meeting man's needs. It can only be a matter of cooperation. And the terms of the cooperation between man and nature are not laid down by man! They are implicit in the totality of things, and possibilities of ordering and rearranging them are limited.[20]

The recognition of the rightness of this vision of the relationship between man and nature grows daily. Before the environmental crisis became a matter of general concern it was possible to write off such an attitude as being bucolic, romantic, unreal. But now a whole division of the natural sciences have affirmed the rightness, indeed the absolute necessity, of this vision. Even the life-styles of many who are wholly committed to a quite different concept of this relationship have been altered as a result. For many, trees have again become more beautiful than billboards!

But how could such a vision become a social reality? It is one thing for a small group to return to the country, away from the concrete cities of man, to work with their hands in the good earth, to weave their own garments and care for the wild creatures. But does not this way belong to a time that is past, irrevocably? The world is too full; there is not enough ground for all men to work with their hands. The economy of the world depends upon a much more efficient working of the ground. Greater and greater machines are needed, more productive techniques for growing wheat and fattening animals, more chemicals, more controlled conditions—*more* mastery, not less!

Yet in that direction lies the omega to which all the signs of the times are pointing. If the earth is worn out from our plundering, its own needs ignored for the sake of ours, can this reasoning be acceptable? And is it after all so impeccable? Is the necessity for more efficient techniques, more chemicals, more mastery based on *authentic* human needs? Or can the needs of men and nations be *qualified* by the needs and the possibilities of the whole environment of which we are a part? Have our needs not been exaggerated out of all proportion by centuries of fancying ourselves gods? Does not the growth economy come down to our refusal to accept, and to adapt ourselves to, such a version of our position in nature? A refusal to be "reduced"? To be limited? Those who have grown accustomed to eating cake can easily persuade themselves that cake is necessary to their very existence.

The vision of a new relationship between man and nature, which comes to us chiefly in the form of an imperative today, threatens us at a level deeper than economics. It requires a whole new understanding of our own identity. Is our life really the eating of cake? Is it possible that life is more than cake alone?

2. A second aspect of the emergent *imago hominis* belongs with the picture of man standing within nature, rather than above it. It is *the search for a new human identity.* How can man imagine himself? If not as master, then what?

The end toward which the concept of human mastery moves with a certain inevitability embodies a form from which all the "unmasterful" elements in human existence have been removed: inefficiency, inconsistency, error, laziness, self-interest, emotion, love, particular loyalties. Inevitably, the machine alone can fulfill these requirements. Men who are moved by the mastery image are impelled by the awareness of their own inadequacies to create more and more complex machinery to achieve the mastery that transcends their own direct grasp. They hope to achieve it indirectly through their technique. But in the process, partly because they have seen their own ambitions realized in the machines in ways that they could never achieve themselves, they have lost sight of the ends for which this mastery was desired. What purpose do they now have for existing, which is not embodied in their machines? "What the hell are people *for?*" (Vonnegut).[21] To be master has come to mean to be the machine, or a whole complex network of machinery called technocracy. The model for the image of mastery was once God, or superhuman beings like those of Greek mythology. The name of Prometheus has been especially associated with this fantasy. But these have long since been replaced by the machine. The only mastery in which contemporary men are interested, which they can believe and respect, is the mastery of the machine. There is nothing human about it. So, ironically, it is in a real sense transcendent: more than the gods ever could be, since they always had anthropomorphic features. (Even Aristotle's God "thought"!)

> Every generation has a definition of man it deserves. But it seems to me that we of this generation have fared worse than we deserve. Accepting a definition is man's way of identifying himself, holding up a mirror in which to see his own face. It is characteristic of the inner situation of contemporary man that the most plausible way to identify himself is to see himself in the image of the machine. "The human machine" is today a more acceptable image of man than the human animal.[22]

The alternative image of himself which expectant man tries now to pursue, in conscious or reflexive abhorrence of the ignominy to which the old *imago* has led, is an attempt to rediscover his animality. Whether he can ever again regard himself as a *"rational animal"* we shall consider in a moment. But clearly the search for a viable humanity today has to lead through the rediscovery of man's basic animality. The influence of the machine as model can only be countered by an awakening to the beauty, grace, and wonder of the human body, and the exploration of its natural potentialities and pleasures.

This attempt to rediscover his animality, so pathetic in many ways, so fraught with dangers, must nevertheless be seen in the context of the struggle against mechanization. Even in the most bizarre and morally questionable experiments—the cults of the body, the fascination for foods that are "natural" to the human organism, the search for sexual abandon, the drugs that dim the mind so the flesh may feel—it is possible to discern this struggle. Much that is connected with this attempt has been complicated and corrupted by the desire for gain. An example is the inroads that pornography has made on account of our inhibitions and reluctance to explore our animal appetites. It is also true that the whole search is conducted on the very brink of disaster, because if man is an animal, he is a very complicated animal. He may long to be "just an animal," especially at times when "to think is to be sad" (Keats). The secret behind the sales of a book such as Desmond Morris' *The Naked Ape* is to be found in that longing, not in the supposedly titillating sexual descriptions; Desmond Morris told man that he *is* what he desperately wants to be. Yet his very longing to be an animal sets him apart from the animals. Moreover, the search for animality is still conducted on the grounds of the old image of mastery: one works at it. But in spite of all that is questionable in it, the attempt to discover his animal identity is an important aspect of contemporary man's search for a new image of himself. It should be respected and cultivated by all who have concern for the race.

For one thing, the possibility of a new relationship between man and nature is dependent upon man's ability to recognize himself as animal—a species among species. So long as he refuses to find the essence of his being in his animality, in his body; so long as he excludes the physical from his view of essential humanity; so long as he seeks to overcome the body as something inferior or evil, he will find it impossible to regard nature as his own "natural" environment. He will always think himself superior to his habitat; he will always create for himself some kind of heaven which he imagines more appropriate to his native grandeur. The sense of mastery grew, after all, in the soil of a corrupted Christianity, which found the essence of man in his soul, to the exclusion of the body. Neither the Renaissance nor the Enlightenment challenged that concept. On the contrary, they took it over, translated it to mean "mind," and sent man on his way building earthly heavens which corresponded precisely to the heavenly heaven of medieval religion. The age of rationality was as much a rejection of earth and of human earthiness as was the age of belief. Only a man persuaded of his essential transcendence of animal creatureliness could have made good an image that placed him above nature as its lord. Similarly, only a man persuaded of his essential involvement in animal creatureliness can be receptive to a view of himself existing *within* nature. The road to such a realization is necessarily dangerous, and there are wrong turnings everywhere. But there can be no talk of a new image of man without it.

3. A third aspect of the image of man that is struggling to take form among us is found in *the search for an alternative to the rationality bequeathed to us by the Enlightenment*. There is a new attempt to understand what it means to understand—to think. For obvious reasons, this attempt is not so widespread as the search for identity with the body. For the majority of men, the body is the more immediate battleground of consciousness. Moreover, thought has for so long been associated with activity, particularly with technical activity, that it is difficult to divorce it from the image of mastery. Besides, by comparison with complex machinery man has rather become embarrassed by the ancient definition of himself as a thinking animal.

At the same time, the very invention of "thinking" machines, which can be trusted for accuracy far beyond man's capacities, has occasioned the question, What is thought? Surely in the whole history of philosophy this question has not been asked so frequently and with such insistence as in the contemporary world. Like the question, What is man? it is a characteristically contemporary question.

Although it is by no means a question for philosophers only, serious philosophy has been preoccupied with it. Existentialism especially has been the articulate front of the revolution of images in this connection. Its most important contribution has been to locate and defend a category of thought that is not only distinct from the mechanistic reasoning but that belongs to man qua man. More than that, existentialism has gone behind modernity to link its understanding of thinking with the rudimentary philosophic tradition, the tradition of Athens, on which our civilization was based. In doing so, it has been a far more diligent midwife to the new image of man than has Christianity, whose roots might also have provided important aid to the struggling *imago hominis* if established Christianity had not been so thoroughly committed to the modern *imago*.

According to existentialism, genuine thought could not be performed by machines, for it involves reflection and decision. It is subjective, and the machine is no subject.

Heidegger finds the essence of man exactly in that form of thought which defies objectification. In his famous Memorial Address on the occasion of the 175th anniversary of the birth of Konradin Kreuzer, he distinguishes between calculative and meditative thought. Calculative thought is necessary for certain kinds of problems. But the danger of our time, says Heidegger, is that it has come to be identified with thought as such. Thought that does not proceed along the lines of calculation tends to be relegated to the realm of the unproductive. It is mere daydreaming. What Ellul calls "the technical state of mind" scorns thought that does not address the solution of problems. Yet, according to Heidegger, that thought which does not aim at solving but at understanding is the quality without which man would not be man. The elimination of meditative thought would mean quite literally the elimination of man, *Homo sapiens*.[23]

What is significant in such distinctions is their implicit indication of a widespread refusal to proceed farther on the lines of rationality established by the Enlightenment and sanctified by modern science. We now understand that if pursued, that line leads to the virtual exclusion of man from the field of rationality. He is too full of self-interest, too immersed in value, and too much subject to error to be entrusted with the pursuit of truth so understood. He must be replaced by processes—certainly including machines—which eliminate the human factor from this pursuit.

In the face of this threat, where it is seen as a threat, men ask again whether thought, reason, truth, and understanding should be allowed, in the first place, to be equated with calculation.

The attempt to discover, or rediscover, a mode of thinking distinct from the thinking that can also be undertaken mechanistically ought not to be limited to the fields of philosophy and art. Behind the quite conscious search for an alternative mode of reasoning on the part of scholars and artists lie countless movements, experiments, and even fads, which have been on the periphery of Western experience for a century or more. Today they have presented themselves at the center of the stage, with the demand that they be taken quite seriously. To the calculator, they can only seem irrational, emotional, Dionysian. The cults of feeling and touch; the quest for a world of color and sensitivity, with or without benefit of drugs; the revival of interest in spiritual religion, especially in the religions of the East; also the attempt to rediscover a *Christian* spirituality which does not either intellectualize faith or turn it into religious activism—all such quests can be quite legitimately criticized. But what critics need to recognize is that in and through them all there runs a search for a mode of thought that does not eliminate the greater substance of human consciousness and personhood. In all of them, and in the larger trends that they have helped to establish, there is an insistence that reason be set free from its Babylonian captivity to technique.

The alternatives presented in this chaotic marketplace of the soul are not all attractive to mature Christianity. Some of them seem obviously demonic, such as those associated with the various new forms of witchcraft. Others—for instance, the reliance on artificial stimuli such as drugs or group manipulation—appear at best questionable substitutes for that thought which Heidegger calls "meditative." At the same time, it is possible to see in and through the confusion certain recurrent themes. One is the almost universal assumption that human rationality pertains to man's whole being; it proceeds from a creature who is also a body, not merely a rather mediocre brain computer, a being whose "rationality" is that of an "animal." Another is the significant recognition, to which the Protestant Reformation tried in its early stages to bear witness, that human thought begins and ends with the involvement of the thinker in what he is thinking about. There is a new dimension in this recognition today. In distinction from the Reformers, it has been given to men today to know from experience that a process which eliminates this involvement from its epistemology will end by eliminating man himself. A third recurrent theme in this diverse experimentation with thought is the tendency to conceive of thought as a process in which a person participates, not merely something that he originates. Like Rodin's Thinker, the man to whom many popular as well as scholarly expressions point in our time is one who is "lost" in reflection. He is not engaged in activity, whether physical or mental, but immersed in something that transcends his own intellect and will.

4. The fourth element in the image of man that is struggling to be born is *the search for community*.

What drives this attempt is the discovery, so obvious that it now requires little insight to perceive it, that the *imago hominis* by which modernity has been inspired leads finally to the dissolution and disintegration of human community. How could it be otherwise? The idea of mastery is no basis for community. That is what the story of the tower of Babel and the pathetic city surrounding it is all about. When men imagine that they can seize the power of heaven for themselves, all they acquire is a profound distrust of one another's power. They can communicate no longer.

The quest for mastery has built into it an insoluble problem of authority. Mastery defies distribution. It moves toward mastery of one over others, of each over his neighbor. It lends itself to schemes of the powerful to lord it over the powerless, the rich to acquire even more riches at the expense of the poor. It assumes that those who best achieve domination have best achieved their human destiny. It is fundamentally individualistic, in the worst sense of that word.

The experience of our own period provides gross and fantastic illustrations of this inability of the technocratic mind-set to offer a basis for genuine human community. It is one of the most pathetic aspects of our life today that so many men and women assume that human community is impossible, on the intimate level of the family or on a global scale. This fatalistic assumption, which lies behind the sighs and the cynicism of the average citizen as he listens to world news or hears of the promises of leaders of state, is a terrible witness to the bankruptcy of the technocratic presuppositions of our culture. There may be no single area of human experience where the essential inhumanity of the technocratic *imago hominis* manifests itself so clearly and with such paralyzing effects. It can no longer be assumed that if each man pursues his own selfish interests, the interests of all will be served. In the light of contemporary experience, particularly with the Third World peoples, such a belief is patent nonsense. When still indulged by men, corporations, and nations, it is in the most explicit sense sinful. Yet what other grounds for community can be found?

Communism represents the most concerted effort of contemporary man to discover a new foundation for human community. In this respect, all who value human brotherhood should recognize in the Communist ideal a genuine response to the plight of mankind. In its better manifestations— as in Cuba or People's China—this dimension of Communism has dominated. Christians feel rightly judged by the extent to which the actual community achieved in these societies approximates the brother-hood espoused in our rhetoric but seldom realized in our society. At the same time, the suppression of individual freedom, the sacrifice of diversity to conformity, and the authoritarian maintenance of order in Communist states causes one to wonder whether any real basis for community has been found by this system of thought. Does it not rest upon a determined application of the imperative, There *must be* community, which begs the question of a foundational indicative? Still, in terms of the contemporary search for community, Communism must certainly be considered a significant instance.

It is nevertheless in the less grandly political experiments that the contemporary search for human community has become more transpar-ent. The competitive, production-oriented world of technocracy having all but destroyed the family, surprising numbers of persons have engaged in experiments intended to recover the communion that once belonged to the "nuclear family." This is especially so in North America. It is not surprising that many of those experiments have gone hand in hand with the attempt to recover a new proximity to nature. For there is an inherent connection between man's recognition of belonging to other men and the recognition that he and his species belong to a larger-than-human community.

Significant also in many of these experiments is the fact that openness to the needs of others is a primary prerequisite for participation. This is also the most difficult, almost impossible, requirement to attain. Quite apart from the egocentrism that is common to all men, it is like asking the leopard to change his spots when a commune insists that its members, most of them thoroughly imbued with the technocratic state of mind, give first consideration to their fellows. It is true that a certain moral rhetoric has kept before us in our world of legalized selfishness the concept that the neighbor's needs are significant. Even a distorted Christianity has always paid lip service to this "golden rule." But the actual way of life imposed upon us by the dominant culture is a direct contradiction of this morality, and its power to convince should not be overestimated. The sense of individual rights, of reward according to performance, of property, is so deeply embedded in us that it defies all morality which proceeds from another understanding of man's destiny, no matter how time-honored. Hence, most of the experiments in human community end in failure, or fall far short of the expectations of their originators. But they are not to be written off, for they point to a vision of human community which, even if it never could succeed, is at least a vantage point from which to understand the evils and inhumanity of a society that at its core militates against the communion of man with man.

MAN AS RECEIVER

These four elements in the *imago hominis* incipient in our time by no means exhaust the possibilities. But they provide sufficient background against which we may ask whether it is possible in any sense to generalize about this emergent image of man.

Following the lead of other commentators on modern Western civilization, we have designated the central idea in the *imago hominis* by which this civilization was moved as the idea of man's mastery over nature. We have observed that this mastery inevitably connotes human mastery over human nature, and thus leads to contradiction. Now we may ask: Is there in the new *imago* struggling to be born among us today any such central, guiding concept? If we can discern such a concept, we shall then be able to inquire how Christian faith might relate to it.

We have drawn attention to the diversity, the uncertainty, and the unformed character of the emergent *imago hominis*. Nevertheless, there seems to me to be a common conviction about the nature of man running throughout this great diversity, and expressing itself in many different ways. Having characterized some of the aspects of the emergent image of man, we may now attempt to name this common conviction. It is something more impressive than random rejection of what prevails. I know of no better single concept for designating this common conviction than the one that Grant and others have already suggested: receptivity.[24]

That a culture based on mastery should be opposed—and possibly superceded—by a culture based on receptivity is perhaps not altogether unpredictable. The pendulum theory of history seems to apply here. The fathers have eaten sour grapes, and the children's teeth are set on edge. In our time, self-confident, self-made, masterful fathers have begotten sons who turn away from all that with loathing and become beings of whom their fathers can only be ashamed—weaklings, dependents, dropouts, beggars! But the explanation of this generation gap is not to be found only in Freud and the pendulum theory. Nor is it merely a social response to a culture which, if it produced "the good life," also produced Vietnam. Behind the move toward receptivity as a style of being, there is that profound, half-conscious awareness that the preservation of the species depends upon it. *Unless* man turns from mastering to serving, from grasping to receiving, from independence to interdependence, he will simply not last very long on the face of the earth. To reiterate: it is not unusual that this awareness should be felt with special keenness by the young, who, after all, bear the hope and the burden of preservation farther into the future than do the fathers.

The concept of receptivity is strongly present in all four of the elements of the new *imago* to which reference has been made.

1. It is obvious in the attempt to achieve a *new relationship between man and nature.* Man's role in this relationship is transformed from that of the lord of nature to nature's listener and protector. He understands himself, not as one who stands above nature, but as one who lives within the natural world and is dependent upon it. He is not *sui generis.* He does not possess his being; he receives it. He receives it, not from some transcendent source—not even from God, if by God is meant a being who is able to sustain the creature man in "unnatural" ways. He receives his being from nature, too. He *is* what he eats, though he is also more than that. He stands within an ecological cycle whose inner working he must respect. He is required by this inherent logic of the natural world to give much, but in the long run, man is for the most part "on the receiving end."

2. The same theme is implicit in *the attempt to recover the sense of humanity* through a new awareness of man's animality. Here, receptivity finds expression in being a body. The body is obviously dependent. It is possible for only a few men—normally for those who are physically powerful or attractive and mentally weak!—to imagine themselves masters from the standpoints of their bodies. Only a civilization that had essentially eschewed the body could raise itself, in its own estimation, to the posture of mastery in the world. Only a mind that had convinced itself that the body to which it was "attached" was accidental could have given itself the airs of a god. Those men and races of men who have been more closely in touch with their bodies have seldom made such pretensions.

If the body is of the essence of man (and Christians, who confess the incarnation of the Word, are bound to say that it is), then it is of the essence of man to *receive* what is necessary for his life. At every point man as body is dependent upon what he can neither make nor master: air, water, earth, fire—the elements of the ancients. Those ancients who worshiped the sun were wiser than modern men who worship nothing beyond the technological works of their own hands—and purchase suntan oils! The ancients at least knew that man's essential condition is that of receiver.

3. In *the attempt to discover ways of knowing and thinking* qualitatively

different from calculation, receptivity is again the central concept. Behind
the hundreds of ways in which man searches for an essentially *human* mode
of thinking there lies an assumption: that upon which thought dwells
(truth, reality, or however it may be designated) precedes and transcends
the minds that seek to know it.

This is true even of those whose aim is specifically self-knowledge. What
is desired to be known is there, in the memory, in the unconscious, and
knowing consists in opening one's consciousness to these internal depths of
the psyche. The suggestion implicit here is not only that what we seek to
know precedes our knowing but that the process of knowing itself involves
movement not only from the knower toward "the truth" but also of "the
truth" toward the knower. To know is to be known. To engage in
"meditative" thought is to open oneself to the truth that "comes to one."
It can only be received, not tracked down and captured. Information,
data, facts can be mastered, used. But the fruit of meditative reason can
finally only be enjoyed. Here are the seeds of an awareness that can and
should be traced to the very roots of our civilization.

4. Finally, receptivity is the most important concept in *the various attempts
to discover new bases for human community*. All these attempts recognize that
authentic community depends upon its members' need for others. They
must receive their life, not only from nature, but from one another. The
idea of mastery sets men apart from one another, and against one another.
However careful the shapers of a society may be to ensure that the race,
the group, or the species, is in control, still the concept of mastery
inevitably tempts men to think of mastery in individual terms. Only
beggars can have community; only they know that they are quite
incapable of independence. The first prerequisite for the communion of
men, as many have discovered in our time, is the willingness to receive.
That is more difficult than the willingness to give, because the giver can
still think of himself as independent. His independence and mastery of the
situation is even confirmed, often subtly, by his giving.

ECHOES OF THE PAST UNRECOGNIZED

The basic and unifying role that receptivity plays in the *imago hominis*
that wavers on our horizon could hardly have come closer to the central
concept of the traditions on which Western civilization is chiefly based.
Both Athens and Jerusalem, as George Grant has shown in his *Time as
History,* depict man as one whose fundamental posture is that of the
recipient. This thought becomes especially provocative when we consider
the institutions in the contemporary world that ostensibly guard and

perpetuate the traditions of Athens and Jerusalem. The university and the church are so thoroughly committed to the modern image of man that they can only recognize the recurrence of the theme of receptivity as an alien and unwelcome threat to our stability! It is a further irony that many to whom the posture of receptivity has most commended itself have bypassed both traditions and sought guidance from the traditions of the East.

It is not claimed that Athens and Jersualem stand for the same understanding of man's being and calling. The differences are evident even to a casual student of the two traditions. The New Testament is a meeting place of the two, and it is by no means certain that it achieves a reconciliation of their basic differences. At best it can perhaps be claimed, with Paul, that in Christ "there is neither . . . Greek nor Jew." However, when the two ancient foundational traditions of Western civilization are compared with the modern view of man, which borrowed elements from both of them, their differences pale in relation to their common divergence from the latter.

Neither the Greek nor the Jew is able to assume man's mastery. Both, indeed, regard the claim to mastery as the height of presumption: *hubris* in the Greek concept, sin (rebellion) in the Hebraic. Both understand well enough that man *tries* to achieve mastery: that is his tragic condition, his fall. But salvation lies in reconciling man to his humanity. He does not have to strain himself to achieve significance. He has only to open himself to what is given, freely and without restraint. For the Greek tradition, this givenness is articulated in ontological terms, whether of the Platonic Reality in which man's soul participates, or the Aristotelian Reason which transcends and informs all that is, or the universal Logos of the Stoics. In the Judeo-Christian tradition, this givenness is expressed in relational categories: love, forgiveness, grace. The fundamental difference between the two ways lies in the distinction between ontological (substantial) and relational concepts. It is not a small thing to consider whether humanity consists in being or in loving (being-with). But beside the modern image of man, which sets humanity in the categories of having and of doing, there appears an exceptional agreement between the ancient views.

It is reasonable to expect that those who have regarded themselves as the guardians of these foundational traditions would recognize a certain affinity between them and the contemporary movements about which we have been speaking, and, moreover, that they would be prepared to assist the coming of the new image of man which *could* emerge out of these movements. But neither of the two institutions that claim these traditions has recognized this affinity or provided the assistance needed.

The university has been even more negligent than the church. It is a long time since the university has given any real evidence of standing within the tradition of Athens. It has cut itself off from that tradition just as conclusively as from the tradition of Jerusalem. At the same time, the university has not *wished* to deny its relation to Athens in the way that it has wished to deny its relation to Jerusalem. In its rhetorical promotion of itself, it has retained this important link with the ancient world. So even if its neglect is not as clear-cut as is that of the church, which announces its ties with the tradition of Jerusalem with every breath it takes, it is still legitimate to ask why the university has so consistently failed to provide any leadership in the countercultural search for a new image of man.

It is precisely the lack of support—the kind of support that could come only from the acquisition of roots—that is causing this incipient *imago hominis* to dissipate itself. It is simply unable to grow, to develop, to take form without such support. Its actual birth depends in great measure upon the presence of concerned and wise midwives. Perhaps it will not be born. Perhaps, on account of the neglect of the midwives, and of the parent culture which fears it, this child has already ceased to live in the womb.

Without the wisdom that could be brought to this widespread revolutionary movement by those who have intellectual connections with the older traditions the protesting movement could simply destroy itself. Destruction can occur from within, through unprofitable internal contradictions, or from without, by incorporation into the dominant culture which knows perfectly well how to smother by adoption. What we have in the multitude of protesting groups, which constitute what we are calling "the revolution of images," is not more than a potentiality: a mass of energy looking for direction and form. It cries out for roots, for a past, for understanding. Without this grounding it can achieve nothing—like the seeds in Jesus' parable that fell on rocky ground and soon capitulated to the elements. In the long run it could produce nothing except a vague dissatisfaction, noise, and occasional anarchy. Given a vital connection with the traditions, the great revolution could acquire direction and a sense of unity. It could at least become sufficiently formed to stand for an image of man powerful enough to rival the modern image of man as technocrat. It is even conceivable that, given strong and intelligent support from the intelligentsia and the religious, it could become the *legitimate* successor of those foundational traditions, over against the modern aberration. There are those within the countercultural movement who have been able to state their purpose in precisely such terms.[25]

Unfortunately neither the university nor the church is willing (or able?)

to provide this recognition and support. On the contrary, they can only be the enemies of the revolutionary movement in their present state. They are not even neutral. They must *resist* the revolution of images (naturally there are exceptions!) because their own identity is no longer distinguishable from the dominant culture's adaptation of the modern *imago*.

It would not be so distressing if this were true only at the level of structures, for new content can burst the most ironclad bureaucratic forms. But it is true also at the more basic level of content. Both of these institutions aim at producing people whose manipulative powers have been cultivated and refined. To confirm this, one has only to ask who are regarded by these institutions as failures. Without a doubt, the failures in both cases are the persons who have not been enabled to "take charge" of themselves, to "become leaders," useful citizens. There is no room in the contemporary university for Plato's wise man, who knows that he is ignorant. Nor is there any room in the churches for Paul's righteous man, who knows that his righteousness is "as filthy rags."

It is this commitment to modernity, and not the more specific issues of authority, curriculum, representative government, which caused Western universities in the 1960's to resist the rebellion from within—sometimes to the point of death.

Theoretically, it is more difficult for the church to derive a consistent and convincing basis for its resistance than it is for the university. For in spite of theological and popular movements to eliminate from the Christian message all elements incompatible with modernity, the confessions, creeds, hymnody and liturgy of the churches, and above all the Scriptures themselves, have made it extremely difficult for the churches to dissociate themselves altogether from the tradition of Jerusalem. It has never been quite possible for the church to be rid of the insistence that *essential* manhood is man receiving the grace of God. And yet the actual life of the churches, particularly in North America and more particularly Protestant North America, has born witness to a quite different way of conceiving of man's essence. It is in reality the direct antithesis of the belief in grace. Ludicrous scenes are repeated Sunday after Sunday. Churches full (but lately not so full) of self-made business and professional people, whose whole life centers around the ideas of work, effort, and mastery, singing hymns about the total dependence of man and the futility of his work! Persons who bear the burden of office, wealth, and power in their communities, listening to such readings as I Cor., chs. 1 and 2: "Not many of you were wise according to worldly standards, not many were powerful, not many were of noble birth; but God chose what is foolish in the world to shame the wise, God chose what is weak in the world to shame the strong, God chose what is low and despised in the world, even things that are not, to bring to nothing things that are, so that no human being might boast in the presence of God." (I Cor. 1:26–30.) The irony is that these scenes were not, and are not, experienced as being in the least ironic! Here and there, there have always been persons who pointed to this incongruity and cried, "Hypocrisy!" We have all known such persons. But the vast majority have been quite undisturbed. Bound up with the middle class, a stratum of society that came into being precisely in response to the technocratic image of man, the churches have been quite unable and unwilling to proclaim the radical message of grace (*sola gratia!*). To do so would have been to call into question, concretely, the whole way of life espoused by their chief "supporters." If they have at the same time been unable to dispense with the idea of grace as the central concept of the tradition of Jerusalem, they have found ways of interpreting it which guarantee its inoffensiveness. Either it is understood as the new basis for a work ethic (Jesus replaces the old law with his own version), or else it is given a pietistic, individualistic interpretation which effectively eliminates it from the everyday world of social and political life.

There is one hopeful element in this situation. While neither the church nor the university has recognized or given support to the great revolution in which the new *imago* struggles to be born, their occasional and halfhearted reference to the older traditions has in some sense kept these traditions alive in the world. Many who have heard the words of Jesus and some of the concepts of Socrates in ways that these institutions did not intend have, on their own, turned to these ancient founding traditions and have discovered in them grist for their mills. Hence it is possible to find many among the young in particular, most of whom have had little association with the churches, defending their rebellion over against their vaguely religious parents and mentors by quoting the Bible and dressing like Jesus. They must, as Theodore Roszak has said, "improvise their maturity," because they have so little help from society and its institutions. But sometimes they stumble upon teachers who regard the pursuit of *truth* as more important than the pursuit of security; who compare men with lilies of the field and birds of the air; who call them to become children again. In spite of themselves, the institutions have maintained sufficient touch with their roots that others, desperately in need of roots, could benefit from them. But this does not excuse the institutions themselves for their inauthenticity and recalcitrance.

PROBLEMATIC OF THE EMERGENT *IMAGO HOMINIS*

The failure of the intellectual and religious segments in our society to recognize and support the echoes of their own deeper traditions in the countercultural revolution of images is only one reason to fear that the embryonic *imago* will fail to mature. Three further difficulties must still be discussed: (1) the entrenched nature of the dominant *imago;* (2) dangers inherent in the emergent *imago;* and (3) the question whether there is time for a new image of man to reach maturity.

The modern *imago hominis,* as we have observed, is deeply entrenched. We must be realistic about the possibilities of a new image of man actually replacing it. The technocratic image of man not only is implicit in our institutions, our values, our goals, but is thoroughly embedded in the presuppositions that abide in the minds and hearts of all of us. These are so basic and so deeply hidden that we act upon them automatically. Even those who rebel against this image of man; even those who are aware of its now demonic and destructive character, are influenced by it in the very depths of their souls. Again and again we revert to basically technocratic assumptions—often in the very attempt to practice things intended to combat those assumptions of our society! It is hard to wage a war, even an intellectual war—without drawing heavily upon the image of man as master! Western man is so totally indoctrinated in the assumptions of mastery that it is only in his contact with other cultures, notably those he designates "primitive," that he even begins to suspect the extent of his captivation.

Beside this established, almost innate way of regarding ourselves and our humanity, the emergent *imago* can only seem fragile, tentative, uncertain of itself, the mere possibility of something new. By its very nature, it is badly equipped for combat. Receptivity is no motto for protest—especially not protest against a highly activistic, inherently militant concept like mastery! It is almost ridiculous to conceive of the confrontation between these two images of man, one impelled by visions of human triumph, the other opening itself to what transcends it and permitting itself to be acted upon. It is like a struggle between a well-equipped police force and a group of flower children, or between peace marchers and soldiers. Can there be any doubt about the outcome? To have hope at all for the emergent *imago* it is necessary at least to conceive of this confrontation in terms to which even Christians (alas!) are entirely unaccustomed: the power of the weak!

Beyond the danger from without, there is an internal danger which is in some ways even more distressing. There are tendencies within the

emergent *imago hominis* which, if they prevailed, could produce a civilization perhaps as questionable from the Christian point of view as the one
based on the quest for mastery. This requires careful elaboration.

Theologically, Christian faith must affirm and support emergent images
of man that *approximate* its own view of man's nature and destiny, but it
ought never to equate any of these images with its own view. For the
Christian, the image of essential manhood can only be found in *imago Dei*.
Whatever else that means (and it has meant a great many different
things), it stands at least for this: man's being, like God's, is fundamentally
a mystery. The confession that man is *imago Dei* contains a methodological
prerequisite for all who seek to understand and define man. It insists that
all attempts at definition and analysis defy systematization, theory,
categorization, and accurate description. And that in a radical sense!
The drive to understand who we are, and why, is given in our being as
such. Christian faith recognizes that. Its pursuit of the knowledge of man
is just as impassioned as its pursuit of the knowledge of God. Moreover, as
Calvin and many others have insisted, the knowledge of God and the
knowledge of man can in no way be undertaken separately. Precisely
because of this primary relationship with the Source of life's mystery,
Christian faith is deeply suspicious of anthropological statements which,
for the sake of completeness, or consistency, or (as is more often the case)
for far less noble reasons, reduce man's being to some of its aspects, and so
destroy the mystery.

On these theological grounds, it is possible to affirm that it was right for
Christians to support, in some measure, the *imago hominis* that emerged in
the modern epoch. Against the background of a system that enslaved man
to natural elements and to the human institutions, including the church,
which benefited from this enslavement, it was theologically obedient to act
and think in behalf of man's liberation from nature and the supernatural.
What we have criticized in this was the willingness of Christian theology,
especially in the New World, to permit the technocratic image of man to
become too uncritically identified with its own view of human nature and
destiny.

Whatever humanizing elements were contained in the earlier forms of
the modern image of man, it has become thoroughly dehumanizing in the
contemporary period. What may have begun as a liberation of man from
bondage to the elements has ended in his bondage to the processes that he
initiated in order to free himself from these elements. Clearly, Christians
are obligated to look for new, counter expressions of the nature and
purpose of human existence, which can perform anew the liberating work.

The mistake of Christian modernism should not be repeated. No incipient *imago hominis*, however wonderfully it may seem to reflect the tradition of Jerusalem, should be identified as a flawless expression of essential manhood. It may contain highly significant qualities which, in our historical context, are desperately in need of support. But to "baptize" a historical image of man, and therefore to hallow the epoch that it generates, is a dangerous undertaking. We should have learned that, as Christians, from other periods besides the modern one. Perhaps we are only now in a position to understand it fully—now that we have come to the end of "the Constantinian era." The illusion of identifying worldly empires with God's Kingdom should no longer so easily tempt us.

Our contention has been that in the emergent image of man, with its concept of receptivity instead of mastery, there is a potential new identity for man, by means of which he might preserve his humanity, and indeed his very life on earth. But in making this strong affirmation in favor of the emergent *imago*, we ought not to overlook the fact that this image of man, too, is only an approximation, for the time being, of what we confess to be *essential* manhood. In the name of the *imago Dei* we may embrace it; in the name of the *imago Dei* we must also be critical of it. There are dangers implicit in this image of man; therefore, while supporting it, we also maintain a certain distance, so that we can, if necessary, become witnesses to the dehumanizing tendencies implicit also in it.

What are these dehumanizing potentialities?

The basic danger is not difficult to ascertain: *"receptivity" could come to mean "passivity."* Obviously neither Jerusalem nor Athens ever intended such a thing. Obviously also many of those in our own time who are seeking new life-styles distinct from the grasping, producing dominant culture are far from merely passive. But there are elements of passivity present already in certain wings of the revolution. For example, there are ecological groups that almost want man to disappear so that the grasshoppers can have a chance!

The concept of receptivity does not automatically lead to passivity—neither in theory nor in historical experience. Christians more than others ought to realize that: To be the recipient of the grace of God, indeed to own that one's whole existence is dependent upon this grace, does *not* mean to become passive. The God who bestows his grace freely upon men sends them out to be vehicles of his grace among men. This is not merely theological theory; it has been the experience of countless men and women and of the church over the centuries.

At the same time, Christians are aware of the ease with which the gospel of "sheer grace" is distorted. "Cheap grace" (Bonhoeffer) has abounded in our centuries-long experience, and the more devastatingly just where the message of *sola gratia* was most consistently announced, e.g., in Lutheran Germany! Given the right circumstances, and the failure to spell out the relationship between active and passive elements in receptivity, the natural danger of this concept is to slide over onto the side of the passive.

Now this danger can be perceived in connection with each of the four aspects of the emergent *imago hominis* mentioned in the preceding discussion:

1. The danger of a *new relationship between man and nature* that would put man back into nature is to lose sight of the fact that man is not only a natural but also a historical being. This is not a theoretical danger. It is already real among many whose identification with nonhuman nature makes them suspicious of any claims for man's distinctiveness as a historical creature. They find it possible to explain man in strictly natural terms. History, with its presupposition of a distinctive freedom, is acceptable only in terms of the history of a species.

2. The danger implicit in *the search for a new human identity* is that receptivity to the body and its needs could lead to a new animalism. The indulgence of the body could displace that difficult but somehow creative tension between body and spirit out of which human greatness has usually been born. The unchallenged pursuit of bodily gratification can only lead to the grossest form of hedonism. Along that path there is no future for a species which knows now that it lives in a limited universe. The rediscovery of the body as an element of the essence of man—and as such "good"—is necessary in an era that has identified value with rationality of the most mechanistic sort. But we should be aware of the tendency of certain countercultural elements to exaggerate the value of the body in reaction to this technocratic threat. Such a tendency contains within itself a threat to humanity which, under certain circumstances, could be just as fatal.

3. The danger implicit in *the search for a new mode of thought* in such concepts as meditation and contemplation is manifold. It could, for example, create a split between ontological reason and technical reason (to use, for the moment, Tillich's categories).[26] A split of this sort would leave technocratic thought without a critique from the side of thinking that has a broader and more transcendent aim. This has already occurred significantly within the modern world. A considerable dimension of our present dilemma concerns precisely this split. It was explored by Sir Charles Snow in his famous work, *The Two Cultures,* but it has already progressed far beyond the situation described by him. It may be assumed for most practical purposes that the "leaderless" (Buber) character of technology today stems in great measure from the withdrawal of religion,

philosophy, and the humanities from the political world and even from consistent social responsibility.[27] What has occurred on the part of these human disciplines is not just a withdrawal, but an attempt to imitate the objectivity and noninvolvement of the sciences.

Another possible danger of pursuing meditative thought would be the advent of an epoch in which technical reason had come to be despised. The circumstances under which such a period could occur are perhaps less probable than the first danger, which would be simply an extension of present conditions. However, they are not unimaginable. As Walter M. Miller has depicted brilliantly in his novel *A Canticle for Leibowitz*,[28] a society whose ruination or near-ruination was clearly linked with science and technology might very well turn against these pursuits with something like puritanical vengeance. There are enough echoes of this vengeance in the air already to make the suggestion far from trite. The *simple* solution to the dilemma of the technological society is the destruction of the machines. That solution, being simple, has occurred to many people who would not dare to express it aloud but who, given other circumstances, might well become latter-day Luddites. Their reaction is understandable enough, since machines *are* the most concrete symbols of the menace to our existence. But they are only symbols—"symptomatic" (Ellul)—and in reality symbols of the most peripheral sort. The technocratic disease is internal. It is a matter of images, of a state of mind. The machinery, even at its most complex, is merely a surface manifestation of this internal social and psychic condition. Besides, the alternative to the technological society is not a society in which there is no technology, but a society in which technology has been made subservient to truly human requirements.[29]

4. The danger implicit in *the search for new bases of community* is that genuine individuality will be extinguished. This is not inevitable, but it is possible—very possible! The possibility has been explored by many contemporary authors, both at the imaginative and at the discursive level. The most provocative treatments of the question, in my opinion, are those by anti-Utopian novelists such as Orwell, Zamiatin, and Huxley.[30]

Individuality ought not to be equated with individualism. The latter is a natural offspring of the technocratic image of man, for that image sets man against man in the competition for mastery. But community that sacrifices individual freedom and potential for the sake of equality is just as destructive of genuine humanity as societies based on competition. What does equality mean if to achieve it gifts must be buried and persons reduced to the lowest common denominator? What does community mean if, in order to be receptive to the others, I must empty myself of my own idiosyncrasies and potentialities, thus putting myself into the strange position of having nothing, really, to *contribute* to the others? Community that does not maintain dialectical balance with a concern for individual identity and destiny is in the last analysis nothing but a great emptiness, from which all riches have been drained. For riches come, not from aggregation, but from variety, from the creative encounter of dissimilarities. To preserve and enhance real individuality is therefore the primary concern of those who want to build authentic community. But the danger of destroying individuality for the sake of commonality is present in every search for community.

In sum, the emergent image of man is, then, fraught with dangers from within. It shares with all other historical images the propensity to dehumanize, even though in the primary sense it is a new bid for humanity against a reigning *imago* that is leading to death. It would not be unthinkable, on the grounds of historical realism, to posit a swing of the pendulum from mastery to receptivity, in which the latter would develop according to its own worst elements. At very least, the emergence of the new image of man will require the guidance of wise and concerned counselors who know its implicit dangers and are not afraid to be critical of what they support. There is reason enough to doubt that such guidance can be found.

Is There Time?

A third reason to fear for the successful emergence of such a new image of man is related to the time factor. Is there time? After all, images of man do not come to be overnight. The technocratic image of man required perhaps three centuries to become universally influential. Even today, when it has reached a certain pinnacle in some areas of the world, notably in the North Atlantic nations, it is *(Deo gratia!)* far from having accomplished its work in the greatest portion of the earth. Part of the confusion that abounds in analyses of the technological society today stems from the tremendous discrepancy between various cultures in terms of their stages of technological development. Those who do not yet enjoy the fruits of the technological mentality are astonished by any criticism whatsoever of these wonders. On the other hand, the most highly developed technological societies (notably from North America, for even most Western Europeans seem fascinated by machinery still) have a growing body of critics who realize that technology does not bring "the good life." But the point is, if even such an attractive and triumphant *imago hominis* has required so long to establish itself, how can anyone reasonably hope that a much less appealing *imago* will be introduced in a few decades?

We are dealing with just that: a few decades. On every side, scientists, economists, social scientists, prophets, and poets are telling us that we must acquire a new attitude, new life-styles, a new "concern for the quality of life." There can be no doubt that all of this means, concretely, that *we must limit ourselves or else we shall be limited.* It is as simple as that. We must discover a new way of being in the world, or else we shall have such a new way thrust upon us by famine, overcrowding, noise, natural resources depleted, wars of global proportions unknown heretofore. And we must find this new way soon, very soon—at once!

Against the pessimistic assumption that there simply is not time to develop such a new conception of our place in the world, it is necessary to put a biological datum: Man has a remarkable ability to adapt to whatever is necessary for his own preservation. It is not impossible, surely, that under duress a new *imago hominis* could inculcate itself quickly, more quickly than ever before in history, for never before in history has it been necessary to be quite so immediate. Necessity is the mother of inventions —also perhaps of images of man. The speed with which the countercultural movements in North America sprang to life in response to the data of despair—and without mentors!—makes the prospect of a swift response seem the more feasible.

On the other side, however, if such a new *imago* did emerge so quickly, would there be time for it to be modified, balanced, corrected? The dangers from within, about which we have already reflected, are almost certainly aggravated by the need for haste. A situation drastic enough to impel the majority of people toward such an image of man could quite conceivably push them to the point of embracing the most questionable dimensions of that image. Like the "Simplifiers" in Miller's *A Canticle for Leibowitz,* they might so turn against everything that Western civilization has produced as to bring about a new "dark age" undreamed of by the age of progress. The sight of bodies charred by nuclear explosion, oceans rendered "dead" by pollution, millions of people dying of starvation and malnutrition, could turn a people not only against machinery but against the whole course of a culture that produced such results. Or, instead of such a reaction, which is after all still a kind of activism, an unduly fast transition to a new image could accentuate the passive elements to such an extent that it would lead to total inactivity and fatalism. For if the life urge is strong in mankind, there is also a concomitant death urge, born of the fear of pain. We can endure a great deal of pain so long as we can still see it in the context of hope. But when experience ceases to give any confirmation of our expectancy, we would rather capitulate.

THE CHALLENGE TO NORTH AMERICA

The question is whether or not expectancy has been too narrowly based. Is there room for an expectancy that comes to be and maintains itself *within* the pain? Is there a hope that, without blessing the pain, finds through it an entree into the future? This is the challenge to mankind today. It is in a special way the challenge to North Americans. I believe there is. But it is an affirmation that requires explanation.

Clearly, in the matter of acquiring a new image of man in the world, North America is in a key position. This is so for a number of reasons.

First, as has already been shown, this continent is the place where the technocratic image of man was most consistently inculcated. It has been, if not the exclusive, at least the dominant mind-set of our people from the outset of the experiment called "America."

Second, because of the long, unchallenged and uninterrupted influence of the technological mentality in North America, this continent is by far the most technologically advanced society in the world. It may be demonstrated that in this or that area of science or technology other peoples (notably the Russians) are ahead of us. But where the general application of technique to all areas of life is concerned, from the kitchen to the concert hall,[31] there is obviously no rival.

Third, this continent is the center from which the technological empire spreads into all the world. We are not referring so much to the so-called imperialistic designs of the greatest member nation of this continent as to the technological pace set by this continent as the model for the rest of the world. Even those nations who regard the United States as their principal political enemy measure their own advances and standard of living by the American pattern. The power of the technological empire of this continent does not lie so much in its wealth and its arms as in its superior application of the technological aims of modernity. Other peoples are captivated by this prowess, and they capitulate to it without the hint of a struggle. (In some important ways, the American "capture" of West Germany is more significant than its conquests in Asia.)

Fourth, this continent seems to be the only place in the modern world where the technological society has been called into question by a significant minority of people. Given the triumph of technique here, as expressed in the preceding three observations, it is highly significant that this is so. For only those who have experienced fully what technology can do—only those who have experienced the *failure* of that dream—are in a position to engage in serious protest and the search for an alternative vision.

In short, North America is in a key position in the matter of the revolution of images. It is the one place in the modern world where the modern *imago* has been able to develop to the point where it can be apprehended as having consequences detrimental to man and society.

This is not to say that North Americans alone can appreciate that fact. The questionable character of the image of man so consistently and exclusively adopted by this continent can also be noticed from the perspective of those who have been subjected to the mastery of this continent. Notably, the peoples of the Third World. From that perspective, this continent has been and is robbing the rest of the world of resources and exploiting other nations and peoples to the point of breaking. From that perspective, too, it is mandatory that North Americans discover a new way of being in the world. We must find new expectations that do not violate the right of *other peoples* to hope!

But from the standpoint of a potential *change* in images, the view "from within" is more important. It is assumed that such a view would be informed, in the most sensitive interpreters, by a knowledge of the image projected by this continent upon the rest of the world, especially upon the world's poor.

To state it in more theoretical terms: a genuine revolution at the level of images can occur only where an old *imago* has expended itself. Only where it has been allowed to develop to a certain maturity, and has demonstrated to a sufficient number of people that it does not deliver what it promised to deliver, can a change occur. The expectations associated with it must be denied by experience. Or to state it in other words, the advent of a new life-style depends upon recognizing that the old life-style does not in fact make for life. This can only occur from within. Those outside North America can with perfect right chastise a small proportion of the world's population which consumes a very great proportion of its raw materials and pollutes the earth beyond all reason. These criticisms can be made, however, without in the least calling into question the state of mind that has produced such a continent. In fact, many who voice this criticism today from the Third World and elsewhere have no better plan than to duplicate the North American life-style at the earliest opportunity! With rare exceptions, only those within the highly developed technological society are able to become sufficiently disenchanted to engage in the radical activity of looking for another image of man.[32] Indeed, as we have maintained, it is only in North America that the revolution of images *has,* thus far, achieved support of a significant and articulate minority. Most of the other revolutions in the present-day world are taking place on the assumption that the technological mentality is right and unassailable.

However, North America is prevented from moving toward a new vision, new expectations, a new image of man, on any scale that could radically affect the world situation and the quality of man's survival.

Why? The reasons for this refusal are numerous. They can be discussed at many different levels. The technocratic assumptions about man and society are deeply entrenched in every facet of our life. It is indeed almost beyond imagination to contemplate how such an image of man as one informed by receptivity could possibly influence us as a people. And yet, what must always be stated on the other side is the equally impossible idea that we should continue along the lines of our own past performance. We must change, or we will be changed.

Why, then, do we hold back? The most fundamental reason why North Americans hold on to expectations whose foundation in experience has almost disappeared is that we cannot admit failure. This is why we refuse to let go of the image of ourselves born of those expectations. And it is why we will hardly recognize, let alone explore, the quite different *imago hominis* into which some of our own children would like to initiate us. As a people, we are simply incapable of facing the experience of negation. We cannot admit that we have failed.

Facing the experience of negation in this context means two things. First, it means facing the bankruptcy of the image of man by which we have been impelled throughout our history. Second, it means adopting a style of life which, from the standpoint of the modern *imago hominis,* can only seem to us something small, weak, niggardly, insignificant, defeatist. It is to us an *imago* born of the death of expectation, in which there could be no vitality, no enthusiasm, no hope.

For us as a people, expectancy is synonymous with progress, expansion, development, production, growth, bigness, victory, the breaking of barriers, the pushing back of frontiers, the refusal to admit limits, the sense of power and success. We even banished death!—and the religion of Jesus helped us to do it. Now we stand at the edge of the Red Sea. We cannot return to the Egypt of the nineteenth-century industrial optimism that made us great. Nor can we walk across the water to some better time. All the same, instead of facing this dilemma, we refuse to admit the impasse. Some talk of holding off the enemy, and some of building bridges. Only a small number of the strangely attired young, with a sprinkling of people from other generations, have begun to walk *into* the sea. They seem to expect a miracle!

THE CHALLENGE TO CHRISTIAN FAITH IN NORTH AMERICA

One of the most perceptive of George Grant's writings is an essay entitled "In Defence of North America." At the end of this essay he writes:

> We live then in the midst of the most realized technological society which has yet been: one which is, moreover, the chief imperial centre from which technique is spread around the world. It might seem then that because we are destined to be so, we might also be the people best able to comprehend what it is to be so. Because we are first and most fully there, the need might seem to press upon us to try to know where we are in this new found land which is so obviously a "terra incognita." [33]

Professor Grant concludes his essay, however, with an expression of grave doubt over the realization of such a possibility. "The very substance of our existing which has made us the leaders in technique stands as a barrier to any thinking which might be able to comprehend technique from beyond its own dynamism." [34]

It would be difficult to imagine a more direct and provocative way of stating the challenge to Christian faith on this continent today. Christian faith announces itself as trust in a Power *(dunamis)* that surpasses the power of this world's kingdoms, systems, fantasies, and principalities. It confesses membership in a Kingdom that transcends the kingdoms of this world and recognizes them for what they are. The test of the authenticity of these claims today is quite simply whether such faith enables men "to comprehend technique from beyond its own dynamism."

At least to comprehend it! Beyond that, it remains to be seen whether such a faith could recognize *alternatives* to the technocratic way, which has become a way of death. Are Christians as bereft of a vantage point for understanding the technological society as are most of the others who constitute this society? Are we, too, so caught up in the spirit of technique—mastering, manipulating—that we are unable to assess what has happened and is happening to man and the world? Have we perhaps interpreted even our own tradition, our life, our faith itself, according to the presuppositions and myths of the technocratic mind-set? Or is there still in this faith the possibility of gaining a perspective?

So far as official Christianity is concerned, there is no reason at all to think that Grant's doubts would have been qualified had he given more serious thought to the religious establishment. As a Christian, Grant himself knows perfectly well what to expect from the churches. Not only have the churches been unable to offer any insightful critique of the technocratic mentality, but they have adapted themselves to it unquestioningly. At the lowest level of adaptation this has meant the pathetic concern for relevance, which asks no questions of the rightness of that to which it seeks to relate. It has also meant incorporating into the churches themselves the most primitive of our society's manipulative techniques, as in the cult of group dynamics. At a higher level of theological sophistication, the naïve notion has prevailed that the problem is the unwise use of technology. It is assumed that technology is itself altogether neutral. There is no understanding of what is meant by such terms as "technique," as Ellul or Grant use it, or "technocracy," as Philip Slater uses it.[35] The sense of the demonic has gone out of contemporary church Christianity, while many outsiders are able to employ Pauline categories ("principalities and powers"!) to describe the technological society.[36] Christian analyses of technology almost invariably and monotonously call for enlightened and humane use of technology. Predictably enough, the employment of technology for ends that are destructive of man and nature are now regularly being decried by directives from Geneva and the head offices of our denominations. (Large universities, governments, industries, foundations, and every red-blooded American can be counted upon for *the same* pronouncements.) Certainly there are individual Christians, and certain minorities within the churches, who seek to delve more deeply into the problem. But there is no reason to single out the churches for special commendation in this connection. The record of scientists and technologists themselves, most of whom have little cultivated connection with the tradition of Jerusalem, is far better. Novelists and artists have been pointing for decades to the dehumanizing trends of technocracy in a way that should make us utterly ashamed to think of ourselves as the inheritors of the prophetic tradition of Israel! If one looks to official Christianity for comprehension of technique "from beyond its own dynamism," then, one will look in vain. In this matter, as in most others, there is no reason to distinguish between religion and culture in North America. On the contrary, the official religion can almost be defined in our context as the most uncritical expression of the dominant culture.

What makes it both possible and necessary to articulate this challenge to Christianity, however, is that the faith which confesses membership in a Kingdom that transcends and judges this world's empires also transcends, potentially, the structures with which it is itself bound up. There is still some reason to hope that, if not in the churches themselves, then at least in the tradition to which, in spite of themselves, they continue to bear witness, it might be possible to find a vantage point from which to discern the signs of the times and discover the courage to live.

In fact, if one has been able to get behind the facade of Christian triumphalism and religiosity to the story itself, the story of the crucified God, one cannot suppress the feeling that this faith is in reality intended precisely for *our time!* In one way, as Grant has said, it is a gigantic step, a regular crossing of the Rubicon, when a man begins to question the basis of modern Western civilization, i.e., the doctrine of progress through human mastery.[37] It is a dizzying prospect to contemplate the possibility that the whole of modernity might have been the indulgence of a fantasy that promised to give us the moon and gave us—the moon. But at the same time, just this step is the precondition for discovering meaning and the courage to be, according to that faith which has always declared that real possibilities emerge only in the midst of impossibilities, only at the edge of the Red Sea. The impatience and anger with which not a few Christians reproach the churches today is born precisely of this sense that many in the contemporary world might really be able to hear the Christian witness now, having come to the edge of night. Meanwhile the churches, avoiding the darkness *and* the light, the depths *and* the heights, stand for halfhearted attempts to revive the failing faith—not in Jesus, really, but in the modern credo of progress and mastery.

There can be no question of turning this sense of the real pertinence of Christian faith today into a new form of triumphalism. The time is long since past when Christians could have interpreted the salvation of humanity as their special prerogative. It belongs to all men of goodwill. Christians must increasingly interpret their own peculiar mission within the context of the greater human struggle for life. They could become in the most Biblical sense a grain of salt, a bit of yeast. The new understanding of man that is striving to manifest itself today is no product of the church or of Christian proclamation. It comes to be only in the mystery of the love of God, who does not will the destruction and condemnation of the earth and man. The church can only recognize something of the dynamics of this mystery and participate in its engagement with the principalities and powers of the established order.

In the present critical movement, there are many ways in which the church, taking its place beside other cultural forces, *could* play a leading role. Rightly aware of its own Biblical roots, it *could* be an important factor in preventing the demonic and dehumanizing elements within the emergent *imago hominis* from becoming dominant. Honestly assessing its own misuse of divine grace, it *could* help to keep the receptivity characteristic of the new *imago* from falling into passivity, quietism, or the sort of half-secular otherworldliness that already informs so many countercultural experiments. From the riches of the dynamic, relational understanding of reality that is present in the tradition of Jerusalem, the church *could* assist in the birth of an image of man which maintained an appropriate dialectical tension between man's natural and historical dimensions; between his physical and spiritual identity; between pragmatic and meditative reason; between the life of the community and the life of the individual. It is indeed of the most serious importance that Christian faith become actively involved in the "midwifery" of this process. It is difficult to see where, apart from Christian influence, help can be found to maintain the necessary dialectical tension between these elements. It is even difficult to discover, outside the Judeo-Christian tradition, that wisdom which is capable of recognizing *the necessity* for maintaining these tensions. For the awareness of that necessity, and of the dangers implicit in systems where one or another element in the dialectical tension is permitted to dominate, is rare not only in the contemporary world but in the whole recorded history of the race! Christianity is challenged, then, to play a significant and "leading" role in the cultural change through which we are passing.

The greater immediate challenge to Christianity in North America, however, does not concern the emergent image of man so much as it does the preparation for its birth. *If* a new life-style is to take shape, a major segment of our society must be made open to it—if not the majority, at least a very creative minority. This is clearly not yet the case. Between that possibility and the present situation, there lies the necessity about which we have spoken. It is a veritable slough of despond. To become open to a new image of themselves, men must have grown consciously, and to some extent articulately, aware of the detrimental character of the old *imago.* And what if that old *imago* is the only one known? What else could have established itself as the highest, the very pinnacle of man's vision of himself? From such heights, every other style of life looks exceedingly small. To face the failure of an image of man is hard enough; to accept another *imago hominis* that from the perspective of the past must seem a very concession to *eternal* failure is something else.

The challenge to faith, then, is not only whether from the treasure-house of the Biblical tradition Christians can bring forth things old and new to give form and direction to the image of man that is struggling to be born. Before that, it is whether we can help men to face the failure of the old *imago hominis* without capitulating to despair.

It is not only whether we can help to provide new light, but, since in any case light can only be seen in the darkness, whether we can help to provide a way into the darkness!

VII

A WAY
INTO THE DARKNESS

"LIGHTEN OUR DARKNESS"

What follows should not be regarded as conclusive. It is the suggestion of a spirit and a method—nothing more. The very nature of the content precludes finality. A theology of the cross is not a theology of answers; it is a theology of the question. Besides, the whole thing is offered, not as light, but as a way into the darkness: the darkness that *is*, the darkness that must become the *known* context in every search for light.

Let us be quite clear: only the light is final. We have no lasting interest in the darkness as such, and certainly no desire to court it. It is necessary to think about it and to enter into it only because it is already there. It is already our condition; and the true light that lightens our darkness can only be apprehended by us as we stand, honestly and knowingly, exactly where we are. Indeed, the true light will itself lead us into our darkness, unlike the false lights of religions and world views. For it is known that only as we become accustomed to the night, the deepening gloom, are we able to see the light that is specifically light for this darkness. Otherwise we are simply deluding ourselves with artificial light.

Concretely, my intention is to offer in broadest outline a theology of the cross that tries to be indigenous to our North American experience as "the most realized technological society which has yet been" (Grant). I shall offer this outline according to three categories of theological thought—theological, ethical, and ecclesiastical. The first, which is the specifically theological statement, gives what I regard as the primary apologetic rationale for the theology of the cross as the appropriate "word" for our situation. The second, the ethical statement, describes the fundamental

203

character of this theology, as the basis from which a political ethic can and must emerge. The third, the ecclesiastical statement, depicts the life and expectations of the people—the church—which offers itself not only as witness to this possibility but as a guide into the darkness.

In connection with each of the three statements, there is an implicit assumption: namely, that what is stated could become meaningful only if it were elaborated and incorporated into the living structures and programs of the church. In professional jargon, the whole is intended in the strictest sense as "practical" theology.

Not everything can be said in any study, and in this study in particular there are reasons why one would eschew even the attempt to say everything. Theology, finally, can only be done by the Christian community. It is not an individual undertaking. Individuals can only propose ways; the means have to be explored corporately—by the body. The three ensuing statements, therefore, should not be judged for their completeness, but for their cogency as directives.

A Paradigm for the Experience of Negation

An indigenous theology of the cross would offer men in the officially optimistic society a paradigm for the experience of negation.

The most tenacious facet of the theological triumphalism we have inherited is our propensity to regard the Christian gospel from a triumphalistic point of view. This kerygmatic triumphalism, as we may name it, remains with people even when they have discarded the more obvious ecclesiastical triumphalism, the imperialism of the church. It is much more difficult to apply the *theologia crucis* to theology than to apply it to the ecclesia and the Christian life. We have already observed this problem in Part Two: There is something about the Christian message that seems to demand its being given the last word—not necessarily in a crass and obvious triumph, as in some of the more militant Christian sects, but all the same a triumph. It is presented as a source of solution for every human problem: it roots out human selfishness and makes love possible; it gives the foundation of a sound family life; it overcomes alienation; it provides a climate of brotherhood among men and nations; it replaces doubt and cynicism with faith, bitterness with gratitude, guilt with forgiveness, despair with hope, anxiety with joy, death with life.

In making this criticism of the implicit triumphalism of so much of the church's preaching and practice in the world, I do not mean to deny the power of the gospel to transform the human condition. But there is a certain modesty in the Biblical witness to the triumph of the gospel which has been almost lost in the Christendom church: the Bible never indulges in the sort of instant overcoming of evil which characterizes so much Christian thought, both on the conservative and on the liberal front. There is always a "Not Yet" in the Biblical witness. Moreover, there is a deep awareness of the way in which the final overcoming of evil involves all of us in a yet more intensive encounter with it. As Christ had himself to be brought into dialogue with Satan, so the Christian is carried off by the Spirit into the wilderness of sin and temptation.

The triumphalistic spirit, on the other hand, banishes the wilderness straightaway, and replaces the dialectical "Already/Not Yet" with a straightforward "Already." It produces a gospel that consists primarily in the *overcoming* of the experience of evil and negation, a gospel whose "Yes" disqualifies the "No" of human existence. This kerygmatic triumphalism so informs the church's thought that most Christians find any other analysis almost pagan—especially one that allows for the continuing reality of evil and a certain fear and trembling about the outcome.

The explicit weakness of kerygmatic triumphalism is that it makes it very difficult, if not quite impossible, to take seriously the evil that is present in life. If real evil has already been overcome, then the evil that manifests itself in our actual existence can only be regarded as unreal. If the triumph over evil is already determined, beyond the shadow of a doubt, then history is no longer to be regarded as the locus of a decisive struggle between good and evil. Human responsibility for the future is virtually set aside. Reality becomes undialectically identified with the proclaimed triumph, and faith is defined as the will to believe this triumph in the face of all obstacles. One lives from expectation; it is not necessary for experience to corroborate it. The experienced "No" is not decisive.

But we have come into a period in history when the "No" of human experience is of another order from that of past epochs. It lives independently of a context of expectation, and it contains within itself a new immunity to the whole idea of overcoming.

While in earlier periods the forms assumed by the "No" of experience were not less productive of disbelief nor more amenable to banishment by the victorious Word of God, in our time the most typical experience of negation is, all the same, more insidious. For it produces an atmosphere wholly unfavorable to the thought of a triumphant "Yes." It is one thing to have one's gospel confronted by the thought of death and the devil, and something else to find it confronted by the experience of the absurd.

In order to appreciate the way in which kerygmatic triumphalism is called into question by the present apologetic situation, we need to study these distinctions more closely. Paul Tillich's analysis in *The Courage to Be* is useful in this connection.

Tillich identifies three forms of anxiety in which nonbeing threatens man: the anxiety of fate and death, the anxiety of guilt and condemnation, and the anxiety of emptiness and meaninglessness. While the three types of anxiety are interdependent, periods of history are normally, according to Tillich, dominated by one of them especially. He concludes, as have many other analyses, that our own period is characterized by the dominance of the anxiety of doubt and meaninglessness.

> Certainly the anxiety of fate and death is not lacking in our time. The anxiety of fate has increased with the degree to which the schizophrenic split of our world has removed the last remnants of former security. And the anxiety of guilt and condemnation is not lacking either. It is surprising how much anxiety of guilt comes to the surface in psychoanalysis and personal counselling. The centuries of Puritan and bourgeois repression of vital strivings have produced almost as many guilt feelings as the preaching of hell and purgatory in the Middle Ages.

> But in spite of these restricting considerations one must say that the anxiety which determines our period is the anxiety of doubt and meaninglessness. One is afraid of having lost or having to lose the meaning of one's existence. The expression of this situation is the Existentialism of today.[38]

At the articulate level, the sense of meaninglessness, the encounter with the absurd, is no doubt experienced by only a few. After all, it is such that most men can deal with it only by repressing it. The fact, however, that the few have been recognized, rightly, as the interpreters of the age indicates the extent to which the sense of the absurd has infected the many. Kafka said of himself that he "had the right to represent his age," because he had so "vigorously absorbed the negative element of his age." [39]

It is normal that the real face of an era becomes visible only in the articulate self-exposure of a few men. When, for example, we speak of "the eighteenth century," we refer not simply to an epoch but to a quite definite world view that developed during that epoch, namely, the world view of the so-called Enlightenment. Only a few men—a mere handful—gave expression to that world view during that chronological period. Yet the entire epoch was somehow summed up in them.

Who can measure, then, the extent to which the sickness of emptiness has infected the fabric of our entire culture? Who, especially in a society like our own, which ekes out its existence by denying, rejecting, and repressing just this sickness? How is it possible to measure the cynicism and self-loathing by which our civilization is infected, when it is cloaked by the continuing rhetoric of progress? May not the technological society in its entirety be explicable, finally, only on the basis of the awareness—carefully concealed but nonetheless present—that there may be no purpose, no goal, no meaning in it all? Could it be that our busy preoccupation with means that are no longer answerable to ends (Buber), that our indefatigable efforts to perfect our machines, especially our war machines,[40] and that flirtation with escape and oblivion that is an unmistakable leitmotiv of our space program—could it not be that all of this adds up to a kind of cosmic death wish on the part of a culture that has discovered its essential meaninglessness?

Confronted by the sense of absurdity as the most radical contemporary form of the experience of negation, we find as Christians that we have no answers. I am speaking of those who really are brought to the point of perceiving, not only in other men but also in themselves, the dimensions of the sense of purposelessness indigenous to our time. We can hardly bring ourselves to entertain it consciously. We expose ourselves to the poets of the absurd with extreme caution—and mostly, it must be confessed, for apologetic purposes: i.e., as those who are seeking to discover what *other men* think! We recognize well enough the threat to our own security. We fear being reduced to disbelief and nihilism ourselves. We know that many of the most promising Christian thinkers have already gone that road, and we tremble for ourselves. What pathetic knights we are! Armed for the battle with death and the devil, we have come upon windmills whirling aimlessly. We have equipped ourselves with answers for the doubts of former generations. We can identify and classify the anxieties of Biblical man, and Reformation man, and nineteenth-century man (including the numerous nineteenth-century men who maintain themselves intact in our ecclesiastical institutions—so we need not go without a living!). But we are without a word in the face of the most radical contemporary form of the experience of negation. For, as Tillich put it, "If life is as meaningless as death, if guilt is as questionable as perfection, if being is no more meaningful than non-being, on what can one base the courage to be?" To engage in open encounter with the negative in its contemporary form of the absurd is a fearful thing.

In practice, few Christians get so far as that. The usual Christian response, which is adept at sensing in advance depths with which it is not equipped to deal, is to seek shelter from that night in lesser depths. Who can live without answers? Who can be a clergyman or a theologian without a gospel that "negates the negation" rather consistently?

The shelters sought by Christians, and found with astonishing regularity, are of two sorts. One is to identify the experience of negation to which the gospel addresses itself with a form of that experience dominant in another period. For example, this was the most interesting aspect of the astonishing popularity, several years ago, of the so-called "death of God" theology. Whatever may have been the intention of the prime movers of this theology (and obviously there was never any unified intention, any consistent "school" of thought), what gave this movement its momentum and made it the special target of all orthodoxy, conservative and liberal alike, was the occasion it provided for diverting attention from the real problem. Apparently identifying the dilemma of contemporary man with the death (or absence) of God, or the impossibility of belief in him, the so-called theology of the death of God was able for a time very successfully to distract the attention of both the religious and the secular onlookers away from the death which *is* at the immediate source of our trouble: the death of man, the death of meaning. It had the effect of putting the religious question back where it belonged—in heaven! One can be very sure that the real problem would never have achieved such a successful press. What killed the "death of God" theology was not the fiery darts of the righteous, but the way in which events (notably the Vietnam war and the environmental crisis) kept bringing people back to the basic question of man, in spite of themselves.

The other shelter that Christians seek when they find themselves in the vicinity of the real problem is the way of outright contradiction. This has been the special genius of the cult of celebration. It comes a little closer to authenticity, insofar as it is clearly a response to the felt presence of the "No" of contemporary experience. But in the final analysis it is an irrelevant response. In the face of the absurd, its only tactic is denial—a denial more of gesture than of thought. Like the existentialist "ethic of courage," the decision to dance in the face of the nihil begs the question of the ground of that act. Is it really the celebration of life against death, as it claims? Or is it a cryptic celebration of death—a fascination for oblivion? That question is by no means irrelevant, if one has ears for the music of the god of the vine, Dionysus, whose pipes can be heard distinctly enough in the background of the Christian cult of celebration as in many other places today.

The theology of the cross rejects both of these alternatives, the alternative of reaction and the alternative of contradiction. It finds them both escapist. It can be a theology *of the cross* only as it does not seek to escape the confrontation with the most radical contemporary manifestation of the nihil. It will not be satisfied with a sheer denial of that which negates. It seeks a confrontation at the level of thought, reasoned dialogue. This means for our time that the theology of the cross requires, as Tillich has said, "a kind of faith which *can exist together with* doubt and meaninglessness." [41] For that is the character of the present-day experience of negation.

To embark on such a theology it would be necessary, in a way that has so far been achieved by very few Christian thinkers, to divest oneself of the last vestiges of that theological triumphalism which has typified our concept of the gospel and of faith. Concretely, in order to reflect and live "the kind of faith which can exist together with doubt and meaninglessness," an indigenous theology of the cross would have to be a theology from which the God who *guarantees* meaning from the outset had been once and for all expelled. More particularly, it would have to have rid itself of an image of man which rules out, *a priori,* the prospect that man may indeed by nothing more than a naked ape.

It would be necessary for such a theology, in short, to have dispensed with the habit of regarding the gospel as a word that meets, answers, conquers, and so annuls the negative. Instead, one would have to look upon the gospel of Jesus Christ as a vantage point from which to *engage* the negative: to engage it, not to overcome it. To live with and in it, not to displace it with a theoretically unassailable positive. To permit it to become the place of conflict, from which expectations could be entertained without at the same time closing one's eyes to experience. [42]

In reality, the gospel can become authentic and believable for men today only if it is able to distinguish itself in the conflict with the absurd. Not as a St. George who slays the dragon of absurdity; but perhaps as a broken knight, or a helpless man like Bernanos' little "country priest," who at least does not have to pretend that the dragon has been slain! What Maurice Friedman writes of any who will to discover meaning in the modern world is applicable also to Christians. "Today," he insists, "meaning can be found, if at all, only through the attitude of the man who is willing to live with the absurd, to remain open to the mystery which he can never hope to pin down." [43] In any case, as soon as Christians have pinned down the mystery and surpassed the experience of the absurd, they have accomplished nothing at all except to remove themselves from the ranks of those who bear authentic witness to the crucified Christ in our time. For they have simply put themselves and their "gospel" entirely out of the reach of the most representative men of our epoch, men who need, not answers, so much as *a place to which to refer their questions.*

We have concentrated in the churches on being an answering theology. This is our undoing in an age when answers can only have a hollow ring.

Now we must concentrate on providing a place to which to refer the questions. Not the overcoming of the negative, but the possibility of engaging it, of encountering it at the level of conscious reflection, of facing it in all its enormity, should be our endeavor. Our culture is sick, and because it is also very powerful its sickness infects the whole world. On the brink of overt nihilism in our public life, and neurotically clinging to the positive in our private existences, we fear above all an open confrontation with the contradiction between our highly optimistic expectations and our increasingly depressing experiences. The repression of this contradiction is costly in life and truth. Its repression at home inevitably means that it breaks out in strange places with names which quickly become household words: Vietnam, Bangladesh, Chile. . . . There can therefore be no more responsible theology, at both the pastoral and the political level, than one that tries to provide a climate in which men and women in this society may feel able to expose themselves to that contradictory state. Is it possible to discover in the tradition of Jerusalem a way through which we may open ourselves to our own failure? Or is Christianity so irrevocably success-oriented that its forays into the twilight zone must always be accompanied by plentiful supplies of light?

The pursuit of such a question would take us inevitably to the very center of the Christian kerygma. For in the last analysis the Christian positivism of our continent, whether in its liberal this-worldly or its conservative otherworldly version, has been determined by the theological decision that the message of and about Jesus is to be received as a statement of triumph over that which negates.

Who could question such a decision? It seems altogether axiomatic! But what *can* and *must* be disputed is the extent to which the Biblical declaration of the triumph of God in Christ has been colored and distorted by its association with the triumphalism native to white Western man. A paper published recently by the World Student Christian Federation introduces the disturbing question as to whether Biblical interpretation has reflected the "class" interests of the interpreters. A more significant question—because more inclusive—would be to ask after the extent to which the *whole language of theology* had been conditioned by Western imperialistic culture, an imperialism taken up by one "Christian" empire after another. What precisely is meant by the "victory" of the Christ?

There can be little doubt concerning the meaning assigned to the resurrection by the positive religion of our society. It has been the primary theological foundation of the cultural assumption that the negative, the nihil, the night, radical evil, is basically unreal, nonexistent, a mere phantom. The fact that the theology of the resurrection has never been able to free itself on this continent from entanglement with the Hellenistic concept of the immortality of the soul is one piece of evidence for this. At the sociological level, so is the fact that Easter Sunday still draws many worldlings who otherwise do not darken the churches' doors. And then the manner in which Easter has been inextricably bound up with the conformity of nature—with lilies! Everything has been done, so to speak, to ensure that this Easter triumph lies not only within the realm of *possibility* but within the realm of *necessity*. That it is not a matter of unheard-of grace, but a matter of nature.

But that has been its nemesis at last, because it now appears quite openly that there is nothing necessarily triumphant in the realm of nature, so far as *Homo sapiens* is concerned. Already nature fails to sustain man in vast sections of the earth. And for us, too, who have been used to plenty, there are signs of the time of leanness. There may well come an Easter when lilies do not blossom.

The critical theological task of an indigenous theology is to extricate the Biblical confession of the divine triumph *pro nobis* from the triumphalistic world view of Western bourgeois society. In the light of the foregoing discussion, it is truly difficult to see how this can be achieved. After sixteen centuries of the marriage of the divine glory with the kingdoms of this world and the glory of them, one has seriously to wonder whether the remnant of Christendom is capable of such a divorce. The disease of triumphalism is chronic with us. In North America it is doubly so, for with us the *de facto* cultural establishment of the Christian religion has been far more effective than the *de jure* administrative establishments of old Europe.

But despite the overwhelming odds, responsible theology must make the attempt to distinguish its subject matter sharply from cultural triumphalism. Every theology that neglects this task in North America today automatically aligns itself with the dominant culture, the way of life that is a way of death.

The test of theological authenticity is whether we can present Jesus *as the crucified*. To be concrete: Can one perceive in the Jesus of this theology a man who knows the meaning of meaninglessness, the experience of negation, the anguish of hopelessness? Does he encounter the absurd, and with trembling? Would a man dare to confess to this Jesus his deepest anxieties, his most ultimate questions? Would such a Jesus comprehend the gnawing care of a generation of parents who live every day with the questions: Will my children be able to survive as human beings in the year 1984, 2001, 2026? Will there be enough to eat? Will they be permitted to have children? Would he, the God-Man of this theology, be able to weep over the dead bodies of little children in Southeast Asia and Brazil, as he wept over his friend Lazarus? Could he participate in the anguish and the anger of those who know *why* the little children died: how it was not *their* sickness unto death that cut them off so early? Would he be able to agonize over the millions of other beings—not-quite-little-children, fetuses—for whom there was no place; and over the mothers, who had been able to convince themselves, with the support of their society, that what was growing in their bodies in any case had no inherent right to a place; and over that society . . . ? Could he share our doubt: doubt about God, about man, about life, about every absolute? Could he understand why we cling to expectations that are no longer affirmed or confirmed by experience, why we repress the most essential questions? Would such a Christ understand failure? Could he participate in *our* failure?

Or is he eternally above all that? Do we have to do with him now only as the risen and glorious One, who has put all that behind him? Magnificent with answers, and himself the Answer, has he ascended far above the misty flats of our questions?

In sum, the test of authenticity in theology today is: Is this "Jesus Christ and him crucified"?

Perhaps the world is closer, sometimes, to the crucified Christ than are those who call themselves his body. If the witnesses are silent, the very stones will cry out! For example: The most significant aspect of the popular rock opera *Jesus Christ Superstar* has been precisely its astonishing capacity to communicate to a generation of young and mostly pagan people the message that Jesus participates in their condition. That he is anxious with their anxiety, uncertain about the future as are they, involved in the ambiguities of loves like theirs, desperate as they are to change the world and men; that he is finally, by all the standards we have taught them, a failure.

The orthodox loudly complain that this piece has no "resurrection." Precisely! They want to have everything answered—made right again. He must after all be presented as a success—a *real* Superstar! The triumphant "Yes" must in the last analysis cancel out the hideous "No." . . . And thus is Jesus Christ removed altogether from *the place where we live.* The religious have their little triumph of orthodoxy, but it has nothing to do with life anymore.

The rock opera spoke to life—and significantly to those for whom life and the future of life is most pressing, the young. It kept us in touch with this world, with experience, because it did not introduce, in conclusion, a false and extravagant expectation. It did not, I think, lack the suggestion of a victory. Not, however, the victory of a *deus ex machina* swooping down to rescue us from this bondage to decay. It was, rather, a victory that left the Christ among us, one of us, hurt enough by life to lead us through the valley of the shadow of death. A victory that did not annul his defeat or leave the cross "empty," a void, a meaningless symbol. A victory that did not remove him from the beggarliness, brokenness, and failure of our own condition.

The basic message communicated to many through this portrayal of the Christ was the message of the incarnate, crucified God. It was not a forthright profession of faith—though it may in the more authentic sense have been a *con*fession of faith. In any case, it did not preach, or teach, but instead it stated: God, if there is a God, would have to be "with us" like this, in the agony and failure of our humanity. If that were so, we would not have to look for meaning beyond our suffering, but in it: in the midst of failure, a way; in the midst of darkness, light; in the midst of despair, hope.

To say that the primary task of an indigenous theology is to provide a frame of reference for the experience of negation could not be better illustrated than by this work of popular art. The fact that it has achieved the response that it has ought to indicate to Christians everywhere that the God the contemporary world *might* believe is "the crucified God." And if not "believe," then at least seek him out by night, like Nicodemus.

It is the same thing, whether one says that our task is to develop a theology of the cross indigenous to our own experience as a people, or on the other hand that we should develop a theology of hope. But on this continent, which has already demonstrated its propensity to turn theologies of hope into new versions of "the national philosophy of optimism" (Hook), it is dangerous to use that precious word "hope." The only hope that would be pertinent to our condition and responsible within the context of the contemporary world would be one that was born out of an encounter with the despair implicit in and emanating from our own "way of life." That is no hope, in the Christian sense, that only shields men a little longer from the meeting with their own failure and despair.

A THEOLOGY OF LIMITS

An indigenous theology of the cross would testify to the limits within which man may pursue the possibilities of his humanity.

We have argued that the appeal of the imported theology of hope in North America has resided in its apparent confirmation of the positive outlook. It seemed to provide a new theological stimulus for that positive thinking which we treasure so much. Although its European and South American originators did not intend this, this theology conveyed to many

North Americans the familiar but now beleaguered and threadbare idea that the world is full of possibilities, if only we would open our eyes and our hearts to them. Such a message is not at all inappropriate in many places in the contemporary world, including Moltmann's Germany, where there is a strong tendency to that peculiarly Lutheran form of fatalism to which we have already made reference. But whoever speaks about possibilities in North America—opportunities awaiting those who have sufficient belief and daring—must at least be aware of the background of official optimism in which he speaks.

In a real sense, our society does have possibilities that it has not discovered. But those possibilities are not the ones that come naturally into the minds of North Americans when they hear of "possibilities," "hope," "openness to the future," and all the language associated with the theology of hope and, latterly, with the theology of liberation. Genuine possibilities are present for us—and present for us in a way that they are not present for any other people. They have rather to do with our potential, as the most realized technological society ever to have been, for comprehending the meaning of this condition. Only in this society is the technological experience sufficiently long and ubiquitous for men to recognize for what they are the redemptive expectations associated with technology in the minds of people all over the world. If we had the wisdom and the courage for it, this continent could play an extremely significant role in the contemporary world by providing an honest testimony to the dangers to humanity inherent in the submission of life to technique. Our real possibilities are bound up with our very failure to realize the salvation dreamed by the modern mind. But there seems to me to be no direct way for us to discover those possibilities. For it means to acknowledge our failure. It means the discovery of our limits.

The discovery of limits can only be for us the most traumatic experience. Our entire continental experiment has been based on the mirage of limitless horizons. Limitless land, limitless resources, limitless opportunities, limitless human know-how, limitless freedom. So thoroughly has the spirit of uncircumscribed potential been absorbed into our North American consciousness that to begin to question it is almost an outrage. Of all the aspects of the optimism that has informed our way of life, perhaps the most unshakable is the belief in limitlessness. Partly, no doubt, because the boundless drive of our frontier forefathers has left its mark on our imaginations. Partly also because strong economic interests are vested in maintaining this particular fantasy. Industry depends upon it. The space program appeals, in part, because in the face of the deadly questions that nature and recent history have raised about this fantasy, space exploration again opens up the possibility of a limitless universe. At the same time, the most significant spin-off of the space program—viz., the picture it has given us of a lonely green planet, exquisitely beautiful but poised tentatively on the edge of a sea of emptiness—has militated against that fantasy powerfully. On the whole, the kind of Promethean vitality we have been able to demonstrate on this continent for two or three centuries has seemed to justify the fondest dreams of the men in whom the concept of mastery first took shape. We see the space program as a continuation of that spirit which confronts nature with "audacity" (Hobbes). Audacity of spirit is indigenous to our experience as a people. We cannot face limits without thinking ourselves cowards.

Official Christianity not only failed seriously to question the spirit of audacity but provided religious sanction and a theological rationale for the belief in man's mastery, the limitless range of his authority, and his own potential as the crown and jewel of creation. From the frontier pulpit which gave man (the white man!) the right to dominate and possess nature (including those "lesser breeds without the law") to that secular theology which celebrated man's emancipation from sacred cows and holy trees, the general impact of the Christian religion on the life of this continent has been to foster and undergird the technocratic image of man. So much so that now, in the midst of an environmental crisis of hardly imaginable proportions, *Christians* find themselves having to answer for an attitude toward man and nature which, no matter how much they may protest their innocence of it, is exactly what men heard them saying during these past three or four centuries. "Modern technology," writes Prof. Lynn White, Jr.,

> is at least partly to be explained as an Occidental voluntarist realization of the Christian dogma of man's transcendence of, and rightful mastery over, nature. . . . Our science and technology have grown out of Christian attitudes towards man's relation to nature which are almost universally held not only by Christians and neo-Christians but also by those who fondly regard themselves as post-Christians.[44]

"Christianity," White concludes, "bears a huge burden of guilt."

It is more difficult to answer this charge than many Christian apologists imagine. When White and others (e.g., the British ecologist Frank Fraser Darling[45]) trace the problem to the Biblical concept of man, especially to the creation narratives of Genesis, it is a relatively easy matter to demonstrate that their exegesis is faulty. As we have already attempted to show, the Biblical estimate of man has certainly not been responsible for the modern vision of man as master of nature and history. In fact, it is a clear contradiction of Biblical theology at its most basic when such a picture is given. Man can only be regarded as master in a world where the mastery (sovereignty) of God has been virtually denied.

At the level of Biblical exegesis critics such as White and Frank Fraser Darling are quite innocent of any real sophistication of insight. However, their charge against Christianity—that it "bears a huge burden of guilt"—should not be dismissed by the Christians as if the exoneration of the Scriptures meant the simultaneous exoneration of the Christian church! The church's interpretation or neglect of these very Scriptures has created an impression so unconditionally supportive of the concept of man's unlimited mastery that the attempt to voice a different view can only be regarded by critics as a belated attempt to provide excuses for a guilty religion.

This failure to distinguish between the Biblical and theological estimate of man on the one hand and the developing modern *imago hominis* on the other is only one indication of the church's uncritical acceptance and sanction of the vision of a limitless world awaiting man's ordering. Christianity paid a great deal of attention to the question of limits and restraints in the realm of personal morality. In North America particularly the churches still live with the reputation of being restrictive and moralistic. But this preoccupation with moral restraint did not carry over into the areas of social and political ethics. It had little to do, in fact, with the image of man that was all the while taking over, the image of an unlimited, Promethean being, who no longer even had to contend with jealous gods! Private morality remained private. There is no better illustration of the triviality of the private morality with which the churches of this continent have occupied themselves than that it had so little influence on the *public* morality that has shaped our people's attitudes toward nature, other races, the poor, economic policies, and women.

In this as in every other area of our life today, expectations are no longer upheld by experience. Expecting to encounter no limits in our role as makers of "the New World," we have suddenly come upon decisive limits. Not even the unthinking can ignore these limits, even though they impinge on many people only in the form of material shortages (e.g., oil). Thinking people, on the other hand, are led to truly frightening reflections as they contemplate the encounter of an economy of unlimited growth with the limits present in the natural environment:

> Surely the twentieth century has presented us with one question
> above all: are there any limits to history making? The question

must be in any intelligent mind whether man's domination of nature can lead to the end of human life on the planet, if not in a catyclysm of bombs, perhaps by the slow perversion of the processes of life.[46]

The experience of limits is for us both new and terrifying. It is perhaps the most conspicuous form of the experience of negation, its cutting edge. Faced with the crisis of the biosphere, we are driven to ask whether there are any limits to our exploitation of the sea, the earth, the air. Confronted with the famines of the East, Africa, South America, and the predictions of global famine during the present decade; with the depletion of our natural resources, crude oil, fresh water, etc.; and with the new awareness of our planet's uniqueness and smallness—we ponder whether the assumption that nature is infinitely resilient may not have been grossly misleading. That private morality, so easily set aside by an order to kill peasant men and women and children, or our own children, drives us to ask whether there are any limits to our freedom. Contemplating the six millions and the mushroom clouds of the "future Hiroshima" (Wiesel), we are compelled to ask whether there are limits to what men and nations may do to one another.

In short, there is occasion today for contemplating Nietzsche's definition of a nihilistic society: a society in which there are no limits. We have been brought up short by our experience both of the limits there are (and will be) and of our incapacity for dealing with the experience of limits. This experience finds no echo in our national philosophy. It is not the stuff out of which the speeches of high school principals and the annual reports of corporations are made. It does not conform at all to the expectations we have been taught to entertain.

How can we face such an experience?

Since our expectations as a people are bound up with the vision of a limitless universe, must we give up hoping because of the experience of limits? Or are our expectations so incorporated into the system that we are powerless, having no alternative expectations, to alter our course? Must we go on with the orgiastic rape and wastage of nature until we have finally met our limits head on in an omega of civilization, or of man, or of earth itself? Is there no way of stopping "progress"? Are we caught in an inescapable whirlwind of technique? The Greeks, Ellul points out,[47] as well as the men of the Renaissance, did not develop their technology to the point of their knowledge. They limited it because they feared that its impact upon society would not conform to their understanding of what was human. Have we lost the possibility of limiting our mastery because we have lost any vision of humanity to which our technique is answerable? Must we then simply wait to *be limited* by ruthless natural and historical forces that are already closing in upon us? It would seem so. "If you want to stop the advance of this juggernaut," said a medical scientist with evident irony, "then you must turn off my ingenuity." "I cannot tell you how it *should* be," said a highly placed technocrat, who professed also to be a Christian. "I can only tell you how it is . . . and will be." The scientist and the technocrat were only repeating in their fashion the terrible utterance of the great Oppenheimer: "If the experiment is sweet, one must pursue it."

The question is not only whether we can be brought to face our limits but whether, in the process of facing them, we can discover *possibilities* that might constitute a new vision of man: a vision strong enough to provide new and authentic norms for *limiting ourselves*.

A theology of glory has fanned the flames of human ambition to give us the vision of man the master in a limitless universe. For the vision of man as a limited creature, discovering his possibilities within those limits, it is necessary to turn to a theology of the cross.

The theology of the cross at its most rudimentary level is in fact a theology of limits. What the theology of the cross provides by way of a foundation for Christian ethics is a statement of the nature and destiny of man as one who may discover the authentic possibilities of his creature-hood only as he is cast upon the limits of his creaturehood. The theology of the cross is innately suspicious of *any* discussion of possibilities which does not emerge out of the definite and, very often, devastating experience of limits. In particular, it rejects that human *superbia* which feeds upon the delusion of mastery. It begins with the frank recognition of our limits. We are not masters. We are beggars.

This recognition of limits does not seek to denigrate man, nor to impose some kind of religious fatalism. It begins there in the name of freedom. It is not interested in limits per se; it intends that we should encounter our limits in order that we may discover our true possibilities. For the whole intention of the gospel of the cross is to release us from captivity to false images of ourselves: to crucify the "unhappy god" (Camus) in us, so that the man ("a man pure and simple"—Bonhoeffer) can be brought to life.

The exposure to limits which is at the heart of this theology is not based on the religious concept that God can only be magnified if man is made little. The aim is not to reduce man to the status of "a worm five feet high" (Calvin), nor to deny his distinctiveness as a creature. Its aim, rather, is to lead him to discover the limits within which he may and must work out his humanity. To put him into the way of that authentic humanity, to preserve him from inauthentic pretension to divinity, the wisdom of the cross subjects man to the humiliating recognition of his limits—not once only, but time and again, for pride is perennial. That it is truly humiliating cannot be denied. "Unhappy gods," even in their unhappiness, do not find begging very appealing! But the end of the subjection to limits is not humiliation. That is not even the end of the last limit, death itself, according to Biblical faith. That death is a great humiliation is not denied by this faith. No one is asked to accept it easily or lightly. The end is not humiliation, but that finally through death in its grim reality we should find something like real life.

Jesus taught his disciples that those who are rich can only enter the Kingdom of God with great suffering. It may well be that we of this continent, who are so endowed with the wealth and spirit of Dives and so little acquainted with the condition of Lazarus the beggar, shall have to suffer unheard-of humiliation before we can receive what is given only to those who beg. There are intimations of this coming great humiliation in many places, not least of all in the eyes of those who ask us for bread. We have yet to comprehend the darkness of our own deeds and the deeds of our fathers. We have been so accustomed to seeing ourselves in the role of Samaritans that it is hard for us to envisage ourselves as thieves. Yet it is in the latter role that most of the peoples of the earth have perceived us. We shall not escape their judgment. Whether at their hands or more subtly as the result of the works of our own hands, "we shall have to live with manifest peril." [48] The limits of our mastery crowd daily in upon us.

The theology of the cross does not rejoice in the prospect of peril. To *seek* suffering, whether for oneself or for others, is not the counsel of this theology. It was in the name of the cross that the early church forbade its members to flirt with martyrdom. But in the midst of peril, or in anticipation of it, which is just as painful, the theology of the cross tries to discern the presence of meaning. It does not desire the death of man—not even of the rich man. That would be sadism, not the wisdom of the cross. It hopes to assist the rich man to understand that in the *loss* of his riches and the threat to his very being there could be the unfolding of a purpose greater than his own continued affluence and well-being. Such a purpose may serve the very survival of the species! It wishes for the rich man in peril—or in his *anticipation* of peril—that he may discover through his proximity to the poverty and pain of Lazarus the reality of his own situation: that he shares a common lot with Lazarus. He is also a beggar.

Against those who seek the death of the sinner—the death, in this case, of the sinful society whose way of life is a way of death—the theology of the cross announces the possibility of good news. It is possible to repent, even when patterns have become deeply entrenched, even at the eleventh hour! Even a society in decay can find grace on the brink of its disintegration. More than anything else, honest exposure to our limits *could*, with some courageous guidance, give us as a people new wisdom and new hope.

The theology of the cross does not court peril. But in its fight against the ultimate peril, the death of expectation, it does not shrink from exposing men to the failure of false expectations. It moves on the assumption that authentic expectation occurs *within* the experience of limits. To have come to the boundaries of our yearning; to be thrust back and rejected—the theology of the cross does not find debilitating. It could be the beginning, not the end. The gospel of the cross tries to interpret the *meaning* of the experience of limits, and to seek through that experience the possibilities that may be inherent in it, or may emerge out of it. It opens men to the prospect that in the experience of thwarted expectations, if entered into with sufficient depth and courage, new and better expectations can be discovered. That is not a law of this theology, but it is a possibility.

THE CHURCH UNDER THE CROSS

An indigenous theology of the cross would call into being a community whose most conspicuous mark would be the frustration of its every attempt to have a theology of glory.

The theology of the cross is not only a theology of limits and of possibilities that may emerge at the edge of the impossible. Beyond that, it calls forth a people whose own vocation is to undergo the experience of limits. And to do so again and again. This is the ecclesiastical statement of this theology, corresponding to the ethical and the theological statements.

The church lives only as it is given over daily to participation in the death of the cross. Only as it is itself denied the glory that it craves can it become the friend of those who can no longer pretend to glory. Only as it is itself denied the expansiveness and power and authority it covets can it be equipped to accompany men and nations into the depths of humiliation. Only as it is brought again and again to the experience of its own limits will it be able to participate in the life of a whole age which has been brought face to face with the limits of human endeavor and the human species. Only as it looks for light in the darkness, hope in the midst of despair, possibilities at the edge of the Red Sea, a way beyond failure, will it be a fit counselor to those who sit in darkness and in the shadow of death.

The mission of the people of "the Way" today is to *go with* men and nations *into the darkness.* They do so not as superior guides; not as experts at maneuvering in shadowy places. Certainly not as the possessors of some inextinguishable light! But, let us say, as those who are at least not surprised by the darkness, as if it were something strange (I Peter 4:12). They expect it—though they do not welcome it or revel in it. Still, they have not ruled it out *a priori,* as if the "dark ages" of the earth were already long behind us.

It is customary to say of this people that its particular task is to bear witness to the light that shines in the darkness and is not overcome. Jürgen Moltmann, for example, concludes his book *Hope and Planning* on just such a note.

> If theology answers for God in the world and for the world before God, then it does not see only night over the world, but has to arouse all the senses for the coming morning. It has to sharpen the sense for responsibility and the capability for anticipation in all disciplines. As Paul said, "The night is far gone, the day is at hand." (Rom. 13:12.)[49]

No one could deny this indubitably Scriptural emphasis. However, the theology of the cross knows that the witness to the true Light is never easily—and seldom straightforwardly—accomplished. For us on this continent which has both enjoyed much light and hardly known the dark, let alone how to handle it, the Christian witness *to the Light* is extremely difficult and fraught with danger. Perhaps in a society that knows and admits its darkness it is necessary for the watchman to cry without further ado that the night is far spent and the day at hand. Such a society was that Germany of 1938, the year of the *Kristallnacht,* when the courageous Jochen Klepper, husband of a Jewish wife and father of Jewish children, wrote the hymn that became a watchword of the Confessional Church:

> Die Nacht ist vorgedrungen,
> Der Tag ist nicht mehr fern,
> So sei nun Lob gesungen
> Dem hellen Morgenstern.[50]

A Christian community that has undergone the cross and the night has the right to announce the dawn.

But that is neither a description of our society nor of the church in it. And when we assume that it is our business here and now to bear witness to the Light, to "arouse the senses [of man] to the coming morning," we are behaving like watchmen who have become nervous at the first signs of sunset.

Of course it would be possible to turn that simile to another purpose. The really perceptive watchman will indeed have discerned how far we have gone into the night! For the most part, however, when we North American Christians grab our lanterns and run out into the streets offering men light, it is not because we, like Nietzsche's madman, have discerned the real depths of our own darkness, but because we are unnerved by the shadows that are being cast on what we regarded as the most enlightened culture of all time. Afraid to let the shadows lengthen, knowing that the darkness will cover our own pious dwelling as well as the houses of the rich men and the Lazaruses, we scurry about the place to find our little candles. But the light we offer men is mostly artificial, for we have not yet exposed ourselves to the darkness. We are using our alleged light to ward *off* the darkness, not to have the possibility of taking a few steps *within* it.

This high-minded witness to the light; this preoccupation with the positive; this readiness to see in every new invention its potential for serving God and man; this mostly uncritical acceptance of the electronic age as though it were bound to release men from boring work and set them on the path of true leisure; this celebration of the space flights and the extension of their already extravagant scientific claims by the addition of spiritual and religious dimensions; and, on the other side, this self-conscious and often self-righteous dissociation from the frankly critical analyses of our society, like those of Ellul, Beckett, and the more articulate young—this so characteristic behavior of the adherents of cultural Christianity in North America indicates how wedded our Christianity is to the spirit and method that Luther called *theologia gloriae.* In recent years, to be sure, some Christians have learned how to speak about the church as "the church of the wilderness," "the pilgrim people," and "the people of the cross." *Ecclesia crucis!* Even in the high places of our major denominations this concept is somewhat understood now. Here and there it has been impressively organized. But what has not been learned is that the theology of the cross applies at the level of *belief, theology, proclamation,* and not only at the level of life-style. Too many of those who have grasped the necessity of being the church under the cross are still suffering under the illusion that it is possible to be such a church while carrying about an unambiguous *theology* of glory under the doctrinal aegis of the resurrection, and a triumphalistic anthropology. They try to be the *ecclesia crucis* with a *theologia gloriae.* The discrepancy is glaring.

An indigenous theology of the cross would call into being a community whose most conspicuous mark would be the frustration of its every attempt to have a *theology* of glory.

Such a community would *try* to have such a theology. It would endeavor, even in the midst of its own poverty and littleness and lack of worldly prestige, to hold on to the sense of its superior, truer, deeper wisdom. Its temptation would be, the smaller and less impressive it became, to regard itself all the more as the bearer of the one true light in the darkness. The *theology* of glory is not so easily expelled. It is easier for the Christian to lose his cloak than to lose an argument! One may be a figure of little glory on the university campus or in suburbia today, but when one opens one's mouth one hopes to command a certain respect.

The people called into being by a theology of the cross indigenous to our experience would have to be denied, not once but again and again, this last vestige of triumphalism: i.e., their own attempt to preserve the belief that their theology—their belief itself—constitutes a certain triumph. Only as they live under the cross at the level of belief and witness will their life under the cross at the level of action and service appear credible. Otherwise, their best efforts to identify with those who really do live in the darkness today (not only the poor, but those who genuinely "understand" —the real "intellectuals") will be belied by the presence of a religious overview which insulates them from direct contact with the darkness and with those who live in it. Subtle Christian apologists with concealed lighting are no less inaccessible to those who most feel the anguish of history than are the old Christian warriors who march in with torches ablaze and battle-axes at the ready!

It is not asked of the people of the cross that they cease to put their trust in the triumph of the Crucified. What is asked is that they let the Crucified and not the bourgeois culture with which they are identified define his triumph. At the most personal, concrete level this means the willingness of the people of the cross to give evidence that they are men whose faith lives only in company with unfaith, whose hope is a dialogue with despair, whose sense of meaning comes out of an ever-renewed confrontation with the sense of meaninglessness and the absurd.

It would be better if, instead of following the familiar description of this people as "witness to the light," we said that an indigenous theology of the cross would call forth a people who could bear witness to the darkness.

No doubt to suburban Christianity such a proposal can be heard only as the final heresy. But to persons who are familiar with the Scriptures it is by no means entirely new. If one follows with care that thin tradition of the *theologia crucis* to which we have looked for precedence, one will not be at all surprised by such a proposal. "The day of the Lord is darkness and not light." Is it so different if one bears witness to the darkness than if one bears witness to the light? What makes the difference, what decides which it shall be? It is the context in which the witness is to be made. To a people who disclaims all traffic with the darkness and loudly announces its own adherence to the light, it is quite obvious that the prophetic voice must again cry: "The day of the Lord is darkness and not light." To prophesy light in the city of light is to court the lie, even if one does not intend to do so. If it is dark, the prophet says that it is dark. Perhaps, like the little child who said the emperor was naked, he is the only one who is not afraid to say so. Then others may be willing to look upon the darkness, and from within it strain for the light that shines there.

To know the darkness and to name it, then, would be the special task of the people of the cross in *this* society.

There could be no glory in that! Especially not when it means knowing and naming the darkness of a technological society in which there are so few of the *usual* marks of deprivation. It is possible to give evidence of the great physical horrors that confront us today, and even to have impressive allies, scientists and others! At that level one could bear witness to the darkness and still experience a somewhat exhilarating sense of glory. But the darkness to which the Christian community must bear *particular* witness—because there are so few who are able to do so—is another matter. It is the darkness which robs man of his manhood while seeming to give him the very substance of the good life. That darkness is more dangerously present in the solutions that men put forward than in the problems they are supposed to solve. To know and to name *that* darkness is to receive no praise, no glory.

But just here there arises the final temptation to a theology of glory: To know the darkness that robs man of his humanity and substitutes mediocrity for the pursuit of excellence, it is necessary to possess a vision of man and a standard of excellence as the basis for making this judgment. That is indisputable. As George Grant has put it, "How can we think of deprivation unless the good which we lack is somehow remembered?" [51] But do not Christians possess precisely such a vision and standard? Are they not defined by their remembering, as by their hoping? Do they not have the *imago Christi,* the image of the true man—*vere homo?* If they have lost something of the vision of the Divine, do they not at least retain Christ's humanity as a norm for distinguishing true from false, authentic from inauthentic, what is human from what is inhuman and dehumanizing?

This is the last temptation to a theology of glory. It still tries to possess an absolute vision, definitive and unassailable. It is altogether true that apart from remembering that one man *(Ecce homo!)* we have no criteria for assessing what is happening to man today. But what about our remembering, our power of recall? Is it so impressive? Does it really give us that kind of clarity of vision which is frequently implied in our very definitive statements about what is human and what is not? Are we still, after all, of the generation of those who knew who Jesus was, and who went out into the world in the confidence of their knowing, to transform the world according to his image?

The koinonia of the cross would have to be denied this attempt at a theology of glory, too. It is perhaps the greatest temptation, for it recognizes that whoever has an authoritative vision of man today, whoever can say something definitive and significant about this beleaguered creature, will find an audience. The history of Biblical scholarship in the past hundred years has made it abundantly plain that our remembering is incredibly biased. Jesus in the nineteenth-century "Lives" was too often only a Victorian gentleman—a mildly Jewish Wilberforce. Do we think we have transcended all that? Are not we ourselves, the citizens of a mass, conforming culture, liable to flounder in the same way? Might not Jesus become for us, if not a Middle American, perhaps an activist of the Zealot sort, or the incarnation of bourgeois love?

In our remembering, too, we are beggars. There is nothing left us but the promise, from his side, that he will be present in our remembering. It is the promise from the cross to that first beggar, that to his remembering there would correspond a remembering from eternity.

Thus at the point where we are most tempted to retain a triumphalist theology, the point of our anthropology, we are brought back under the cross. The people of the cross, who name the darkness, can summon no absolute light, no unsullied vision, whether of God or of man. It becomes for them, as for all who in the past have been grasped by this logic of the cross, a matter of faith.

CONCLUSION

THE COURAGE
TO HAVE FAILED

WE BEGAN by noticing that human life is a dialogue between expectation and experience. Civilization flounders, life fails—not when these two elements are in conflict, for conflict is of the essence of their discourse, but when they no longer inform each other, that is, when the contradiction between them is so great that they must proceed along separate lines.

It has been our conviction throughout that human life *depends* on this dialogue. Whether at the individual-personal level or at the social-political level, the state of contradiction between expectancy and experience can only be a temporary one. It cannot endure as a permanent way of life. Especially in the actual circumstances of our social condition, to carry on with the expectations we have been conditioned to have, without subjecting them to the scrutiny of experience, is suicidal.

Our expectations as a civilization have failed. We have not been able to sustain the dream called "America" dreamed by European optimism of the Renaissance and its aftermath. We have floundered conspicuously and notoriously.

The complicating thing is that, of all peoples of the earth, we are the least capable of facing failure. We seem to be locked into the mind-set of modernity, unable to question it seriously, unable to think through alternatives. The state of contradiction seems chronic with us. For until we have permitted ourselves to admit the failure of old expectations, we cannot be open to new ones.

At the same time, the importance of living through this experience at the conscious level, allowing ourselves to feel the failure of our dreams and seeking the meaning of this failure, cannot be overestimated. For what is "America," what is "the New World," but the dream of man that he can

227

produce the perfect kingdom within the terms of his own mastery. The world is still full of people who dream this very dream; they call it by various names and they give it many nuances, but it is still the same dream whether it is dreamed in Moscow or Peking or the jungles of Africa.

It is a highly dangerous dream. If it is not criticized, if it is not severely altered, it can spell the end of the human race.

We North Americans have long dreamed the dream. We have had time for it to take hold of us at the deepest levels of the psyche. It has shaped our life. It has driven us to a level of technical achievement, unimagined even by our own forebears. Time and the will of man, prosperity, the absence of war, and the abundance of nature have all indulged the dream. We have taken it—rather, have been taken by it—beyond the reaches so far experienced by any people. And it has failed.

Other peoples looking on see that we are immersed today in failure, in a state of impossible contradiction. For the most part, however, they do not understand that it has been the dream itself that failed. They think in their naïvety that *we* have failed the dream; that in their hands it would be otherwise—just let them have their chance! Only we can know, with something like the wisdom of experience, that the failure lies in the dream itself: the dream of mastery.

But in our state of anxiety, hidden dread, we cannot and dare not and will not expose ourselves to that failure. We would rather think that *we* had failed than that the failure was all along inherent in the dream. We are still trying to pretend that we can yet make it work. If not the present generation, then future generations will pick it up and start over again to build "the New World"! Meantime, the "future generations" have already given notice, in significant numbers, that they will not buy that dream wholesale. With an earnestness born of biological drives that transcend their powers of rationality, they cry out for new expectations. They are right: we need new expectations. There can be no civilization of men without them.

But the most precious and needed expectations can only emerge among us if we courageously and rigorously investigate the failure of the old ones. New expectations must, as did the phoenix, arise out of the ashes of the old. Without that purging, what advertises itself as new is usually no more than a variation of the old—perhaps its antithesis, which is also a variation.

There is nothing in our sojourn as a people—neither in our expectations nor in our experience—to give us insight and courage for the facing of failure. Amongst us, to be sure, there are pockets of those who, because they have been forced by our standards of success to regard themselves as failures, can be of special assistance in these times: the blacks, the native Indian peoples, the French Canadians, and a few others. But our way of life has been the way of "success." Nobody ever told us what to do in case of failure—least of all our religion. "Christianity," as it has been called, functioned more precisely to turn into successes all the failures that could not otherwise be handled by education, business, technology, and the other institutions of our society.

Nevertheless, that same "Christianity" carried along with it—usually as a matter of considerable embarrassment—a version of human existence quite strictly out of keeping with the dominant image of man, the dream of mastery. That version was symbolized by the Man on the cross. Despite its truly olympian efforts, cultural Christianity was never quite able to make the cross as empty as it wished to make it. The symbol has endured—a symbol of failure.

Now it has turned up for some of us as the only symbol left out of that world-conquering Christian religion that can make sense to a failing people, a failing civilization that is part of a failing species. It becomes for us a point of entry—not only to Christian faith but to hope itself, simple, human hope. It means, if one can believe it, that real hope sometimes becomes possible in the midst of despair. Authentic expectations are never far from the experience of failure. The best works of man were born in the night (Wiesel).

Cultural Christianity ceased to be pertinent to mankind a long time ago; it ceased to be the meeting place of the real expectations and the real experiences of man. For the conflict of that encounter it substituted the "peace, peace" of expectations unsullied by contradictory experience.

The thin tradition carried along in the wake of cultural Christianity, unwanted, unawares, could become a saving presence in our time. A faith that knows failure, and even begins in failure, can touch the lives of many today who otherwise do not have the courage to have failed.

NOTES

PREFACE

1. Reinhold Niebuhr, *The Nature and Destiny of Man* (Charles Scribner's Sons, 1953), Vol. II, pp. 307 f. (Italics added.)

2. "Christian faith fully appreciates the threat of meaninglessness which comes into history by the corruption of human freedom. But it does not succumb to the despairing conclusion that history is merely a chaos of competing forces." Reinhold Niebuhr, *Faith and History* (Charles Scribner's Sons, 1959), p. 22.

3. "Our thinking is not wholly serious until we come to the end of our know-how. Our age must learn that some things are beyond 'doing.'" Karl Jaspers, *The Future of Mankind* (The University of Chicago Press, Phoenix Books, 1961), p. viii.

4. Douglas John Hall, *Hope Against Hope: Towards an Indigenous Theology of the Cross* (Geneva: World Student Christian Federation, Vol. 1, No. 3, 1971).

INTRODUCTION

1. Perhaps it is this methodological similarity which explains why Marxism and existentialism sometimes meet in the same soul. But they have hardly ever enjoyed a happy alliance, because at the level of content the two systems take up antithetical emphases (witness the cases of Brecht and Sartre).

2. The use of the word "problematic" as a noun is proper in other languages. It means more than problems: it means that many problems are bound up in one great bundle and can only be properly seen in their interrelatedness. This usage in English is growing in the fields of science and philosophy.

3. Jean-Paul Sartre, *Nausea*, tr. by Lloyd Alexander (New Directions Paperbook, 1964), pp. 95–96.

4. Eugène Ionesco, *La Vase* (Paris: Cahiers des Saisons, 1956).

5. David Brower (ed.), *Not Man Apart* (Sierra Club, Ballantine Books, 1969), p. 100.

6. This is not to deny the authenticity of the critique which both systems bring to our expectations and experiences as a civilization. Existentialism is right in calling into question many of our aspirations as Western peoples: they are fraught

with pretension, arrogance, and pomposity. Marxism is right, too, in pointing out that much in contemporary human experience is unnecessary, and unnecessarily negating. Nothing could be more insidious in the realm of theory, including theological theory, than the insinuation that specific *forms* of evil are necessary or inevitable (e.g., war, poverty, disease and early death). But existentialism tends to deny the habit of expectation as such, and doctrinaire Marxism denies that the experience of negation belongs to life. In this they are two questionable interpretations of existence, from the Christian perspective.

PART ONE
Positive Christianity and the Experience of Negation

1. Sidney Hook. See Robert L. Heilbroner, *The Future as History* (Harper & Brothers, Harper Torchbooks, 1959), cover.

2. Barbara W. Tuchman, *The Atlantic*, Vol. 232, No. 3 (Sept. 1973).

3. *Ibid.*, p. 39.

4. Quoted by Basil Willey, *The Seventeenth Century Background* (Doubleday & Company, Inc., Anchor Books, 1953), pp. 95–96.

5. René Descartes, *Discourse on Method*, tr. by Laurence J. Lafleur (The Liberal Arts Press, 1950), p. 40.

6. George P. Grant, *Philosophy in the Mass Age* (Toronto: The Copp Clark Publishing Company, Ltd., 1966), Chapter IV.

7. Quoted in Sidney Pollard, *The Idea of Progress: History and Society* (Harmondsworth: Penguin Books, Ltd., 1968), p. 7.

8. *Ibid.*

9. *Ibid.*

10. See Reinhold Niebuhr, *Faith and History*, p. 3.

11. See Josef Pieper, *Leisure: The Basis of Culture*, tr. by Alexander Dru (Toronto: The New American Library of Canada Limited, 1952).

12. Reinhold Niebuhr, *Faith and History*, p. 3.

13. *Ibid.*, pp. 2–4.

14. *Ibid.*

15. Heilbroner, *op. cit.*, pp. 33 f.

16. *Ibid.*, p. 34.

17. Norman Mailer, *Of a Fire on the Moon* (The New American Library, Inc., Signet Books, 1971).

18. George P. Grant, *Time as History* (Toronto: Canadian Broadcasting Corporation Learning Systems, 1969), p. 31. The wording here is taken from the lectures as broadcast, and is slightly different from the printed text.

19. Mailer, *op. cit.*, p. 48.

20. Reinhold Niebuhr, *Faith and History*, p. 8.

21. Paul van Buren, *Theological Explorations* (London: SCM Press, Ltd., 1968), p. 7.

22. Garrett Hardin (ed.), *Population, Evolution, and Birth Control* (W. H. Freeman and Company, 1972), p. 368.

23. Sonia Orwell and Ian Angus (eds.), *The Collected Essays: Journalism and Letters of George Orwell*, Vol. 2, *My Country Right or Left* (Penguin Books, Inc., 1970), p. 30.

24. Elie Wiesel, *Legends of Our Time* (Holt, Rinehart & Winston, Inc., 1968), pp. 180, 190. (Italics added.)

25. Elie Wiesel, *The Gates of the Forest*, tr. by Frances Frenaye (Avon Books, 1969), pp. 123–124.

26. See Emil L. Fackenheim, *God's Presence in History: Jewish Affirmations and Philosophical Reflections* (Harper & Row, Publishers, Inc., Harper Torchbooks, 1970).

27. The German word means literally *un-* (ent) *being* (wesen), i.e., "the process of robbing living organisms of their being." Cf. Pierre Joffroy, *A Spy for God: The Ordeal of Kurt Gerstein*, tr. by Norman Denny (London: William Collins Sons & Co., Ltd., 1971), p. 141.

28. Herbert Marcuse, *One-Dimensional Man* (Beacon Press, Inc., 1964), p. 247.

29. *Time*, Oct. 31, 1969, p. 75.

30. *Life*, July 24, 1970, p. 2.

31. Josef Pieper, *Hope and History* (Herder & Herder, Inc., 1969), p. 76.

32. Saint-Simon, quoted in Pollard, *The Idea of Progress*, p. 7.

33. James Klugmann, "The Marxist Hope," in G. B. Caird, Wolfhart Pannenberg, *et al.*, *The Christian Hope* (London: S.P.C.K., 1970), p. 65. Mr. Klugmann is editor of *Marxism Today*.

34. See, e.g., Marshall I. Goldman, *The Spoils of Progress: Environmental Pollution in the Soviet Union* (The MIT Press, 1972).

35. The same point can be made from another angle. Whenever Christian spokesmen announce what appears to be a relaxation of this "higher Christian morality," the general outcry that follows comes from many quarters in society, not only from conservative Christians. There is today a considerable social pressure, felt in the churches, to maintain this "higher" morality intact. Thus the "new" morality is criticized as much by the totally secular as by the religious. Its "newness" seems on careful examination to consist chiefly in its questioning of the alliance between Christian and bourgeois morality. An ethic that introduces the "radical" idea that love alone can be the basis and norm of *Christian* morality is rightly seen as inaugurating an essential difference between Christianity and cultural morality. The entire debate over the "new" morality illustrates the extent to which the real establishment of the churches on this continent has involved a subordination of the church to the culture—not at the level of legislation and administration, but at the more basic level of the gospel itself.

36. Heidegger did not derive his concept *Mitsein* out of thin air. To *be* in the Hebraic meaning is to *be with;* its antithesis is not non-being, but being-against or being-alone. It is not accidental that the New Testament names the incarnate God "Emmanuel" ("God with us").

37. Martin Buber, *I and Thou* (Edinburgh: T. & T. Clark, 1937), pp. 7–8.

38. From the text of a public relations film produced by a large hydroelectric company. The rest of the text is heavily interspersed with Scriptural quotations.

39. This distinction not only informs pious conservative Christianity, but is to be found at the heart of Christian liberalism as well. See, e.g., Friedrich Schleiermacher, *The Christian Faith* (Edinburgh: T. & T. Clark, 1929), Proposition 66, pp. 71 ff.

40. We are just beginning today to realize the extent of the objection. It includes impressive names: Blake, Thoreau, Emerson, Schopenhauer, Dickens— even Tolstoy. Too few are specifically *Christian spokesmen*.

41. Whatever one may think of the strange case of the Luddites, one thing emerges from it with crystal clarity: the absolute unanimity of established

Christianity with the industrialists. See selections from the transcript of the trial of the Luddites reproduced in John G. Burke (ed.), *The New Technology and Human Values* (Wadsworth Publishing Company, Inc., 1966), pp. 8–9.

42. There can be no doubt that the new *imago hominis* is bound up with the emergence of this class. The noted French historian Georges Lefebvre has given the following analysis: "The bourgeois of the West—first among the middle class of England—had worked out a conception of life and society that was no doubt suited to its origins and its role, but which in its eyes was valid for all mankind. In the Middle Ages the Church, without reproving the search for well-being, emphasized preparation for death and the future life, the essential unimportance of material conditions of existence, the merit to be gained by renunciation and ascetic living. Here was a conception of life and society that may be called static, for scientific and technical progress, to say the least, was unavailing for the salvation of souls. The bourgeoisie put its emphasis on earthly happiness and on the dignity of man; it urged the necessity of increasing the former and elevating the latter, through the control of natural forces by science and utilizing of them to augment the general wealth. The means, it was believed, consisted in granting entire freedom to investigation, invention, and enterprise, for which the incentive was personal gain, or the charm of discovery, struggle and risk. The conception was dynamic, calling upon all men, without distinction of birth, to enter into a universal competition from which the progress of mankind was to follow without end. The ideas appeared in a confused way in the France of the Renaissance; subsequently Descartes inaugurated a new humanism by opening up a magnificent perspective, the domination of nature by science; finally, the writers of the eighteenth century, encouraged by English and American influences—here we must note Voltaire, the encyclopedists, the economists—set forth with spectacular success the principles of the new order, and the practical conclusions that it seemed fitting to deduce." Georges Lefebvre, *The Coming of the French Revolution*, tr. by R. R. Palmer (Vintage Books, Inc., 1947), p. 42.

The consequences for a Christianity that identified itself with this new power are obvious from the outset.

43. Although on the one hand modern Christianity, especially in North America, became strangely interwoven with the religion of nature, this connection seems to pertain chiefly at the level of sentiment. If it is a form of pantheism, it is in the last analysis a very ineffectual form. For the hard economic and political realities of the ecclesiastical identification with the middle class, whose existence depends upon the exploitation of nature, basically betrays it. Hence those who really do feel a certain divinity in the natural world would have found the "Christian" variety of pantheism at best self-deceptive and at worst a sham to hide the steel fist of technique under the velvet glove of lilies in the sanctuary.

44. It is important to grasp, however, that the failure of modern Christianity at this juncture is not *exclusively* related to the doctrine of sin. The dialectical tension in the relationship between man and nature is already present in and integral to the Christian doctrine of creation. To associate this tension with sin and the fall of man exclusively is quite erroneous. It suggests that Christians regard the limits and conflicts that man experiences in his approach to nature to be due only to the *distortion* of his creaturehood; they belong to his fallenness, and not also to his "original righteousness." On the contrary, man in the intention of God—man the creature—is man existing in a dynamic tension with nature. A *dynamic* relation is

one in which there is always a give-and-take, a certain conflict, and, above all, the experience of limits. In the dynamic relation between man and the world as ordained by the Creator, man must necessarily encounter nature's limits of his freedom. That is an important part of the symbolic significance of the divine prohibition to eat from "the tree which is in the midst of the garden."

45. Students of Christian theology who did not participate in the heyday of liberal optimism cannot even comprehend the extent to which the theologians whom we have come to regard as the "giants" of our epoch (Barth, Niebuhr, Tillich, Bultmann, *et al.*) were at first rejected and regarded as very monsters from the depths on account of their analysis of the human condition in terms of sin. The term "neo-orthodoxy" still bears some of the earmarks of that reaction. The only explanation that could be offered for these monsters, with their dark quotations from Paul and Luther, was that they represented a return to that bleak orthodoxy which had been surpassed by enlightened Christian scholarship. Through these "giants" and their successors, the concept of sin is now more familiar to us. Yet the reality for which it stands is hardly better known or more acceptable in the churches. In the year 1972, it was still possible for an eminent psychiatrist to write a book with the title *Whatever Became of Sin?* (Karl Menninger; Hawthorn Books, Inc., 1973).

46. Dietrich Bonhoeffer, *Temptation*, tr. by Kathleen Downham (The Macmillan Company, 1955).

47. For the Jesus of the Gospels, especially the Synoptics, the prospect of overwhelming nature is always seen as *temptation*. Even the miracles, which seem upon a superficial reading to deny this, are reported for a quite different purpose—and usually with a certain reluctance, as if their misuse over two thousand years had been anticipated! The primary thing is that Jesus' *humanity* be believable. The New Testament knows this, and therefore it presents him as one who is subject to natural necessities and limitations. Accounts of his life that did not conform to just this insight were rejected from the canon. But the New Testament also intends to present him as one who *wills* to subject himself to natural necessities and limits. Therefore it has him say, on various occasions, that while he does not *have to* do something, he wills to do it. Being a man means not only being subject to nature; it means being "content and glad" (Barth) to be subject to nature, and not to rebel against this. That Jesus did not grasp at equality with God (Phil., ch. 2) means at once that he did not try to rise above his biological affinity with *adamah*.

48. Like all the primary concepts of Biblical faith, even being (see n. 36), the concept of sin is relational. Obviously this presupposes personhood: that against which I rebel is not an object but a subject, a Thou. Hence sin in this tradition is primarily associated with God and the neighbor, and its expiation means *reconciliation* with these two counterparts of my existence. However, nature, the inarticulate creation, is by no means relegated to the sidelines in this faith, as if it were quite devoid of whatever could constitute relationship. To be sure, in comparison with those religions which actually attribute subjectivity or personality to nature, Christianity is rightly seen as a very secular statement about nature. At the same time, it is quite wrong to identify Biblical religion with the scientific-technical attitude toward the natural world. Nature is not merely "objective," either. In the case of the animals, it is *almost* possible within the framework of Judeo-Christian thought to speak of personality (e.g., the naming of the beasts in

Gen., ch. 2; the descriptive passages of God's answer to Job; the many references to
the creatures in the optimistic Wisdom Literature; the laws protecting animals in
the Old Testament). Even inanimate nature can evoke the sense of relationship, as
Buber has shown. Thus at the very least one must say that nature, if it is not in
itself capable of relationship, becomes again and again the meeting place between
God and man, man and man. The voice speaks from a bush; cloud and fire
become the Presence; the ground will not receive the blood of the righteous; a tree
becomes the primary symbol of the divine identification with man; etc.

49. This insight has always been present in the classical traditions of Christianity. (See, e.g., Rom. 8:18 ff.: "The creation waits with eager longing. . . . The
creation was subjected to futility, not of its own will but by the will of him who
subjected it in hope; because the creation itself will be set free from its bondage to
decay.") But this dimension of the doctrine of sin has been obscured by the *religious*
interpretation of sin, which concentrates on man's rebellion against the Creator.
Modern Christianity further robbed the doctrine of sin of its cosmic/natural
connotations by giving it a moralistic and individualistic definition. But the crises
of our times evoke the original Biblical insight that the church through the
centuries has lost. The fall of man, in New as well as Old Testament theology,
involves at once and as a central thrust the teaching concerning man's violation of
nature.

50. In a moving passage of the *Church Dogmatics*, Barth speaks of man in the
intention of God as man in solidarity with his environment, and "content and
glad" to be so: "Of all creatures the Christian is the one which not merely is a
creature, but actually says Yes to being a creature. Innumerable creatures do not
seem to be even asked to make this affirmation. Man is asked. But man as such is
neither able nor willing to make it. From the very first man as such has continual
illusions about himself. He wants always to be more than a creature. He does not
want merely to be under the universal lordship of God. But the Christian makes
the affirmation that is demanded of man. . . . And as such he is availing himself
of a permission and invitation. He is going through an open door, . . . into a
banqueting hall. And there he willingly takes his place under the table, in the
company of publicans, in the company of beasts and plants and stones, accepting
solidarity with them." Helmut Gollwitzer (ed.), *Karl Barth's Church Dogmatics*, tr. by
G. W. Bromiley (Edinburgh: T. & T. Clark, 1961), pp. 155–157.

51. The Biblical myths of the Fall can be read at many levels. The tale of Babel
certainly has something to do with language origins and the whole question of
communication; it also has a peripheral interest in the explanation of the ziggurat.
But what has transformed the ancient story in its Hebrew retelling is its deep
recognition of man's rejection of creation, including his own creaturehood, and his
attempt to create an alternative. In that alternative, the primary thing he wants to
achieve is *securitas*, i.e., translation beyond the necessities and vicissitudes of
biological existence. Cf. Jacques Ellul, *The Meaning of the City* (Wm. B. Eerdmans
Publishing Company, 1970).

52. From the recording, *Brecht on Brecht: Selections from the Author's Works*
(Columbia 02L 278 [0L 5832-5832], 1964).

53. If the humanities that came to life in the modern epoch had not from the
outset rejected all that the dogma of original sin stood for, they might not today be
cut off from the natural sciences so pathetically. At least the sciences, in their
always implicit determinism, have unwittingly retained something of the awareness of man's ancient and tragic struggle to overcome nature.

54. It is not simply a matter of setting to work on it! The same story which insists that our condition is one of "no return" throws up to us the thought that our very efforts to return are part of our tragic situation. They are part of the alienation we attempt, through our work, to overcome. The modern era hallowed the concept of work. Ironically, it learned that concept from that same Protestantism which insisted that man's salvation could only be a matter of pure grace, not work. This has been explained in these days by an embarrassed Protestantism as if it had been an unfortunate misunderstanding. Modern secular man took from Calvinism and elsewhere the work ethic, it is said, without the theological context of the ethic. These explanations are never quite satisfactory, however, because the background against which they are offered is a Christianity that had lost all track of connection between work and *sin*. Indeed, a Christianity that was glad to discover that in respect to the question of work it had something in common with the modern vision. Modernity was able to consecrate the doctrine of work because Christianity was no longer interested in bearing witness to the sin of work.

55. The modern world was willing to hear of sin so long as it meant a lack: imperfection, not measuring up to potential. It is unfortunate that the main New Testament word for sin *(hamartano)* could be used to support just such an idea. The Hebrew concept, however, which the New Testament writers were trying to convey through the use of this limited Greek word which had been borrowed from archery, was much more dynamic and thoroughly relational: *pesha* means rebellion or apostasy. That man exists in a state of active and passive contradiction vis-à-vis the others; that he is a rebel; that he participates in a brokenness of life's essential relationships and is fundamentally distorted—such ideas were not amenable to the modern mind. It is this Hebraic concept of sin which modern Christianity dispensed with.

56. After all, as a few decades have easily demonstrated, Christianity and the modern world could be reconciled on points of cosmology. It could be shown that Christian belief was not *dependent* on the belief in a three-story universe, or creation in seven days. Thus however bitter were struggles between Christians and the representatives of the new science, there could be a certain openness about them. The majority of Christians, whether theologically sophisticated or not, were willing to accept changes of cosmological interpretation.

57. To challenge the new Prometheus in terms of *power* might indeed have been wrong at this juncture in history. A church which had aligned itself with powers that had kept man in submission to structures and institutions that had nothing to do with the gospel had no right to question his attempts to free himself from those powers. But the question about man's goodness as prerequisite for his authority in nature belongs to the church's essential witness.

58. Friedrich Nietzsche, *Thus Spoke Zarathustra*, Second Part: "On the Tarantulas," in Walter Kaufmann (ed.), *The Portable Nietzsche* (The Viking Press, Inc., 1954), pp. 211 ff.

59. "Love is a spendthrift . . . and God is love." Paul Scherer, *Love Is a Spendthrift: Meditations for the Christian Year* (Bantam Books, Inc., 1972), inside leaf.

60. The constant attempt on the part of the disciples to become first and to be in a position of authority is held up as the precise antithesis of the Way of the Christ. The "essential" man of Scripture as distinct from the fallen, "existential" man is the servant *(doulos)*.

61. Isa. 11:6: "The wolf shall dwell with the lamb, and the leopard shall lie down with the kid, and the calf and the lion and the fatling together, and a little child shall lead them. . . . They shall not hurt or destroy in all my holy mountain." (See also Isa. 65:25.)

62. See Douglas John Hall, *The Reality of the Gospel and the Unreality of the Churches* (The Westminster Press, 1975).

63. Again this is most conspicuous in North America. The most popular denominations have been those which found it easier, by reason of "democratic" forms of government, the control of the purse by the laity, and a more "liberal" spirit, to discard elements of "the tradition" which conflicted with the basis and aims of the new dominant class. Catholicism offers some special problems in this connection. But almost without exception the *non*-Roman Catholic churches that contained conspicuous ties with older traditions and images have had to take a back seat, while nonconformists of the Old World have increasingly found their way to the front. The Anglican communion is the best example of the former. This has nothing whatever to do with the vivacity of the nonconformist gospel as compared with that of the older traditions (a nice fiction believed by many nonconformists). It is purely a reflection of the basic *conformity* of the message and practices of the newer "denominations" with the new controlling culture. In North America, the nonconformists have become the conformists *par excellence.*

PART TWO
IN SEARCH OF A LOST TRADITION

1. Nietzsche, *Thus Spoke Zarathustra,* First Part: "On Free Death," p. 185.

2. The theology of the cross is by no means an exclusively New Testament approach. Its real roots are in the Old Testament—in the J writer, the Psalmist, Jeremiah, Amos, Hosea, Isaiah, Koheleth, Job, and elsewhere. It is in fact a distinctively *Hebraic* theology, for it is the affirmation that God suffers in the suffering of man, and demands of his "elect" that they also participate in this suffering.

To attempt to rediscover the theology of the cross is therefore at the same time to rediscover the theology of Israel. Whenever Christianity got very far away from its Hebraic roots, it became a *theologia gloriae.* By and large, that is the story of Western Christendom. There is a real connection between the theology of glory and the anti-Semitism of Western Christendom. No better illustration could be provided of this than is visible in the art of the Middle Ages. Everywhere in Europe, two figures are to be found on the facades of the great Gothic cathedrals and churches. (Notre-Dame de Paris is a very good instance.) On the one side, a female figure, dejected, crushed, usually with broken staff, often blindfolded, perhaps with crown askew: "The Jewish Religion." The counterpart of this figure is altogether predictable: a regal lady, stern, powerful, banner flying—a secular queen after the image of Elizabeth I of England: "The Christian Religion."

No adequate theology of the cross can be worked out in the church today that does not emerge out of dialogue with the Jewish faith and experience, including in a special way the contemporary experience of Judaism. The final product of Christian triumphalism was Auschwitz. To learn the true theology of the cross, we Christians have to return to Auschwitz and trace our progress from a militant theology of resurrection triumph to the captains of the death factories.

3. Helmut T. Lehmann (ed.), *Luther's Works, Sermons I* (Muhlenberg Press, 1959), Vol. LI, p. 14.

4. Written on Tuesday, Feb. 16, 1546, after he had dealt with his relationship to the Bible. He died on Feb. 18.

5. Quoted by Gordon Rupp, *The Righteousness of God* (London: Hodder & Stoughton, Ltd., 1953), p. 227.

6. Ernst Käsemann, "The Pauline Theology of the Cross," *Interpretation*, Vol. XXIV, No. 2 (April 1970), p. 151.

7. Cf. Gustaf Aulén, *Christus Victor*, tr. by A. G. Hebert (London: S.P.C.K., 1953).

8. Käsemann even goes so far as to insist that Paul himself has to be understood through Luther's basic grasp of this category: "It cannot be too strongly emphasized that Paul, historically and theologically, must be understood according to this insight of the Reformation." Käsemann, "The Pauline Theology of the Cross," p. 151.

9. Harold J. Grimm and Helmut T. Lehmann (eds.), *Luther's Works*, Vol. XXXI, pp. 40–41.

10. *Ibid.*, p. 225.

11. Paul Althaus, *The Theology of Martin Luther* (Fortress Press, 1966), p. 34.

12. Paul Tillich, *The Courage to Be* (London: James Nisbet & Co., Ltd., 1952), p. 161.

13. E. Gordon Rupp *et al.* (ed.), The Library of Christian Classics, Vol. XVII, *Luther and Erasmus: Free Will and Salvation* (The Westminster Press, 1969), p. 138.

14. Ernst Käsemann, *Jesus Means Freedom* (Fortress Press, 1969), p. 68.

15. Käsemann, "The Pauline Theology of the Cross," p. 177.

16. *Ibid.*

17. Shakespeare, *Macbeth*, Act V.

18. Søren Kierkegaard, *The Gospel of Suffering*, tr. by David Swenson and L. M. Swenson (Augsburg Publishing House, 1948), p. 31.

19. Søren Kierkegaard, *The Sickness Unto Death*, tr. by Walter Lowrie (Princeton University Press, 1951), p. 25.

20. *Ibid.*, p. 32.

21. *Ibid.*, p. 28.

22. *Ibid.*, p. 70.

23. *Ibid.*, p. 49.

24. *Ibid.*, p. 51.

25. *Ibid.*, pp. 164–165.

26. *Ibid.*, p. 144.

27. *Ibid.*, p. 139.

28. *Ibid.*, pp. 58–59.

29. Søren Kierkegaard, *Attack Upon Christendom*, tr. by Walter Lowrie (Beacon Press, Inc., 1944), p. 157.

30. Kierkegaard, *Sickness Unto Death*, p. 199.

31. Robert Bretall (ed.), *A Kierkegaard Anthology* (Princeton University Press, 1951), p. 220.

32. *Ibid.*, p. 411.

33. *Ibid.*, p. 339.

34. Paul Tillich, *Perspectives on 19th and 20th Century Protestant Theology*, ed. by Carl E. Braaten (Harper & Row, Publishers, Inc., 1967), p. 163.

35. Kierkegaard, *Attack Upon Christendom*, p. 117.

36. *Ibid.*, p. 33.

37. *Ibid.*, p. 212.

38. *Ibid.*

39. *Ibid.*, p. 277.

40. *Ibid.*, p. 31.

41. *Ibid.*, p. 286.

42. *Ibid.*, p. 287.

43. *Ibid.*

44. *Ibid.*, p. 17.

45. *Ibid.*, p. 41.

46. *Ibid.*, p. 280.

47. Cf. Dietrich Bonhoeffer, *The Cost of Discipleship*, tr. by R. H. Fuller, revised and unabridged edition (London: SCM Press, Ltd., 1959).

48. Bretall (ed.), *op. cit.*, p. 411.

49. G. K. Berkouwer, *The Triumph of Grace in the Theology of Karl Barth* (Wm. B. Eerdmans Publishing Company, 1956), p. 202.

50. Karl Barth, *Church Dogmatics*, Vol. I/1 (Edinburgh: T. & T. Clark, 1936), p. 15.

51. Karl Barth, *The Word of God and the Word of Man* (Harper & Brothers, Harper Torchbooks, 1957), pp. 144 ff.

52. *Ibid.*, pp. 144–149.

53. *Ibid.*, pp. 151–152.

54. *Ibid.*, pp. 167–168.

55. H. R. Mackintosh, *Types of Modern Theology: Schleiermacher to Barth* (London: James Nisbet & Co., Ltd., 1937), p. 296.

56. Karl Barth, *Epistle to the Romans* (London: Oxford University Press, 1933), p. 341.

57. Barth, *Church Dogmatics*, Vol. I/1, p. 22.

58. Mackintosh, *op. cit.*, p. 296.

59. Werner Pelz, *Irreligious Reflections on the Christian Church* (London: SCM Press, Ltd., 1959), p. 21.

60. "The same solitude, the same silence. And no hope this time of forcing or turning away the obstacle. Besides, there isn't any obstacle. Nothing. God! I breathe, I inhale the night, the night is entering into me by some inconceivable, unimaginable gap in my soul. I, myself, am the night." Georges Bernanos, *The Diary of a Country Priest* (The Macmillan Company, 1937), p. 96.

61. Barth, *The Word of God and the Word of Man*, p. 169.

62. *Ibid.*, p. 179.

63. *Ibid.*, pp. 169–170.

64. Berkouwer, *op. cit.*, p. 37.

65. Dietrich Bonhoeffer, *Letters and Papers from Prison*, ed. by Eberhard Bethge, tr. by R. H. Fuller (London: SCM Press, Ltd., 1953), p. 126. Although it is specifically Barth's "positivist" doctrine of revelation that Bonhoeffer refers to here, his underlying complaint is against the triumphalism in the *theology* of the later Barth.

66. Barth, *Church Dogmatics*, Vol. IV/4, p. vi.

67. Barth, *Church Dogmatics*, Vol. IV/1, p. 343.

68. "I belong to the generation that lived through the end of World War II, the

collapse of a state with all its institutions, the tyranny and the shame of its own people, and a long imprisonment. . . . Perhaps behind the barbed wire, we had discovered the power of hope." Jürgen Moltmann, "Politics and the Practice of Hope," *The Christian Century,* Vol. 87, No. 10 (March 11, 1970), p. 288.

69. Albert Camus, *The Rebel* (Vintage Books, Inc., 1956), p. 45.

70. I have in mind Solzhenitsyn's definition of a citizen in his *August 1914,* tr. by Michael Glenny (London: The Bodley Head, Ltd., 1971), p. 51, where he describes the headmistress of a girls' boarding school in these words: "She and her late husband regarded it as the chief aim of education to bring up young people as citizens, that is to say as individuals with an inherent mistrust of authority."

71. Käsemann, *Jesus Means Freedom,* p. 177.

72. Käsemann, "The Pauline Theology of the Cross," p. 177.

73. *Ibid.*

74. Cf. Karl Rahner, *Mission and Grace,* Vol. I, tr. by Cecily Hastings (London: Sheed & Ward, Ltd., 1963), pp. 20 ff.

75. Jürgen Moltmann has assumed this from the outset, but it has become explicit in his most recent work, the purpose of which is precisely to demonstrate the dependence of the theology of hope on the theology of the cross. See *Der gekreuzigte Gott: Das Kreuz als Grund und Kritik christlicher Theologie* (Munich: Chr. Kaiser Verlag, 1972).

76. Paul Lehmann, *Ethics in a Christian Context* (Harper & Row, Publishers, Inc., 1963). See especially Ch. 3.

PART THREE
An Indigenous Theology of the Cross

1. Charles A. Reich, *The Greening of America* (Bantam Books, Inc., 1971).

2. Grant, *Time as History,* p. 45.

3. J. R. R. Tolkien, "On Fairy Stories," in *The Tolkien Reader* (Ballantine Books, 1966), pp. 64–65.

4. "We live in a secular world. To adapt to this world the child abdicates its ecstasy. . . . Having lost our experience of the spirit, we are expected to have faith. But this faith comes to be a belief in a reality which is not evident. There is a prophecy in Amos that there will be a time when there will be famine in the land, 'not a famine of bread nor a thirst for water, but of *hearing* the words of the Lord.' That time has now come to pass. It is the present age." R. D. Laing, *The Politics of Experience and the Bird of Paradise* (Penguin Books, Inc., 1967), p. 118.

5. Paul R. Ehrlich and Anne H. Ehrlich, *Population, Resources, Environment: Issues in Human Ecology* (W. H. Freeman and Company, 1970), p. 324.

6. See George P. Grant, *Technology and Empire: Perspectives on North America* (Toronto: House of Anansi, 1969), p. 118.

7. Paul Tillich, *Theology of Culture* (Oxford University Press, 1959), p. 43.

8. *Ibid.,* pp. 43–44.

9. *Ibid.,* p. 44.

10. *Ibid.,* p. 45.

11. *Ibid.*

12. *Ibid.,* pp. 45–46.

13. *Ibid.,* p. 46.

14. *Ibid.,* pp. 46–47.

15. Commenting on Napoleon's propensity for self-glorification, Sir Kenneth Clark remarks: "Painfully reminiscent of Hitler and Wagner. And yet one can't resist the exhilaration of Napoleon's glory. Communal enthusiasm may be a dangerous intoxicant; but if human beings were to lose altogether the sense of glory, I think we should be the poorer, and when religion is in decline it is an alternative to naked materialism." (Kenneth Clark, *Civilisation: A Personal View*, p. 304; London: British Broadcasting Corporation and John Murray, 1969, p. 304.) The truth of the observation is obvious. At the same time, if the price of such glory is survival itself, it would seem the better part of valor to question it!

16. Reinhold Niebuhr, *The Nature and Destiny of Man*, Vol. II, pp. 305–306.

17. The language of "overcoming," in the perspective of the cross, depends for its authenticity upon the context in which it is used. It is one thing for the oppressed of the world, like the American black community, to sing the triumphant "We Shall Overcome." It is something else when this same spiritual is sung by a white Anglo-Saxon Protestant congregation in an affluent neighborhood!

18. Reinhold Niebuhr, *The Nature and Destiny of Man*, Vol. II, p. 306.

19. Without doubt the negative factor (shortages of fuel, awareness of pollution, etc.) has played an important part in all such legislation. However, by itself the negative factor is not a sufficient explanation. Without some guiding vision, however tentative, lawmakers have no alternative from which to derive the rationale of and support for their laws.

20. The extent to which the modern *imago hominis* has captured the imaginations of the majority is demonstrated in a great deal of literature today, including Christian literature. Over against what they regard as dangerous tendencies of ecological and other groups, Christian commentators will point out (rightly enough) that man is not merely a "natural" being but also a "historical" being: "We rise out of nature. The word we use for this process of human ascent is 'civilization.' To be civilized is to be free of nature's strictures, to escape from the 'mere becoming' of natural change into the freedom of true history." Thomas Sieger Derr, *Ecology and Human Need* (The Westminster Press, 1975), p. 75.

However, concern for the uniqueness of man seems to have blinded many Christian commentators to the darker side of the Biblical and traditional Christian testimony to man's arrogance and spoliation of the world. "If nature is morally neutral," writes Derr, "then it is no wonder that men regard it unromantically as capricious, ambivalent, in need of altering or healing, as half friend, half enemy. It is the distinction from nature, the acceptance of dominion, that makes us human." *(Ibid.)* This is said as if what the tradition calls the Fall in no way alters the character of man's "dominion."

Nor does it take account of the fact that the Fall, in the classical version of Gen., ch. 3, consists precisely in a symbolic act of the exercise of human "dominion" which transgresses the *limits* of "our birthright."

It would be unfortunate if, in the struggle for a new image of man, Christians could only manage the sort of exegetical imagination that ends by giving Biblical warranty to precisely the *sort* of "dominion" technologism wants to uphold. Surely it is not necessary to overlook the demonic dimensions of fallen man's pretension to power over nature in order to maintain his distinctiveness as a creature.

21. See Kurt Vonnegut, Jr., *God Bless You, Mr. Rosewater: Or Pearls Before Swine* (Dell Publishing Co., Inc., Delta Books, 1974), pp. 29–30.

22. Abraham Heschel, *Who Is Man?* (Stanford University Press, 1966), p. 15.

23. Martin Heidegger, *Discourse on Thinking,* tr. by John M. Anderson and E. Hans Freund (Harper & Row, Publishers, Inc., Harper Torchbooks, 1966). This distinction between two types of thinking can be noted in much contemporary philosophical, theological, and literary work. Karl Jaspers, e.g., distinguishes between "intellectual thought" and "rational thought": "*Intellectual thought* is the inventor and maker. Its precepts can be carried out and can multiply the making by infinite repetition. The result is a world in which a few minds devise the mechanics, creating, as it were, a second world in which the masses then assume the operative function. *Rational thought,* on the other hand, does not provide for the carrying-out of mass directives but requires each individual to do his own thinking, original thinking. Here, truth is not found by a machine reproducible at will, but by decision, resolve, and action whose self-willed performance, by each on his own, is what creates a common spirit." (Karl Jaspers, *The Future of Mankind,* p. 7; The University of Chicago Press, 1961.) For Paul Tillich, the distinction is between "ontological reason" and "technical reason" (Tillich, *Systematic Theology,* Vol. I, pp. 71 ff.; The University of Chicago Press, 1951.) And Rubem Alves says that reason in the technological society has ceased to have a "creative function" and becomes merely "descriptive" (Rubem Alves, "Some Thoughts on a Programme for Ethics," *Union Theological Seminary Quarterly Review,* Vol. XXVI, No. 2 [Winter 1971], p. 163).

24. Grant, *Time as History,* Ch. 5.

25. "One can flippantly construe this exodus as the contemporary version of running off with the circus; but the more apt parallel might be the quest of third-century Christians (a similarly scruffy, uncouth, and often half-mad lot) for escape from the corruptions of Hellenistic society." Theodore Roszak, *The Making of a Counter-Culture: Reflections on the Technocratic Society and Its Youthful Opposition* (Doubleday & Company, Inc., Anchor Books, 1969), p. 34.

26. Cf. the sermon "By What Authority?" in Paul Tillich, *The New Being* (London: SCM Press, Ltd., 1956), pp. 86 ff. Tillich suggests that the end of intellectual authority in the contemporary world is related to just such a split.

27. It is one of the best features of Marxist thought that it has called attention precisely to the withdrawal of the intelligentsia from the sphere of social responsibility—a withdrawal so complete that it is regarded by many in our universities as a positive virtue.

The Marxist thinker Paul A. Baran regards such an attitude as belonging to the "intellectual worker" as distinct from the genuine intellectual:

"What marks the intellectual and distinguishes him from the intellect workers and indeed from all others is that his concern with the entire historical process is not a tangential interest but permeates his thought and significantly affects his work. To be sure, this does not imply that the intellectual in his daily activity is engaged in the study of all historical development. This would be a manifest impossibility. But what it does mean is that the intellectual is systematically seeking to relate whatever specific area he may be working in to other aspects of human existence. Indeed, it is precisely this effort to *interconnect* things which, to intellectual workers operating within the framework of capitalist institutions and steeped in bourgeois ideology and culture, necessarily appear to lie in strictly separate compartments of society's knowledge and society's labor—it is this effort to interconnect which constitutes one of the intellectual's outstanding characteristics. And it is likewise this effort which identifies one of the intellectual's principal functions in society: to serve as a symbol and as a reminder of the fundamental fact that the seeming autonomous, disparate and disjointed morsels of social existence under capitalism—literature, art, politics, the economic order, science, the cultural and psychic condition of people—can all be understood (and influenced) only if they are clearly visualized as parts of the comprehensive totality of the historical process." Paul A. Baran, "The Commitment of the Intellectual," *The Monthly Review, An Independent Socialist Magazine,* Pamphlet Series No. 25, 1966; reprinted from Vol. 13, No. 1 of *The Monthly Review,* May 1961.

All who have maintained some explicit contact with the traditions of Athens and Jerusalem are bound to recognize in this statement some essential (not to say apostolic!) succession of insight.

28. Walter M. Miller, Jr., *A Canticle for Leibowitz* (Montreal: Bantam Books of Canada, Ltd., 1959).

29. The concept of "small" or "appropriate" technology is frequently written off by North Americans, including North American Christians, whose captivity to the technological mentality seems not to permit even minor modification of the technocratic "process." But it is both an imaginative and a logical alternative to the present domination of society by technique, and one that does not indulge in merely "romantic" longing for the pastoral past. See E. F. Schumacher, *Small Is Beautiful: Study of Economics as if People Mattered* (Harper & Row, Publishers, Inc., Harper Torchbooks, 1973).

30. Although not as well known as the works of Orwell and Huxley, Zamiatin's *We* is both earlier than *1984* and *Brave New World* and, in my opinion, more profound in its treatment of the reduction of society to the mass. It is not accidental that this book was written by a Russian who, at first, had been carried along by the spirit of the Revolution.

31. The subservience of art to technique is in itself a vast study. To refer to only one art form: the Canadian pianist Glenn Gould announced in a television interview that his refusal to give large concerts stems from his awareness of the distorting effects of highly technicized sound equipment. He insists that what the audience hears, finally, is not the performance of the artist but an interpretation superimposed on his performance by technical manipulation.

32. This appears to me the most logical explanation of the fact that the works of Jacques Ellul, Josef Pieper, and other Europeans who are critical of the technological society, sell much better in North America than in Europe. Europeans are regularly amazed that these thinkers are taken so seriously on this continent.

33. Grant, *Technology and Empire,* p. 40.

34. *Ibid.*

35. Grant writes: "We can hold in our minds the enormous benefits of technological society, but we cannot so easily hold the ways in which it may have deprived us, because technique is ourselves. All descriptions or definitions of technique which place it outside ourselves hide from us what it is. This applies to the simplest accounts which describe technological advance as new machines and inventions as well as to the more sophisticated which include within their understanding the whole hierarchy of interdependent organizations and their methods. Technique comes forth from and is sustained in our vision of ourselves as creative freedom, making ourselves, and conquering the chances of an indifferent world." Grant, *Technology and Empire,* p. 137.

Ellul: "Technique is the translation into action of man's concern to master things by means of reason, to account for what is subconscious, make quantitative what is qualitative, make clear and precise the outlines of nature, take hold of chaos and put order into it." Jacques Ellul, *The Technological Society* (Alfred A. Knopf, Inc., 1964), p. 43.

Slater: "One cannot avoid a feeling of skepticism when it is proposed that institutional change alone will bring about motivational change. Closing down gambling casinos may reduce the volume of gambling but it does not end it. Institutions, like technology, are materializations of the fantasies of a past generation, inflicted on the present. Unless there is reason to believe that these fantasies have changed there is little point in trying to change the institutions, since they will simply reemerge. On the other hand, one can no longer approach the problem psychologically once the fantasies have achieved institutional form, since they now represent reality—a reality in which subsequent fantasies will be rooted." Philip E. Slater, *The Pursuit of Loneliness: American Culture at the Breaking Point* (Beacon Press, Inc., 1970), pp. 124–125.

36. A rare exception to the rule is Rubem Alves, who understands very clearly that technology in the modern world is no "neutral" entity: "One can change at will those who seem to be in power and shift from one party to another. It makes no difference. Because those who seem to be in charge are not really in charge. They are nothing more than transistors in a network of power, executives plugged into a system. And ultimately it is the system that programs the course of operations. Individuals are expendable, disposable. Paul already knew this political reality better than we. 'For our fight is not against human foes, but against cosmic powers, against authorities and potentates of this dark world, against the superhuman forces of evil in the heavens.' (Eph. 6:12.)" (Rubem Alves, *Tomorrow's Child*, p. 20; Harper & Row, Publishers, Inc., 1972.) Again: "The idea of neutrality of science and technology is no longer tenable." (*Ibid.*, p. 14.)

37. "It is hard indeed to overrate the importance of faith in progress through technology to those brought up in the main stream of North American life. It is the very ground of their being." Grant, *Philosophy in the Mass Age*, pp. vi–vii.

38. Tillich, *The Courage to Be*, p. 164.

39. Maurice Friedman, *To Deny Our Nothingness: Contemporary Images of Man* (Dell Publishing Co., Inc., Delta Books, 1968), p. 345.

40. "Nothing equals the perfection of our war machines." Ellul, *The Technological Society*, p. 16.

41. Tillich, *The Courage to Be*, p. 165.

42. John Dillenberger defines the theology of the cross as descriptive of that kind of faith which makes it possible "to live with a dimension of trust which leaves unanswered the mystery of [one's] own life, but also . . . does not reduce [one's] life to meaninglessness." John Dillenberger, *God Hidden and Revealed* (Muhlenberg Press, 1953), p. 57, para. 28.

43. Friedman, *To Deny Our Nothingness*, p. 345.

44. Lynn White, Jr., "The Historical Roots of Our Ecologic Crisis," *Science*, Vol. 155, March 10, 1967, pp. 27 ff.

45. Frank Fraser Darling in his third Reith Lecture (reprinted in *The Listener*, Nov. 27, 1969) stated: "Our Greek derivation in Western civilization gave us the reason which has guided our sciences, but the Judaic-Christian background gave

us a man-centred world. Our technology is a monument to the belief that Jehovah created us in his image, a belief which of course had to be put that way to express the truth that man created Jehovah in *his* own image. The resources of the planet were for man, without a doubt. They could have no higher end than to serve man at the behest of Jehovah. There could be no doubt of the rightness of technology."

46. Grant, *Philosophy in the Mass Age,* p. 78.

47. Ellul, *The Technological Society,* pp. 28 ff. Lewis Mumford makes the same point: "Leonardo da Vinci suppressed his invention of the submarine because he considered man to be 'too devilish to be entrusted with such an invention.' " Lewis Mumford, *Values for Survival* (Harcourt, Brace and Company, 1936), p. 67.

48. Jaspers, *The Future of Mankind,* p. ix.

49. Jürgen Moltmann, *Hope and Planning* (London: SCM Press, Ltd., 1971), p. 220.

50. "The night is far spent,
  The day is not far off;
 Let praises be sung
  To the bright Morning Star."

51. Grant, *Technology and Empire,* p. 141.

INDEX